ANNOTATED

Gene

MARK

Professor of English
The Queen's University of Belfast

and

DEREK ROPER
University of Sheffield

Editorial Board

BRIAN W. DOWNS
Professor Emeritus and sometime Master of
Christ's College, Cambridge

KENNETH MUIR
Professor of English Literature, University of Liverpool

F. W. BATESON
Fellow and University Lecturer in English
Corpus Christi College, Oxford

M. L. BURCHNALL
Senior English Master, Winchester College

M & E ANNOTATED STUDENT TEXTS

M & E ANNOTATED STUDENT TEXTS

EDWARD THOMAS

Poems and Last Poems

(ARRANGED IN CHRONOLOGICAL ORDER OF COMPOSITION)

Edited by
EDNA LONGLEY
Queen's University of Belfast

MACDONALD AND EVANS

MACDONALD AND EVANS LTD.
Estover, Plymouth PL6 7PZ

First published 1973
Reprinted 1978

Printed in Great Britain
William Collins Sons & Co Ltd, Glasgow

Contents

Acknowledgements

The Editor and Publishers make grateful acknowledgement to the following for permission to include copyright material as stated: Mrs Myfanwy Thomas for references to MSS. and for quotations from the unpublished letters of Edward Thomas to Robert Frost; Mrs Myfanwy Thomas and Faber & Faber Ltd. for extracts from *Collected Poems* by Edward Thomas, *As It Was* and *World without End* by Helen Thomas, and *The Childhood of Edward Thomas* by Edward Thomas; Mrs Myfanwy Thomas and Jonathan Cape Ltd. for extracts from *The Last Sheaf* by Edward Thomas; Mrs Myfanwy Thomas, Mr Gervase Farjeon and Oxford University Press for extracts from *Edward Thomas: The Last Four Years* by Eleanor Farjeon; Mrs Myfanwy Thomas, the Editor and Oxford University Press for extracts from *Letters from Edward Thomas to Gordon Bottomley* edited by R. G. Thomas; Mrs Myfanwy Thomas and A. D. Peters for extracts from *The Life and Letters of Edward Thomas* by John Moore.

The Executors of the Robert Frost Estate, Jonathan Cape Ltd. and Holt, Rinehart and Winston Inc. for extracts from *Selected Letters* of Robert Frost edited by Lawrance Thompson; the Executors of the Robert Frost Estate and J. M. Dent and Sons Ltd. for quotation of a letter included in *Edward Thomas: A Biography and A Bibliography* by R. P. Eckert; Holt, Rinehart and Winston Inc. and Jonathan Cape Ltd. for quotations from *The Complete Poems of Robert Frost*; H. Coombes and Chatto & Windus Ltd. for extracts from *Edward Thomas*; William Cooke and Faber & Faber Ltd. for extracts from *Edward Thomas: A Critical Biography*; F. R. Leavis, Chatto & Windus and Penguin Books Ltd. for an extract from *New Bearings in English Poetry*; Vernon Scannell, Longman Group Ltd. and The British Council for extracts from *Edward Thomas*; Robert Graves, Laura Riding and A. P. Watt & Son for an extract from *A Survey of Modernist Poetry*; the Trustees of the John Middleton Murry Estate for an extract from *Aspects of Literature*; John Press and Oxford University Press for extracts from *A Map of Modern English Verse*; Robert H. Ross and Faber & Faber Ltd. for quotations from *The Georgian Revolt*; James

ACKNOWLEDGEMENTS

Reeves and Penguin Books Ltd. for a quotation from *Georgian Poetry*; Robin Skelton and Hutchinson and Co. Ltd. for an extract from *Selected Poems* by Edward Thomas; C. K. Stead, Hutchinson and Co. Ltd. and Penguin Books Ltd. for quotations from *The New Poetic*; C. Day Lewis and The Royal Society of Literature for extracts from 'The Poetry of Edward Thomas' in *Essays by Divers Hands, XXVIII*; R. George Thomas and The English Association for quotations from 'Edward Thomas, Poet and Critic' in *Essays and Studies*, 1968.

The Trustees of the Hardy Estate and Macmillian and Co. Ltd. for quotations from *The Collected Poems of Thomas Hardy*; The Society of Authors as the literary representatives of the Housman Estate and Jonathan Cape Ltd., Publishers of A. E. Housman's *Collected Poems*; the author's literary Trustees, The Society of Authors and Faber & Faber Ltd. for quotations from *Collected Poems* by Walter de la Mare; Mrs H. M. Davies and Jonathan Cape Ltd. for quotations from *The Complete Poems of W. H. Davies*; Robert Graves and Cassel and Co. Ltd. for 'The Door' from *Collected Poems*; Philip Larkin and the Marvell Press for quotations from 'Born Yesterday' and 'Lines on a Young Lady's Photograph Album' from *The Less Deceived*; George Allen and Unwin Ltd. for quotation of 'To Edward Thomas' from *Selected Poetry and Prose* by Alun Lewis; Ted Hughes and Faber & Faber Ltd. for seven lines of 'November' from *Lupercal*; Brian Jones and Alan Ross for a line from 'A Garland for Edward Thomas' from *Poems and a Family Album* (London Magazine Editions 1972); Derek Walcott and Jonathan Cape Ltd. for two lines of 'Homage to Edward Thomas' from *The Gulf*.

Acknowledgement is also made to the following libraries: The Berg Collection of the New York Public Library; The Bodleian Library; The British Museum; Dartmouth College Library; The Lockwood Memorial Library of the State University of New York at Buffalo; The Library of the University College of South Wales and Monmouthshire.

Note on the Text
of this Edition

EDWARD THOMAS'S POEMS were all written within the space
of two years, from December 1914 to December 1916. In
January 1917 he completed arrangements for publishing
Poems, the first considerable selection from his work. *Poems*
was in the press when Thomas was killed at the Battle of
Arras in April 1917. All but six of the pieces omitted from
Poems were later collected and published in 1918 as *Last
Poems*. The present edition includes the contents of both
Poems and *Last Poems*.

To have reprinted these volumes as they stood would not
have genuinely fulfilled the aim of this series and presented
the poems in true literary and historical context. *Last Poems*,
which looks like a sequel, is simply work excluded by
Thomas from *Poems*. The collections are contemporary
rather than consecutive; and it has been decided to depart
from the normal practice of the series by combining the
poems from both volumes into a single chronological
sequence. Thomas's poems can for the first time be read, in
the order in which they were written. Our knowledge of
this order derives from the dated MSS. Thomas left in all
but a few cases. (For details of MSS., and the placing of
undated poems, see p. 145.) Edward Thomas developed as
much in two years as many poets do in twenty. The nature
of his achievement is better understood if the progressive
use of certain figures, situations, and themes can be easily
studied. The contents of the two original volumes are
listed in Appendix C.

The text of this edition has been checked against all
earlier and subsequent printings of the poems, particularly
Collected Poems by Edward Thomas (C.P.). By generously
permitting inspection of MS. material, Mrs. Myfanwy
Thomas has provided a yardstick against which to measure
the soundness of the printed versions.

Editor's Preface

'the dream
Emerging from the fact that folds a dream'
(Alun Lewis, *To Edward Thomas*)

EDWARD THOMAS (1878–1917) is at last coming into his own as a major twentieth-century poet. In *Aspens* he identifies his poetic method with 'the whisper of the aspens.' Significantly, however, this whisper 'is not drowned' and Thomas has progressively made himself heard above louder voices. For fellow-poets his poetry has often provided a touchstone: in 1927 W. H. Auden and C. Day Lewis included Thomas in the 'extremely short' list of 'contemporary poets whom we had little or no hope of ever equalling.' Derek Walcott, with *Homage to Edward Thomas*, and Brian Jones, with *A Garland for Edward Thomas,* have most recently extended a long tradition of poems addressed to him. Walcott salutes 'lines' previously 'dismissed as tenuous/because they would not howl or overwhelm,' Jones 'an honesty that shirked a specious noise.' Poets have not only revered the integrity of Thomas's achievement, but come to acknowledge its centrality. Alun Lewis found him a valid Muse and model in the context of the Second World War. The poet Vernon Scannell, discussing *Over the Hills*, notices that 'Thomas uses rhyme and . . . half-rhyme very much in the way that a poet of the fifties or sixties like Philip Larkin uses it.' Both Philip Larkin and Ted Hughes, two of the best contemporary English poets, might easily trace an ancestry back to different aspects of Edward Thomas. 'Nature poetry' flourishes again. The development of poetry in England since the First World War has in fact proved the innovations of Ezra Pound and T. S. Eliot less influential

9

than anticipated. More conspicuous than the triumph of free verse has been a revitalisation of traditional forms. *Poems* and *Last Poems*, once a prophecy of this, are now a reminder. They constitute the kind of unobtrusive landmark Thomas himself celebrates, whose real significance is not recognised until later.

The terms in which Thomas acclaimed Robert Frost's *North of Boston* (1914) are appropriate to his own achievement: 'This is one of the most revolutionary books of modern times, but one of the quietest and least aggressive. It speaks, and it is poetry.' Between them Robert Frost and Edward Thomas may have effected a 'quiet' and unaggressive poetic revolution as important as the more publicised *coup d'état* of Pound and Eliot. William Cooke has compared this review of Frost to Wordsworth's Preface to the *Lyrical Ballads*—particularly as regards Thomas's emphasis on language: 'These poems are revolutionary because they lack the exaggeration of rhetoric, and even at first sight appear to lack the poetic intensity of which rhetoric is an imitation. Their language is free from the poetical words and forms that are the chief material of secondary poets. The metre avoids not only the old-fashioned pomp and sweetness, but the later fashion also of discord and fuss. In fact, the medium is common speech and common decasyllables. . . .' In reintroducing poetry to its origins in 'common speech,' in going 'back through the paraphernalia of poetry into poetry again,' Frost and Thomas paralleled and continued the effort of Wordsworth and Coleridge. Thomas specifically followed Wordsworth, for instance, in hoping that folk songs and the recovery of old ballads would again 'give a vigorous impulse to a new school of poetry'; and also found a fresh source of linguistic strength in traditional idioms and proverbs. He absorbed Frost's free blank verse (as significant an innovation as free verse), while carrying over its logic into a greater variety of lyric forms. In insisting on speech-rhythm as the basis

of poetic utterance—'absolute fidelity to the postures
which the voice assumes in the most expressive intimate
speech'—Frost and Thomas 'revolutionised' what is
possibly more fundamental than content or imagery—the
rhythm, the movement of poetry.

The complex genesis of 'modern poetry' is today being
re-examined, and in the search for origins one road leads to
Edward Thomas as to his own 'Lob.' Like Lob Thomas was
both conservative and radical, standing for evolution rather
than total change, for a *via media* between 'old-fashioned
pomp and sweetness' and the 'discord and fuss' of un-
talented experimenters (see Appendix B). Having already
drawn blood from Ezra Pound, he could have been an
important creative and critical counter-weight to Modernism (in England) during the twenties. One ground of
difference is that Thomas's poetry assumes continuity,
rather than breakdown, between ourselves and the past.
He explored and imagined the past in order to discover
resources for facing the future: 'In some places history has
wrought like an earthquake, in others like an ant or mole;
everywhere, permanently; so that if we but knew or cared,
every swelling of the grass, every wavering line of hedge or
path or road were an inscription, brief as an epitaph, in
many languages and characters' (*The South Country*).
Thomas knew and cared; he also knew and cared about folk
lore, folk tales, folk songs, nursery rhymes, place names.
His poetry manifests a faith that language and tradition
need not be new-minted but can be 'worn new' (*Words*).
Like Yeats, he forged a poetic idiom and rhythm which
bridges the nineteenth and twentieth centuries. Like
Yeats, he revived myths and modes which had been dying
or static to consummate certain aspects of the Romantic
movement. Thomas had deeply absorbed much of Wordsworth and some of Keats. He developed their symbolism of
Nature to a point where it could reflect more intimately

than ever before the psychology and situation of the individual.

Urban imagery is no necessary badge of the modern poet. Thomas used Nature to define, and sometimes heal, the isolation of urban man, of 'those modern people who belong nowhere' (*The South Country*):

> Rain, midnight rain, nothing but the wild rain
> On this bleak hut, and solitude, and me
> Remembering again that I shall die
> And neither hear the rain nor give it thanks
> For washing me cleaner than I have been
> Since I was born into this solitude. . . . (*Rain*)

Thomas thus tackles one theme regarded as peculiarly 'modern' in the poetry of, say, T. S. Eliot. In *The Other* he explores on a large scale the 'unknown' within us and without us; our alienation from ourselves and the universe. *Lob*, like *The Other*, is a main pillar of Thomas's poetic edifice. There he exhibits another modern preoccupation connected with the quest for the self—the quest for tradition. His strong imaginative roots in English literature and the English countryside enabled Thomas to discover more than T. S. Eliot's cosmopolitan 'fragments,' to establish a genuinely organic continuity:

> . . . This is tall Tom that bore
> The logs in, and with Shakespeare in the hall
> Once talked, when icicles hung by the wall. . . .

Edward Thomas had little opportunity to interpret or defend his poetry. After the First World War it suffered devaluation along with that of the Georgians (see Appendix B). In *New Bearings in English Poetry* (1932) F. R. Leavis pioneeringly detached Thomas from the Georgians to declare him 'a very original poet who devoted great technical subtlety to the expression of a distinctively modern sensibility.' H. Coombes admirably filled out Leavis's insight in *Edward Thomas* (1956). Only with considerable reluctance and qualification does Coombes attach to Thomas the label 'minor.' The latest book on Thomas, William Cooke's *Edward Thomas: A Critical Biography* (1970), makes no explicit claims for Thomas's major status, but implies it by demonstrating the scope of his vision from a new angle. Cooke stresses the formative importance of Thomas's response to the First World War; arguing that far from being a wholly pastoral or personal poet 'he faced the tragedy of war, the waste and the pity, with an awareness beyond most of his contemporaries.'

The growth of Thomas's reputation has been slowed up by the modesty of the poetry itself, and by the sudden disappearance of its immediate cultural context. Two other impediments have been the fascination of his life and the volume of his prose. Thomas's life is a genuine mystery: the 'strange complex temperament'; the years of literary hackwork; the transformation of the 'hurried & harried prose man' into a poet 'at 36 in the shade'; the tragic death after only two years of creative fulfilment. Biographical material still preponderates over critical—letters, three biographies, the beautiful memoirs of Helen Thomas. Even in 1970 Cooke does not wholly abandon the life for the work.

Thomas's poetry is of course, as Professor R. George Thomas points out in a note on *The Happy-Go-Lucky Morgans*, the culmination of an 'intense desire to interpret his spiritual autobiography.' But the narrow boundary between the life and the poetry makes it all the more important to separate them and judge the point at which Thomas's experience becomes transmuted or objective. The prose, too, should be both assimilated and subordinated. Professor Thomas, who emphasises 'the unity that exists between Edward Thomas's prose and his verse,' observes: 'the poetry, like some rediscovered classical torso or, more precisely, like the prominent tip of an iceberg, gains in depth and power when it is read in the light of the fifteen years of continuous writing that preceded its sudden emergence in the autumn of 1914.' This edition tries to suggest, yet keep in its proper place, the hidden portion of the iceberg by quoting extensively in the Notes from Thomas's prose. As this is not widely available, one motive is to indicate its characteristic flavour and frequently high quality. There are very many prose anticipations of individual poems: I have not been able to include, or probably to trace, them all. These not only show how Thomas worked towards a definitive utterance, but often illuminate points of imagery, mood, and meaning. Other prose passages valuably exemplify his 'philosophy' or the general temper and furniture of his imagination. Edward Thomas is his own best commentator.

Principal Dates of Thomas's Life

1878 Philip Edward Thomas born on 3 March at Lambeth in London, the eldest child of 'mainly Welsh' parents who subsequently have five other sons.

1883–93 Changes school several times. Exploration of London commons; holidays in Wales and Wiltshire; naturalist hobbies; country walks with congenial friends; discovery of books, especially those of Richard Jefferies.

1894–95 Attends, rather unhappily, a public school (St. Paul's, Hammersmith). Frequents (from summer 1894) the Wandsworth home of writer and critic James Ashcroft Noble, who encourages his writing ambitions. Attracted to Noble's second daughter, Helen.

1896 Death of James Ashcroft Noble. Helen Noble leaves home because of her mother's opposition to the friendship with Edward.

1897 *The Woodland Life*, prose descriptions of a year in the countryside, published. Premarital 'honeymoon' with Helen at Swindon (September). Goes up to Oxford, having previously repudiated his father's ambition for him to enter the Civil Service.

1899 Marries Helen at Fulham Registry Office on 20 June.

1900 Mervyn Thomas born (January). Edward takes a second class degree and begins to live by his pen.

1901 The Thomases move to Rose Acre Cottage near Bearsted in Kent.

1902 Begins correspondence with Gordon Bottomley (September). *Horae Solitariae* published (June). Bronwen Thomas born (October). Edward writes essays and reviews and becomes a regular reviewer for the *Daily Chronicle*.

1903 Forced to canvas for literary work in London (February). Rescued by commission to write *Oxford*. The Thomases move to Ivy Cottage in the village of Bearsted.

1904 They move to Elses Farm in the Weald of Kent near Sevenoaks. Thomas commissioned to write *Beautiful Wales*.

1905–6 Befriends W. H. Davies (October 1905) and finds him a cottage near Elses Farm. Obtains books and money for Davies and arranges publication of Davies's *Autobiography of a Super-Tramp*. *The Heart of England* published. The Thomases move to Berryfield Cottage, Ashford, near Petersfield in Hampshire. Edward becomes a regular reviewer for the *Morning Post*.

1907–8 Makes friends with Walter de la Mare. Completes *Richard Jefferies* and *The South Country*.

1909 Reviews favourably Ezra Pound's *Personae* but later recants. The Thomases move into a new house built specially for them by Geoffrey Lupton in the same locality (Wick Green).

1910–12 Produces twelve books, including *Feminine Influence on the Poets*, *Maurice Maeterlinck*, *The Icknield Way*, *George Borrow*, and *Algernon Charles Swinburne*. Birth of Myfanwy Thomas (August 1910). Edward has nervous breakdown (September 1911). Begins *The Happy-Go-Lucky Morgans*. Meets Eleanor Farjeon

1913 Fieldwork for *In Pursuit of Spring*. Begins *Four-and-Twenty Blackbirds* and *Keats*. The Thomases move another short distance to Yewtree Cottage in the village of Steep, Petersfield. Edward meets Robert Frost (October). Begins his autobiography (*The Childhood of Edward Thomas*).

1914 Reviews Frost's *North of Boston* enthusiastically. The Thomases and Frosts holiday at Ledington on the Gloucestershire/Herefordshire border (August). Edward preparing anthology, *This England*, and writing articles about the impact of war on the people of England and on himself. Begins to write poetry (December).

1915 Writing poetry. Includes *The Manor Farm* and *Haymaking* in *This England* under pseudonym 'Edward Eastaway.' Abandons plan to follow Frosts to America and enlists in the Artists' Rifles (July). Sent to Hare

Hall Camp, Gidea Park, Romford, Essex as a map-reading instructor.

1916 Writing poetry. Still at Hare Hall Camp. Poems considered for publication by Selwyn & Blount (later accepted). Posted to Royal Artillery School, Handel Street, London as officer-cadet (August). Commissioned Second Lieutenant. *Six Poems* by Edward Eastaway published (November). Volunteers for service overseas. Writes *Out in the Dark* during Christmas leave at a new cottage in Epping Forest (High Beech).

1917 Goes to France. *An Annual of New Poetry* containing eighteen poems by Edward Eastaway published (March). Thomas sees mainly favourable *T.L.S.* review of his poems (4 April). Killed by the blast of a shell at the beginning of the Battle of Arras (9 April).

POEMS AND LAST POEMS

NOVEMBER

November's days are thirty:
November's earth is dirty,
Those thirty days, from first to last;
And the prettiest things on ground are the paths
With morning and evening hobnails dinted,   5
With foot and wing-tip overprinted
Or separately charactered,
Of little beast and little bird.
The fields are mashed by sheep, the roads
Make the worst going, the best the woods   10
Where dead leaves upward and downward scatter.
Few care for the mixture of earth and water,
Twig, leaf, flint, thorn,
Straw, feather, all that men scorn,
Pounded up and sodden by flood,   15
Condemned as mud.

But of all the months when earth is greener
Not one has clean skies that are cleaner.
Clean and clear and sweet and cold,
They shine above the earth so old,   20
While the after-tempest cloud
Sails over in silence though winds are loud,
Till the full moon in the east

Looks at the planet in the west
And earth is silent as it is black,   25
Yet not unhappy for its lack.
Up from the dirty earth men stare:
One imagines a refuge there
Above the mud, in the pure bright
Of the cloudless heavenly light: 30
Another loves earth and November more dearly
Because without them, he sees clearly,
The sky would be nothing more to his eye
Than he, in any case, is to the sky;
He loves even the mud whose dyes   35
Renounce all brightness to the skies.

MARCH

Now I know that Spring will come again,
Perhaps tomorrow: however late I've patience
After this night following on such a day.

While still my temples ached from the cold burning
Of hail and wind, and still the primroses   5
Torn by the hail were covered up in it,
The sun filled earth and heaven with a great light
And a tenderness, almost warmth, where the hail
      dripped,
As if the mighty sun wept tears of joy.
But 'twas too late for warmth. The sunset piled   10
Mountains on mountains of snow and ice in the west:
Somewhere among their folds the wind was lost,
And yet 'twas cold, and though I knew that Spring
Would come again, I knew it had not come,
That it was lost too in those mountains chill.   15

What did the thrushes know? Rain, snow, sleet, hail,
Had kept them quiet as the primroses.
They had but an hour to sing. On boughs they sang,
On gates, on ground; they sang while they changed
    perches
And while they fought, if they remembered to fight: 20
So earnest were they to pack into that hour
Their unwilling hoard of song before the moon
Grew brighter than the clouds. Then 'twas no time
For singing merely. So they could keep off silence
And night, they cared not what they sang or
    screamed;   25
Whether 'twas hoarse or sweet or fierce or soft;
And to me all was sweet: they could do no wrong.
Something they knew—I also, while they sang
And after. Not till night had half its stars
And never a cloud, was I aware of silence   30
Stained with all that hour's songs, a silence
Saying that Spring returns, perhaps tomorrow.

OLD MAN

Old Man, or Lad's-love,—in the name there's nothing
To one that knows not Lad's-love, or Old Man,
The hoar-green feathery herb, almost a tree,
Growing with rosemary and lavender.
Even to one that knows it well, the names   5
Half decorate, half perplex, the thing it is:
At least, what that is clings not to the names
In spite of time. And yet I like the names.

The herb itself I like not, but for certain
I love it, as some day the child will love it   10
Who plucks a feather from the door-side bush

Whenever she goes in or out of the house.
Often she waits there, snipping the tips and shrivelling
The shreds at last on to the path, perhaps
Thinking, perhaps of nothing, till she sniffs   15
Her fingers and runs off. The bush is still
But half as tall as she, though it is as old;
So well she clips it. Not a word she says;
And I can only wonder how much hereafter
She will remember, with that bitter scent,   20
Of garden rows, and ancient damson trees
Topping a hedge, a bent path to a door,
A low thick bush beside the door, and me
Forbidding her to pick.
                  As for myself,
Where first I met the bitter scent is lost.   25
I, too, often shrivel the grey shreds,
Sniff them and think and sniff again and try
Once more to think what it is I am remembering,
Always in vain. I cannot like the scent,
Yet I would rather give up others more sweet,   30
With no meaning, than this bitter one.

I have mislaid the key. I sniff the spray
And think of nothing; I see and I hear nothing;
Yet seem, too, to be listening, lying in wait
For what I should, yet never can, remember: 35
No garden appears, no path, no hoar-green bush
Of Lad's-love, or Old Man, no child beside,
Neither father nor mother, nor any playmate;
Only an avenue, dark, nameless, without end.

THE SIGNPOST

The dim sea glints chill. The white sun is shy,
And the skeleton weeds and the never-dry,
Rough, long grasses keep white with frost
At the hilltop by the finger-post;
The smoke of the traveller's-joy is puffed   5
Over hawthorn berry and hazel tuft.
I read the sign. Which way shall I go?
A voice says: You would not have doubted so
At twenty. Another voice gentle with scorn
Says: At twenty you wished you had never been born.   10

One hazel lost a leaf of gold
From a tuft at the tip, when the first voice told
The other he wished to know what 'twould be
To be sixty by this same post. 'You shall see,'
He laughed—and I had to join his laughter—   15
'You shall see; but either before or after,
Whatever happens, it must befall,
A mouthful of earth to remedy all
Regrets and wishes shall freely be given;
And if there be a flaw in that heaven   20
'Twill be freedom to wish, and your wish may be
To be here or anywhere talking to me,
No matter what the weather, on earth,
At any age between death and birth,—
To see what day or night can be,   25
The sun and the frost, the land and the sea,
Summer, Autumn, Winter, Spring,—
With a poor man of any sort, down to a king,
Standing upright out in the air
Wondering where he shall journey, O where?'   30

23

INTERVAL

Gone the wild day:
A wilder night
Coming makes way
For brief twilight.

Where the firm soaked road   5
Mounts and is lost
In the high beech-wood
It shines almost.

The beeches keep
A stormy rest,   10
Breathing deep
Of wind from the west.

The wood is black,
With a misty steam.
Above, the cloud pack   15
Breaks for one gleam.

But the woodman's cot
By the ivied trees
Awakens not
To light or breeze.   20

It smokes aloft
Unwavering:
It hunches soft
Under storm's wing.

It has no care   25
For gleam or gloom:
It stays there
While I shall roam,

Die, and forget
The hill of trees,   30
The gleam, the wet,
This roaring peace.

AFTER RAIN

The rain of a night and a day and a night
Stops at the light
Of this pale choked day. The peering sun
Sees what has been done.
The road under the trees has a border new   5
Of purple hue
Inside the border of bright thin grass:
For all that has
Been left by November of leaves is torn
From hazel and thorn   10
And the greater trees. Throughout the copse
No dead leaf drops
On grey grass, green moss, burnt-orange fern,
At the wind's return:
The leaflets out of the ash tree shed   15
Are thinly spread
In the road, like little black fish, inlaid,
As if they played.
What hangs from the myriad branches down there
So hard and bare   20
Is twelve yellow apples lovely to see
On one crab tree.
And on each twig of every tree in the dell
Uncountable
Crystals both dark and bright of the rain   25
That begins again.

THE OTHER

The forest ended. Glad I was
To feel the light, and hear the hum
Of bees, and smell the drying grass
And the sweet mint, because I had come
To an end of forest, and because   5
Here was both road and inn, the sum
Of what's not forest. But 'twas here
They asked me if I did not pass
Yesterday this way. 'Not you? Queer.'
'Who then? and slept here?' I felt fear.   10

I learnt his road and, ere they were
Sure I was I, left the dark wood
Behind, kestrel and woodpecker,
The inn in the sun, the happy mood
When first I tasted sunlight there.   15
I travelled fast, in hopes I should
Outrun that other. What to do
When caught, I planned not. I pursued
To prove the likeness, and, if true,
To watch until myself I knew.   20

I tried the inns that evening
Of a long gabled high street grey,
Of courts and outskirts, travelling
An eager but a weary way,
In vain. He was not there. Nothing   25
Told me that ever till that day
Had one like me entered those doors,
Save once. That time I dared: 'You may
Recall'—but never-foamless shores
Make better friends than those dull boors.   30

Many and many a day like this
Aimed at the unseen moving goal
And nothing found but remedies
For all desire. These made not whole;
They sowed a new desire, to kiss   35
Desire's self beyond control,
Desire of desire. And yet
Life stayed on within my soul.
One night in sheltering from the wet
I quite forgot I could forget.   40

A customer, then the landlady
Stared at me. With a kind of smile
They hesitated awkwardly:
Their silence gave me time for guile.
Had anyone called there like me,   45
I asked. It was quite plain the wile
Succeeded. For they poured out all.
And that was naught. Less than a mile
Beyond the inn, I could recall
He was like me in general.   50

He had pleased them, but I less.
I was more eager than before
To find him out and to confess,
To bore him and to let him bore.
I could not wait: children might guess   55
I had a purpose, something more
That made an answer indiscreet.
One girl's caution made me sore,
Too indignant even to greet
That other had we chanced to meet.   60

I sought then in solitude.
The wind had fallen with the night; as still
The roads lay as the ploughland rude,

Dark and naked, on the hill.
Had there been ever any feud   65
'Twixt earth and sky, a mighty will
Closed it: the crocketed dark trees,
A dark house, dark impossible
Cloud-towers, one star, one lamp, one peace
Held on an everlasting lease: 70

And all was earth's, or all was sky's;
No difference endured between
The two. A dog barked on a hidden rise;
A marshbird whistled high unseen;
The latest waking blackbird's cries   75
Perished upon the silence keen.
The last light filled a narrow firth
Among the clouds. I stood serene,
And with a solemn quiet mirth,
An old inhabitant of earth.   80

Once the name I gave to hours
Like this was melancholy, when
It was not happiness and powers
Coming like exiles home again,
And weaknesses quitting their bowers,   85
Smiled and enjoyed, far off from men,
Moments of everlastingness.
And fortunate my search was then
While what I sought, nevertheless,
That I was seeking, I did not guess.   90

That time was brief: once more at inn
And upon road I sought my man
Till once amid a tap-room's din
Loudly he asked for me, began
To speak, as if it had been a sin,   95
Of how I thought and dreamed and ran

After him thus, day after day:
He lived as one under a ban
For this: what had I got to say?
I said nothing. I slipped away.   100

And now I dare not follow after
Too close. I try to keep in sight,
Dreading his frown and worse his laughter.
I steal out of the wood to light;
I see the swift shoot from the rafter   105
By the inn door; ere I alight
I wait and hear the starlings wheeze
And nibble like ducks: I wait his flight.
He goes: I follow: no release
Until he ceases. Then I also shall cease.   110

THE MOUNTAIN CHAPEL

Chapel and gravestones, old and few,
Are shrouded by a mountain fold
From sound and view
Of life. The loss of the brook's voice
Falls like a shadow. All they hear is   5
The eternal noise
Of wind whistling in grass more shrill
Than aught as human as a sword,
And saying still:
"'Tis but a moment since man's birth   10
And in another moment more
Man lies in earth
For ever; but I am the same
Now, and shall be, even as I was
Before he came;   15
Till there is nothing I shall be.'

29

Yet there the sun shines after noon
So cheerfully
The place almost seems peopled, nor
Lacks cottage chimney, cottage hearth: 20
It is not more
In size than is a cottage, less
Than any other empty home
In homeliness.
It has a garden of wild flowers   25
And finest grass and gravestones warm
In sunshine hours
The year through. Men behind the glass
Stand once a week, singing, and drown
The whistling grass   30
Their ponies munch. And yet somewhere,
Near or far off, there's a man could
Live happy here,
Or one of the gods perhaps, were they
Not of inhuman stature dire,   35
As poets say
Who have not seen them clearly, if
At sound of any wind of the world
In grass-blades stiff
They would not startle and shudder cold   40
Under the sun. When gods were young
This wind was old.

BIRDS' NESTS

The summer nests uncovered by autumn wind,
Some torn, others dislodged, all dark,
Everyone sees them: low or high in tree,
Or hedge, or single bush, they hang like a mark.

Since there's no need of eyes to see them with   5
I cannot help a little shame
That I missed most, even at eye's level, till
The leaves blew off and made the seeing no game.

'Tis a light pang. I like to see the nests
Still in their places, now first known,   10
At home and by far roads. Boys knew them not,
Whatever jays and squirrels may have done.

And most I like the winter nests deep-hid
That leaves and berries fell into:
Once a dormouse dined there on hazel-nuts,   15
And grass and goose-grass seeds found soil and grew.

THE MANOR FARM

The rock-like mud unfroze a little and rills
Ran and sparkled down each side of the road
Under the catkins wagging in the hedge.
But earth would have her sleep out, spite of the sun;
Nor did I value that thin gilding beam   5
More than a pretty February thing
Till I came down to the old Manor Farm,
And church and yew tree opposite, in age
Its equals and in size. The church and yew
And farmhouse slept in a Sunday silentness.   10
The air raised not a straw. The steep farm roof,
With tiles duskily glowing, entertained
The midday sun; and up and down the roof
White pigeons nestled. There was no sound but one.
Three cart-horses were looking over a gate   15
Drowsily through their forelocks, swishing their tails
Against a fly, a solitary fly.

The Winter's cheek flushed as if he had drained
Spring, Summer, and Autumn at a draught
And smiled quietly. But 'twas not Winter—   20
Rather a season of bliss unchangeable
Awakened from farm and church where it had lain
Safe under tile and thatch for ages since
This England, Old already, was called Merry.

AN OLD SONG

I was not apprenticed nor ever dwelt in famous
        Lincolnshire;
I've served one master ill and well much more than
        seven year;
And never took up to poaching as you shall quickly
        find;
    But 'tis my delight of a shiny night in the season of
        the year.

I roamed where nobody had a right but keepers and
        squires, and there   5
I sought for nests, wild flowers, oak sticks, and moles,
        both far and near;
And had to run from farmers, and learnt the Lincoln-
        shire song:
    'Oh, 'tis my delight of a shiny night in the season of
        the year.'

I took those walks years after, talking with friend or
        dear,
Or solitary musing; but when the moon shone clear   10
I had no joy or sorrow that could not be expressed
    By "Tis my delight of a shiny night in the season of
        the year.'

Since then I've thrown away a chance to fight a game-
    keeper;
And I less often trespass, and what I see or hear
Is mostly from the road or path by day: yet still I
    sing: 15
   'Oh, 'tis my delight of a shiny night in the season of
    the year.'

For if I am contented, at home or anywhere,
Or if I sigh for I know not what, or my heart beats
    with some fear,
It is a strange kind of delight to sing or whistle just:
   'Oh, 'tis my delight of a shiny night in the season of
    the year.'   20

And with this melody on my lips and no one by to
    care,
Indoors, or out on shiny nights or dark in open air,
I am for a moment made a man that sings out of his
    heart:
   'Oh, 'tis my delight of a shiny night in the season of
    the year.'

AN OLD SONG

The sun set, the wind fell, the sea
Was like a mirror shaking:
The one small wave that clapped the land
A mile-long snake of foam was making
Where tide had smoothed and wind had dried   5
The vacant sand.

  li ght   divided the swollen clouds
And lay most perfectly

Like a straight narrow footbridge bright
That crossed over the sea to me;   10
And no one else in the whole world
Saw that same sight.

I walked elate, my bridge always
Just one step from my feet:
A robin sang, a shade in shade: 15
And all I did was to repeat:
'I'll go no more a-roving
With you, fair maid.'

The sailors' song of merry loving
With dusk and sea-gull's mewing   20
Mixed sweet, the lewdness far outweighed
By the wild charm the chorus played:
'I'll go no more a-roving
With you, fair maid:
A-roving, a-roving, since roving's been my ruin,   25
I'll go no more a-roving with you, fair maid.'

In Amsterdam there dwelt a maid—
Mark well what I do say—
In Amsterdam there dwelt a maid
And she was a mistress of her trade: 30
I'll go no more a-roving
With you, fair maid:
A-roving, a-roving, since roving's been my ruin,
I'll go no more a-roving with you, fair maid.

THE COMBE

The Combe was ever dark, ancient and dark.
Its mouth is stopped with bramble, thorn, and briar;
And no one scrambles over the sliding chalk
By beech and yew and perishing juniper
Down the half precipices of its sides, with roots   5
And rabbit holes for steps. The sun of Winter,
The moon of Summer, and all the singing birds
Except the missel-thrush that loves juniper,
Are quite shut out. But far more ancient and dark
The Combe looks since they killed the badger there, 10
Dug him out and gave him to the hounds,
That most ancient Briton of English beasts.

THE HOLLOW WOOD

Out in the sun the goldfinch flits
Along the thistle-tops, flits and twits
Above the hollow wood
Where birds swim like fish—
Fish that laugh and shriek—   5
To and fro, far below
In the pale hollow wood.

Lichen, ivy, and moss
Keep evergreen the trees
That stand half-flayed and dying,   10
And the dead trees on their knees
In dog's-mercury and moss:
And the bright twit of the goldfinch drops
Down there as he flits on thistle-tops.

THE NEW YEAR

He was the one man I met up in the woods
That stormy New Year's morning; and at first sight,
Fifty yards off, I could not tell how much
Of the strange tripod was a man. His body,
Bowed horizontal, was supported equally   5
By legs at one end, by a rake at the other:
Thus he rested, far less like a man than
His wheelbarrow in profile was like a pig.
But when I saw it was an old man bent,
At the same moment came into my mind   10
The games at which boys bend thus, *High-cocolorum*,
Or *Fly-the-garter*, and *Leap-frog*. At the sound
Of footsteps he began to straighten himself;
His head rolled under his cape like a tortoise's;
He took an unlit pipe out of his mouth   15
Politely ere I wished him 'A Happy New Year,'
And with his head cast upward sideways muttered—
So far as I could hear through the trees' roar—
'Happy New Year, and may it come fastish, too,'
While I strode by and he turned to raking leaves.   20

THE SOURCE

All day the air triumphs with its two voices
Of wind and rain
As loud as if in anger it rejoices,
Drowning the sound of earth
That gulps and gulps in choked endeavour vain   5
To swallow the rain.

Half the night, too, only the wild air speaks
With wind and rain,

Till forth the dumb source of the river breaks
And drowns the rain and wind,   10
Bellows like a giant bathing in mighty mirth
The triumph of earth.

THE PENNY WHISTLE

The new moon hangs like an ivory bugle
In the naked frosty blue;
And the ghylls of the forest, already blackened
By Winter, are blackened anew.

The brooks that cut up and increase the forest,   5
As if they had never known
The sun, are roaring with black hollow voices
Betwixt rage and a moan.

But still the caravan-hut by the hollies
Like a kingfisher gleams between: 10
Round the mossed old hearths of the charcoal-burners
First primroses ask to be seen.

The charcoal-burners are black, but their linen
Blows white on the line;
And white the letter the girl is reading   15
Under that crescent fine;

And her brother who hides apart in a thicket,
Slowly and surely playing
On a whistle an old nursery melody,
Says far more than I am saying.   20

A PRIVATE

This ploughman dead in battle slept out of doors
Many a frozen night, and merrily
Answered staid drinkers, good bedmen, and all bores:
'At Mrs. Greenland's Hawthorn Bush,' said he,
'I slept.' None knew which bush. Above the town,   5
Beyond 'The Drover,' a hundred spot the down
In Wiltshire. And where now at last he sleeps
More sound in France—that, too, he secret keeps.

SNOW

In the gloom of whiteness,
In the great silence of snow,
A child was sighing
And bitterly saying: 'Oh,
They have killed a white bird up there on her nest,   5
The down is fluttering from her breast!'
And still it fell through that dusky brightness
On the child crying for the bird of the snow.

ADLESTROP

Yes. I remember Adlestrop—
The name, because one afternoon
Of heat the express-train drew up there
Unwontedly. It was late June.

The steam hissed. Someone cleared his throat.   5
No one left and no one came
On the bare platform. What I saw
Was Adlestrop—only the name

And willows, willow-herb, and grass,
And meadowsweet, and haycocks dry,   10
No whit less still and lonely fair
Than the high cloudlets in the sky.

And for that minute a blackbird sang
Close by, and round him, mistier,
Farther and farther, all the birds   15
Of Oxfordshire and Gloucestershire.

TEARS

It seems I have no tears left. They should have
    fallen—
Their ghosts, if tears have ghosts, did fall—that day
When twenty hounds streamed by me, not yet combed
    out
But still all equals in their rage of gladness
Upon the scent, made one, like a great dragon   5
In Blooming Meadow that bends towards the sun
And once bore hops: and on that other day
When I stepped out from the double-shadowed
    Tower
Into an April morning, stirring and sweet
And warm. Strange solitude was there and silence.   10
A mightier charm than any in the Tower
Possessed the courtyard. They were changing guard,
Soldiers in line, young English countrymen,
Fair-haired and ruddy, in white tunics. Drums
And fifes were playing 'The British Grenadiers.'   15
The men, the music piercing that solitude
And silence, told me truths I had not dreamed,
And have forgotten since their beauty passed.

OVER THE HILLS

Often and often it came back again
To mind, the day I passed the horizon ridge
To a new country, the path I had to find
By half-gaps that were stiles once in the hedge,
The pack of scarlet clouds running across   5
The harvest evening that seemed endless then
And after, and the inn where all were kind,
All were strangers. I did not know my loss
Till one day twelve months later suddenly
I leaned upon my spade and saw it all,   10
Though far beyond the sky-line. It became
Almost a habit through the year for me
To lean and see it and think to do the same
Again for two days and a night. Recall
Was vain: no more could the restless brook   15
Ever turn back and climb the waterfall
To the lake that rests and stirs not in its nook,
As in the hollow of the collar-bone
Under the mountain's head of rush and stone.

THE LOFTY SKY

Today I want the sky,
The tops of the high hills,
Above the last man's house,
His hedges, and his cows,
Where, if I will, I look   5
Down even on sheep and rook,
And of all things that move
See buzzards only above:—
Past all trees, past furze
And thorn, where nought deters   10

The desire of the eye
For sky, nothing but sky.

I sicken of the woods
And all the multitudes
Of hedge-trees. They are no more   15
Than weeds upon this floor
Of the river of air
Leagues deep, leagues wide, where
I am like a fish that lives
In weeds and mud and gives   20
What's above him no thought.
I might be a tench for aught
That I can do today
Down on the wealden clay.
Even the tench has days   25
When he floats up and plays
Among the lily leaves
And sees the sky, or grieves
Not if he nothing sees:
While I, I know that trees   30
Under that lofty sky
Are weeds, fields mud, and I
Would arise and go far
To where the lilies are.

THE CUCKOO

That's the cuckoo, you say. I cannot hear it.
When last I heard it I cannot recall; but I know
Too well the year when first I failed to hear it—
It was drowned by my man groaning out to his sheep
    'Ho! Ho!'

Ten times with an angry voice he shouted   5
'Ho! Ho!' but not in anger, for that was his way.
He died that Summer, and that is how I remember
The cuckoo calling, the children listening, and me
    saying, 'Nay.'

And now, as you said, 'There it is,' I was hearing
Not the cuckoo at all, but my man's 'Ho! Ho!'
    instead.   10
And I think that even if I could lose my deafness
The cuckoo's note would be drowned by the voice of
    my dead.

SWEDES

They have taken the gable from the roof of clay
On the long swede pile. They have let in the sun
To the white and gold and purple of curled fronds
Unsunned. It is a sight more tender-gorgeous
At the wood-corner where Winter moans and drips   5
Than when, in the Valley of the Tombs of Kings,
A boy crawls down into a Pharaoh's tomb
And, first of Christian men, beholds the mummy,
God and monkey, chariot and throne and vase,
Blue pottery, alabaster, and gold.   10

But dreamless long-dead Amen-hotep lies.
This is a dream of Winter, sweet as Spring.

THE UNKNOWN BIRD

Three lovely notes he whistled, too soft to be heard
If others sang; but others never sang
In the great beech-wood all that May and June.
No one saw him: I alone could hear him
Though many listened. Was it but four years   5
Ago? or five? He never came again.

Oftenest when I heard him I was alone,
Nor could I ever make another hear.
La-la-la! he called, seeming far off—
As if a cock crowed past the edge of the world,   10
As if the bird or I were in a dream.
Yet that he travelled through the trees and sometimes
Neared me, was plain, though somehow distant still
He sounded. All the proof is—I told men
What I had heard.

            I never knew a voice,   15
Man, beast, or bird, better than this. I told
The naturalists; but neither had they heard
Anything like the notes that did so haunt me;
I had them clear by heart and have them still.
Four years, or five, have made no difference. Then   20
As now that La-la-la! was bodiless sweet:
Sad more than joyful it was, if I must say
That it was one or other, but if sad
'Twas sad only with joy too, too far off
For me to taste it. But I cannot tell   25
If truly never anything but fair
The days were when he sang, as now they seem.
This surely I know, that I who listened then,
Happy sometimes, sometimes suffering
A heavy body and a heavy heart,   30
Now straightway, if I think of it, become
Light as that bird wandering beyond my shore.

THE MILL-POND

The sun blazed while the thunder yet
Added a boom:
A wagtail flickered bright over
The mill-pond's gloom:

Less than the cooing in the alder   5
Isles of the pool
Sounded the thunder through that plunge
Of waters cool.

Scared starlings on the aspen tip
Past the black mill   10
Outchattered the stream and the next roar
Far on the hill.

As my feet dangling teased the foam
That slid below
A girl came out. 'Take care!' she said—   15
Ages ago.

She startled me, standing quite close
Dressed all in white:
Ages ago I was angry till
She passed from sight.   20

Then the storm burst, and as I crouched
To shelter, how
Beautiful and kind, too, she seemed,
As she does now!

MAN AND DOG

"'Twill take some getting.' 'Sir, I think 'twill so.'
The old man stared up at the mistletoe
That hung too high in the poplar's crest for plunder
Of any climber, though not for kissing under:
Then he went on against the north-east wind—   5
Straight but lame, leaning on a staff new-skinned,
Carrying a brolly, flag-basket, and old coat,—
Towards Alton, ten miles off. And he had not
Done less from Chilgrove where he pulled up docks.
'Twere best, if he had had 'a money-box,'   10
To have waited there till the sheep cleared a field
For what a half-week's flint-picking would yield.
His mind was running on the work he had done
Since he left Christchurch in the New Forest, one
Spring in the 'seventies,—navvying on dock and line 15
From Southampton to Newcastle-on-Tyne,—
In 'seventy-four a year of soldiering
With the Berkshires,—hoeing and harvesting
In half the shires where corn and couch will grow.
His sons, three sons, were fighting, but the hoe   20
And reap-hook he liked, or anything to do with trees.
He fell once from a poplar tall as these:
The Flying Man they called him in hospital.
'If I flew now, to another world I'd fall.'
He laughed and whistled to the small brown bitch   25
With spots of blue that hunted in the ditch.
Her foxy Welsh grandfather must have paired
Beneath him. He kept sheep in Wales and scared
Strangers, I will warrant, with his pearl eye
And trick of shrinking off as he were shy,   30
Then following close in silence for—for what?
'No rabbit, never fear, she ever got,
Yet always hunts. Today she nearly had one:

She would and she wouldn't. 'Twas like that. The bad
    one!
She's not much use, but still she's company,   35
Though I'm not. She goes everywhere with me.
So Alton I must reach tonight somehow:
I'll get no shakedown with that bedfellow
From farmers. Many a man sleeps worse tonight
Than I shall.' 'In the trenches.' 'Yes, that's right.   40
But they'll be out of that—I hope they be—
This weather, marching after the enemy.'
'And so I hope. Good luck.' And there I nodded
'Good night. You keep straight on.' Stiffly he plodded;
And at his heels the crisp leaves scurried fast,   45
And the leaf-coloured robin watched. They passed,
The robin till next day, the man for good,
Together in the twilight of the wood.

BEAUTY

What does it mean? Tired, angry, and ill at ease,
No man, woman, or child alive could please
Me now. And yet I almost dare to laugh
Because I sit and frame an epitaph—
'Here lies all that no one loved of him   5
And that loved no one.' Then in a trice that whim
Has wearied. But, though I am like a river
At fall of evening while it seems that never
Has the sun lighted it or warmed it, while
Cross breezes cut the surface to a file,   10
This heart, some fraction of me, happily
Floats through the window even now to a tree
Down in the misting, dim-lit, quiet vale,
Not like a pewit that returns to wail
For something it has lost, but like a dove   15

That slants unswerving to its home and love.
There I find my rest, and through the dusk air
Flies what yet lives in me. Beauty is there.

THE GYPSY

A fortnight before Christmas Gypsies were everywhere:
Vans were drawn up on wastes, women trailed to the
    fair.
'My gentleman,' said one, 'you've got a lucky face.'
'And you've a luckier,' I thought, 'if such a grace
And impudence in rags are lucky.' 'Give a penny   5
For the poor baby's sake.' 'Indeed I have not any
Unless you can give change for a sovereign, my dear.'
'Then just half a pipeful of tobacco can you spare?'
I gave it. With that much victory she laughed content.
I should have given more, but off and away she went   10
With her baby and her pink sham flowers to rejoin
The rest before I could translate to its proper coin
Gratitude for her grace. And I paid nothing then,
As I pay nothing now with the dipping of my pen
For her brother's music when he drummed the tam-
    bourine   15
And stamped his feet, which made the workmen passing
    grin,
While his mouth-organ changed to a rascally Bacchanal
    dance
'Over the hills and far away.' This and his glance
Outlasted all the fair, farmer, and auctioneer,
Cheap-jack, balloon-man, drover with crooked stick,
    and steer,   20
Pig, turkey, goose, and duck, Christmas corpses to be.
Not even the kneeling ox had eyes like the Romany.
That night he peopled for me the hollow wooded land,

More dark and wild than stormiest heavens, that I
    searched and scanned
Like a ghost new-arrived. The gradations of the dark   25
Were like an underworld of death, but for the spark
In the Gypsy boy's black eyes as he played and
    stamped his tune,
'Over the hills and far away,' and a crescent moon.

AMBITION

Unless it was that day I never knew
Ambition. After a night of frost, before
The March sun brightened and the South-west blew,
Jackdaws began to shout and float and soar
Already, and one was racing straight and high   5
Alone, shouting like a black warrior
Challenges and menaces to the wide sky.
With loud long laughter then a woodpecker
Ridiculed the sadness of the owl's last cry.
And through the valley where all the folk astir   10
Made only plumes of pearly smoke to tower
Over dark trees and white meadows happier
Than was Elysium in that happy hour,
A train that roared along raised after it
And carried with it a motionless white bower   15
Of purest cloud, from end to end close-knit,
So fair it touched the roar with silence. Time
Was powerless while that lasted. I could sit
And think I had made the loveliness of prime,
Breathed its life into it and were its lord,   20
And no mind lived save this 'twixt clouds and rime.
Omnipotent I was, nor even deplored
That I did nothing. But the end fell like a bell:
The bower was scattered; far off the train roared.

But if this was ambition I cannot tell.   25
What 'twas ambition for I know not well.

HOUSE AND MAN

One hour: as dim he and his house now look
As a reflection in a rippling brook,
While I remember him; but first, his house.
Empty it sounded. It was dark with forest boughs
That brushed the walls and made the mossy tiles   5
Part of the squirrels' track. In all those miles
Of forest silence and forest murmur, only
One house—'Lonely!' he said, 'I wish it were lonely'—
Which the trees looked upon from every side,
And that was his.

          He waved good-bye to hide   10
A sigh that he converted to a laugh.
He seemed to hang rather than stand there, half
Ghost-like, half like a beggar's rag, clean wrung
And useless on the briar where it has hung
Long years a-washing by sun and wind and rain.   15

But why I call back man and house again
Is that now on a beech tree's tip I see
As then I saw—I at the gate, and he
In the house darkness,—a magpie veering about,
A magpie like a weathercock in doubt.   20

PARTING

The Past is a strange land, most strange.
Wind blows not there, nor does rain fall:
If they do, they cannot hurt at all.
Men of all kinds as equals range

The soundless fields and streets of it.   5
Pleasure and pain there have no sting,
The perished self not suffering
That lacks all blood and nerve and wit,

And is in shadow-land a shade.
Remembered joy and misery   10
Bring joy to the joyous equally;
Both sadden the sad. So memory made

Parting today a double pain:
First because it was parting; next
Because the ill it ended vexed   15
And mocked me from the Past again,

Not as what had been remedied
Had I gone on,—not that, oh no!
But as itself no longer woe;
Sighs, angry word and look and deed   20

Being faded: rather a kind of bliss,
For there spiritualized it lay
In the perpetual yesterday
That naught can stir or strain like this.

FIRST KNOWN WHEN LOST

I never had noticed it until
'Twas gone,—the narrow copse
Where now the woodman lops
The last of the willows with his bill.

It was not more than a hedge overgrown.   5
One meadow's breadth away
I passed it day by day.
Now the soil is bare as a bone,

And black betwixt two meadows green,
Though fresh-cut faggot ends   10
Of hazel made some amends
With a gleam as if flowers they had been.

Strange it could have hidden so near!
And now I see as I look
That the small winding brook,   15
A tributary's tributary, rises there.

MAY THE TWENTY-THIRD

There never was a finer day,
And never will be while May is May,—
The third, and not the last of its kind;
But though fair and clear the two behind
Seemed pursued by tempests overpast;   5
And the morrow with fear that it could not last
Was spoiled. Today ere the stones were warm
Five minutes of thunderstorm
Dashed it with rain, as if to secure,
By one tear, its beauty the luck to endure.   10
At midday then along the lane

51

Old Jack Noman appeared again,
Jaunty and old, crooked and tall,
And stopped and grinned at me over the wall,
With a cowslip bunch in his button-hole   15
And one in his cap. Who could say if his roll
Came from flints in the road, the weather, or ale?
He was welcome as the nightingale.
Not an hour of the sun had been wasted on Jack.
'I've got my Indian complexion back,'   20
Said he. He was tanned like a harvester,
Like his short clay pipe, like the leaf and bur
That clung to his coat from last night's bed,
Like the ploughland crumbling red.
Fairer flowers were none on the earth   25
Than his cowslips wet with the dew of their birth,
Or fresher leaves than the cress in his basket.
'Where did they come from, Jack?' 'Don't ask it,
And you'll be told no lies.' 'Very well:
Then I can't buy.' 'I don't want to sell.   30
Take them and these flowers, too, free.
Perhaps you have something to give me?
Wait till next time. The better the day . . .
The Lord couldn't make a better, I say;
If he could, he never has done.'   35
So off went Jack with his roll-walk-run,
Leaving his cresses from Oakshott rill
And his cowslips from Wheatham hill.

'Twas the first day that the midges bit;
But though they bit me, I was glad of it: 40
Of the dust in my face, too, I was glad.
Spring could do nothing to make me sad.
Bluebells hid all the ruts in the copse,
The elm seeds lay in the road like hops,
That fine day, May the twenty-third,   45
The day Jack Noman disappeared.

THE BARN

They should never have built a barn there, at all—
Drip, drip, drip!—under that elm tree,
Though then it was young. Now it is old
But good, not like the barn and me.

Tomorrow they cut it down. They will leave   5
The barn, as I shall be left, maybe.
What holds it up? 'Twould not pay to pull down.
Well, this place has no other antiquity.

No abbey or castle looks so old
As this that Job Knight built in '54,   10
Built to keep corn for rats and men.
Now there's fowls in the roof, pigs on the floor.

What thatch survives is dung for the grass,
The best grass on the farm. A pity the roof
Will not bear a mower to mow it. But   15
Only fowls have foothold enough.

Starlings used to sit there with bubbling throats
Making a spiky beard as they chattered
And whistled and kissed, with heads in air,
Till they thought of something else that mattered.   20

But now they cannot find a place,
Among all those holes, for a nest any more.
It's the turn of lesser things, I suppose.
Once I fancied 'twas starlings they built it for.

HOME

Not the end: but there's nothing more.
Sweet Summer and Winter rude
I have loved, and friendship and love,
The crowd and solitude:

But I know them: I weary not;   5
But all that they mean I know.
I would go back again home
Now. Yet how should I go?

This is my grief. That land,
My home, I have never seen;   10
No traveller tells of it,
However far he has been.

And could I discover it,
I fear my happiness there,
Or my pain, might be dreams of return   15
Here, to these things that were.

Remembering ills, though slight
Yet irremediable,
Brings a worse, an impurer pang
Than remembering what was well.   20

No: I cannot go back,
And would not if I could.
Until blindness come, I must wait
And blink at what is not good.

THE OWL

Downhill I came, hungry, and yet not starved;
Cold, yet had heat within me that was proof
Against the North wind; tired, yet so that rest
Had seemed the sweetest thing under a roof.

Then at the inn I had food, fire, and rest,   5
Knowing how hungry, cold, and tired was I.
All of the night was quite barred out except
An owl's cry, a most melancholy cry

Shaken out long and clear upon the hill,
No merry note, nor cause of merriment,   10
But one telling me plain what I escaped
And others could not, that night, as in I went.

And salted was my food, and my repose,
Salted and sobered, too, by the bird's voice
Speaking for all who lay under the stars,   15
Soldiers and poor, unable to rejoice.

THE CHILD ON THE CLIFFS

Mother, the root of this little yellow flower
Among the stones has the taste of quinine.
Things are strange today on the cliff. The sun shines so
    bright,
And the grasshopper works at his sewing-machine
So hard. Here's one on my hand, mother, look;   5
I lie so still. There's one on your book.

But I have something to tell more strange. So leave
Your book to the grasshopper, mother dear,—

Like a green knight in a dazzling market-place,—
And listen now. Can you hear what I hear   10
Far out? Now and then the foam there curls
And stretches a white arm out like a girl's.

Fishes and gulls ring no bells. There cannot be
A chapel or church between here and Devon,
With fishes or gulls ringing its bell,—hark!—   15
Somewhere under the sea or up in heaven.
'It's the bell, my son, out in the bay
On the buoy. It does sound sweet today.'

Sweeter I never heard, mother, no, not in all Wales.
I should like to be lying under that foam,   20
Dead, but able to hear the sound of the bell,
And certain that you would often come
And rest, listening happily.
I should be happy if that could be.

THE BRIDGE

I have come a long way today:
On a strange bridge alone,
Remembering friends, old friends,
I rest, without smile or moan,
As they remember me without smile or moan.   5

All are behind, the kind
And the unkind too, no more
Tonight than a dream. The stream
Runs softly yet drowns the Past,
The dark-lit stream has drowned the Future and the
      Past.   10

No traveller has rest more blest
Than this moment brief between
Two lives, when the Night's first lights
And shades hide what has never been,
Things goodlier, lovelier, dearer, than will be or have
    been.   15

GOOD-NIGHT

The skylarks are far behind that sang over the down;
I can hear no more those suburb nightingales;
Thrushes and blackbirds sing in the gardens of the town
In vain: the noise of man, beast, and machine prevails.

But the call of children in the unfamiliar streets   5
That echo with a familiar twilight echoing,
Sweet as the voice of nightingale or lark, completes
A magic of strange welcome, so that I seem a king

Among man, beast, machine, bird, child, and the ghost
That in the echo lives and with the echo dies.   10
The friendless town is friendly; homeless, I am not lost;
Though I know none of these doors, and meet but
    strangers' eyes.

Never again, perhaps, after tomorrow, shall
I see these homely streets, these church windows alight,
Not a man or woman or child among them all: 15
But it is All Friends' Night, a traveller's good-night.

BUT THESE THINGS ALSO

But these things also are Spring's—
On banks by the roadside the grass
Long-dead that is greyer now
Than all the Winter it was;

The shell of a little snail bleached   5
In the grass; chip of flint, and mite
Of chalk; and the small birds' dung
In splashes of purest white:

All the white things a man mistakes
For earliest violets   10
Who seeks through Winter's ruins
Something to pay Winter's debts,

While the North blows, and starling flocks
By chattering on and on
Keep their spirits up in the mist,   15
And Spring's here, Winter's not gone.

THE NEW HOUSE

Now first, as I shut the door,
    I was alone
In the new house; and the wind
    Began to moan.

Old at once was the house,   5
    And I was old;
My ears were teased with the dread
    Of what was foretold,

58

Nights of storm, days of mist, without end;
  Sad days when the sun   10
Shone in vain: old griefs and griefs
  Not yet begun.

All was foretold me; naught
  Could I foresee;
But I learned how the wind would sound   15
  After these things should be.

THE BARN AND THE DOWN

    It stood in the sunset sky
    Like the straight-backed down,
    Many a time—the barn
    At the edge of the town,

    So huge and dark that it seemed   5
    It was the hill
    Till the gable's precipice proved
    It impossible.

    Then the great down in the west
    Grew into sight,   10
    A barn stored full to the ridge
    With black of night;

    And the barn fell to a barn
    Or even less
    Before critical eyes and its own   15
    Late mightiness.

    But far down and near barn and I
    Since then have smiled,

Having seen my new cautiousness
By itself beguiled   20

To disdain what seemed the barn
Till a few steps changed
It past all doubt to the down;
So the barn was avenged.

SOWING

It was a perfect day
For sowing; just
As sweet and dry was the ground
As tobacco-dust.

I tasted deep the hour   5
Between the far
Owl's chuckling first soft cry
And the first star.

A long stretched hour it was;
Nothing undone   10
Remained; the early seeds
All safely sown.

And now, hark at the rain,
Windless and light,
Half a kiss, half a tear,   15
Saying good-night.

MARCH THE THIRD

Here again (she said) is March the third
And twelve hours' singing for the bird
'Twixt dawn and dusk, from half-past six
To half-past six, never unheard.

'Tis Sunday, and the church-bells end   5
When the birds do. I think they blend
Now better than they will when passed
Is this unnamed, unmarked godsend.

Or do all mark, and none dares say,
How it may shift and long delay,   10
Somewhere before the first of Spring,
But never fails, this singing day?

And when it falls on Sunday, bells
Are a wild natural voice that dwells
On hillsides; but the birds' songs have   15
The holiness gone from the bells.

This day unpromised is more dear
Than all the named days of the year
When seasonable sweets come in,
Because we know how lucky we are.   20

TWO PEWITS

Under the after-sunset sky
Two pewits sport and cry,
More white than is the moon on high
Riding the dark surge silently;
More black than earth. Their cry   5

Is the one sound under the sky.
They alone move, now low, now high,
And merrily they cry
To the mischievous Spring sky,
Plunging earthward, tossing high,   10
Over the ghost who wonders why
So merrily they cry and fly,
Nor choose 'twixt earth and sky,
While the moon's quarter silently
Rides, and earth rests as silently.   15

WILL YOU COME?

Will you come?
Will you come?
Will you ride
So late
At my side?   5
O, will you come?

Will you come?
Will you come
If the night
Has a moon,   10
Full and bright?
O, will you come?

Would you come?
Would you come
If the noon   15
Gave light,
Not the moon?
Beautiful, would you come?

Would you have come?
Would you have come   20
Without scorning,
Had it been
Still morning?
Beloved, would you have come?

If you come   25
Haste and come.
Owls have cried;
It grows dark
To ride.
Beloved, beautiful, come.   30

THE PATH

Running along a bank, a parapet
That saves from the precipitous wood below
The level road, there is a path. It serves
Children for looking down the long smooth steep,
Between the legs of beech and yew, to where   5
A fallen tree checks the sight: while men and women
Content themselves with the road and what they see
Over the bank, and what the children tell.
The path, winding like silver, trickles on,
Bordered and even invaded by thinnest moss   10
That tries to cover roots and crumbling chalk
With gold, olive, and emerald, but in vain.
The children wear it. They have flattened the bank
On top, and silvered it between the moss
With the current of their feet, year after year. 15
But the road is houseless, and leads not to school.
To see a child is rare there, and the eye
Has but the road, the wood that overhangs

And underyawns it, and the path that looks
As if it led on to some legendary   20
Or fancied place where men have wished to go
And stay; till, sudden, it ends where the wood ends.

THE WASP TRAP

This moonlight makes
The lovely lovelier
Than ever before lakes
And meadows were.

And yet they are not,   5
Though this their hour is, more
Lovely than things that were not
Lovely before.

Nothing on earth,
And in the heavens no star,   10
For pure brightness is worth
More than that jar,

For wasps meant, now
A star—long may it swing
From the dead apple-bough,   15
So glistening.

A TALE

There once the walls
Of the ruined cottage stood.
The periwinkle crawls
With flowers in its hair into the wood.

In flowerless hours   5
Never will the bank fail,
With everlasting flowers
On fragments of blue plates, to tell the tale.

WIND AND MIST

They met inside the gateway that gives the view,
A hollow land as vast as heaven. 'It is
A pleasant day, sir.' 'A very pleasant day.'
'And what a view here! If you like angled fields
Of grass and grain bounded by oak and thorn,   5
Here is a league. Had we with Germany
To play upon this board it could not be
More dear than April has made it with a smile.
The fields beyond that league close in together
And merge, even as our days into the past,   10
Into one wood that has a shining pane
Of water. Then the hills of the horizon—
That is how I should make hills had I to show
One who would never see them what hills were like.'
'Yes. Sixty miles of South Downs at one glance.   15
Sometimes a man feels proud of them, as if
He had just created them with one mighty thought.'
'That house, though modern, could not be better planned
For its position. I never liked a new
House better. Could you tell me who lives in it?'   20
'No one.' 'Ah—and I was peopling all
Those windows on the south with happy eyes,
The terrace under them with happy feet;
Girls——' 'Sir, I know. I know. I have seen that house
Through mist look lovely as a castle in Spain,   25
And airier. I have thought: ''Twere happy there
To live.' And I have laughed at that

Because I lived there then.' 'Extraordinary.'
'Yes, with my furniture and family
Still in it, I, knowing every nook of it   30
And loving none, and in fact hating it.'
'Dear me! How could that be? But pardon me.'
'No offence. Doubtless the house was not to blame,
But the eye watching from those windows saw,
Many a day, day after day, mist—mist   35
Like chaos surging back—and felt itself
Alone in all the world, marooned alone.
We lived in clouds, on a cliff's edge almost
(You see), and if clouds went, the visible earth
Lay too far off beneath and like a cloud.   40
I did not know it was the earth I loved
Until I tried to live there in the clouds
And the earth turned to cloud.' 'You had a garden
Of flint and clay, too.' 'True; that was real enough.
The flint was the one crop that never failed.   45
The clay first broke my heart, and then my back;
And the back heals not. There were other things
Real, too. In that room at the gable a child
Was born while the wind chilled a summer dawn:
Never looked grey mind on a greyer one   50
Than when the child's cry broke above the groans.'
'I hope they were both spared.' 'They were. Oh yes!
But flint and clay and childbirth were too real
For this cloud-castle. I had forgot the wind.
Pray do not let me get on to the wind.   55
You would not understand about the wind.
It is my subject, and compared with me
Those who have always lived on the firm ground
Are quite unreal in this matter of the wind.
There were whole days and nights when the wind
    and I   60
Between us shared the world, and the wind ruled
And I obeyed it and forgot the mist.

My past and the past of the world were in the wind.
Now you may say that though you understand
And feel for me, and so on, you yourself   65
Would find it different. You are all like that
If once you stand here free from wind and mist:
I might as well be talking to wind and mist.
You would believe the house-agent's young man
Who gives no heed to anything I say.   70
Good morning. But one word. I want to admit
That I would try the house once more, if I could;
As I should like to try being young again.'

A GENTLEMAN

'He has robbed two clubs. The judge at Salisbury
Can't give him more than he undoubtedly
Deserves. The scoundrel! Look at his photograph!
A lady-killer! Hanging's too good by half
For such as he.' So said the stranger, one   5
With crimes yet undiscovered or undone.
But at the inn the Gipsy dame began:
'Now he was what I call a gentleman.
He went along with Carrie, and when she
Had a baby he paid up so readily   10
His half a crown. Just like him. A crown'd have been
More like him. For I never knew him mean.
Oh! but he was such a nice gentleman. Oh!
Last time we met he said if me and Joe
Was anywhere near we must be sure and call.   15
He put his arms around our Amos all
As if he were his own son. I pray God
Save him from justice! Nicer man never trod.'

67

LOB

At hawthorn-time in Wiltshire travelling
In search of something chance would never bring,
An old man's face, by life and weather cut
And coloured,—rough, brown, sweet as any nut,—
A land face, sea-blue-eyed,—hung in my mind   5
When I had left him many a mile behind.
All he said was: 'Nobody can't stop 'ee. It's
A footpath, right enough. You see those bits
Of mounds—that's where they opened up the barrows
Sixty years since, while I was scaring sparrows.   10
They thought as there was something to find there,
But couldn't find it, by digging, anywhere.'

To turn back then and seek him, where was the use?
There were three Manningfords,—Abbots, Bohun,
    and Bruce:
And whether Alton, not Manningford, it was,   15
My memory could not decide, because
There was both Alton Barnes and Alton Priors.
All had their churches, graveyards, farms, and byres,
Lurking to one side up the paths and lanes,
Seldom well seen except by aeroplanes;   20
And when bells rang, or pigs squealed, or cocks
    crowed,
Then only heard. Ages ago the road
Approached. The people stood and looked and turned,
Nor asked it to come nearer, nor yet learned
To move out there and dwell in all men's dust.   25
And yet withal they shot the weatherock, just
Because 'twas he crowed out of tune, they said:
So now the copper weathercock is dead.
If they had reaped their dandelions and sold
Them fairly, they could have afforded gold.   30

Many years passed, and I went back again
Among those villages, and looked for men
Who might have known my ancient. He himself
Had long been dead or laid upon the shelf,
I thought. One man I asked about him roared   35
At my description: "'Tis old Bottlesford
He means, Bill.' But another said: 'Of course,
It was Jack Button up at the White Horse.
He's dead, sir, these three years.' This lasted till
A girl proposed Walker of Walker's Hill,   40
'Old Adam Walker. Adam's Point you'll see
Marked on the maps.'

                    'That was her roguery,'
The next man said. He was a squire's son
Who loved wild bird and beast, and dog and gun
For killing them. He had loved them from his birth,   45
One with another, as he loved the earth.
'The man may be like Button, or Walker, or
Like Bottlesford, that you want, but far more
He sounds like one I saw when I was a child.
I could almost swear to him. The man was wild   50
And wandered. His home was where he was free.
Everybody has met one such man as he.
Does he keep clear old paths that no one uses
But once a lifetime when he loves or muses?
He is English as this gate, these flowers, this mire.   55
And when at eight years old Lob-lie-by-the-fire
Came in my books, this was the man I saw.
He has been in England as long as dove and daw,
Calling the wild cherry tree the merry tree,
The rose campion Bridget-in-her-bravery;   60
And in a tender mood he, as I guess,
Christened one flower Love-in-idleness,
And while he walked from Exeter to Leeds
One April called all cuckoo-flowers Milkmaids.

From him old herbal Gerard learnt, as a boy,   65
To name wild clematis the Traveller's-joy.
Our blackbirds sang no English till his ear
Told him they called his Jan Toy "Pretty dear."
(She was Jan Toy the Lucky, who, having lost
A shilling, and found a penny loaf, rejoiced.)   70
For reasons of his own to him the wren
Is Jenny Pooter. Before all other men
'Twas he first called the Hog's Back the Hog's Back.
That Mother Dunch's Buttocks should not lack
Their name was his care. He too could explain   75
Totteridge and Totterdown and Juggler's Lane:
He knows, if anyone. Why Tumbling Bay,
Inland in Kent, is called so, he might say.

'But little he says compared with what he does.
If ever a sage troubles him he will buzz   80
Like a beehive to conclude the tedious fray:
And the sage, who knows all languages, runs away.
Yet Lob has thirteen hundred names for a fool,
And though he never could spare time for school
To unteach what the fox so well expressed,   85
On biting the cock's head off,—Quietness is best,—
He can talk quite as well as anyone
After his thinking is forgot and done.
He first of all told someone else's wife,
For a farthing she'd skin a flint and spoil a knife   90
Worth sixpence skinning it. She heard him speak:
"She had a face as long as a wet week"
Said he, telling the tale in after years.
With blue smock and with gold rings in his ears,
Sometimes he is a pedlar, not too poor   95
To keep his wit. This is tall Tom that bore
The logs in, and with Shakespeare in the hall
Once talked, when icicles hung by the wall.
As Herne the Hunter he has known hard times.

On sleepless nights he made up weather rhymes   100
Which others spoilt. And, Hob being then his name,
He kept the hog that thought the butcher came
To bring his breakfast. "You thought wrong," said Hob.
When there were kings in Kent this very Lob,
Whose sheep grew fat and he himself grew merry,   105
Wedded the king's daughter of Canterbury;
For he alone, unlike squire, lord, and king,
Watched a night by her without slumbering;
He kept both waking. When he was but a lad
He won a rich man's heiress, deaf, dumb, and sad,   110
By rousing her to laugh at him. He carried
His donkey on his back. So they were married.
And while he was a little cobbler's boy
He tricked the giant coming to destroy
Shrewsbury by flood. "And how far is it yet?"   115
The giant asked in passing. "I forget;
But see these shoes I've worn out on the road
And we're not there yet." He emptied out his load
Of shoes for mending. The giant let fall from his spade
The earth for damming Severn, and thus made   120
The Wrekin hill; and little Ercall hill
Rose where the giant scraped his boots. While still
So young, our Jack was chief of Gotham's sages.
But long before he could have been wise, ages
Earlier than this, while he grew thick and strong   125
And ate his bacon, or, at times, sang a song
And merely smelt it, as Jack the giant-killer
He made a name. He too ground up the miller,
The Yorkshireman who ground men's bones for flour.

'Do you believe Jack dead before his hour?   130
Or that his name is Walker, or Bottlesford,
Or Button, a mere clown, or squire, or lord?
The man you saw,—Lob-lie-by-the-fire, Jack Cade,
Jack Smith, Jack Moon, poor Jack of every trade,

Young Jack, or old Jack, or Jack What-d'ye-call,   135
Jack-in-the-hedge, or Robin-run-by-the-wall,
Robin Hood, Ragged Robin, lazy Bob,
One of the lords of No Man's Land, good Lob,—
Although he was seen dying at Waterloo,
Hastings, Agincourt, and Sedgemoor too,—   140
Lives yet. He never will admit he is dead
Till millers cease to grind men's bones for bread,
Not till our weathercock crows once again
And I remove my house out of the lane
On to the road.' With this he disappeared   145
In hazel and thorn tangled with old-man's-beard.
But one glimpse of his back, as there he stood,
Choosing his way, proved him of old Jack's blood,
Young Jack perhaps, and now a Wiltshireman
As he has oft been since his days began.   150

DIGGING

Today I think
Only with scents,—scents dead leaves yield,
And bracken, and wild carrot's seed,
And the square mustard field;

Odours that rise   5
When the spade wounds the root of tree,
Rose, currant, raspberry, or goutweed,
Rhubarb or celery;

The smoke's smell, too,
Flowing from where a bonfire burns   10
The dead, the waste, the dangerous,
And all to sweetness turns.

It is enough
To smell, to crumble the dark earth,
While the robin sings over again   15
Sad songs of Autumn mirth.

LOVERS

The two men in the road were taken aback.
The lovers came out shading their eyes from the sun,
And never was white so white, or black so black,
As her cheeks and hair. 'There are more things than
    one
A man might turn into a wood for, Jack,'   5
Said George; Jack whispered: 'He has not got a gun.
It's a bit too much of a good thing, I say.
They are going the other road, look. And see her
    run.'—
She ran.—'What a thing it is, this picking may!'

IN MEMORIAM (EASTER, 1915)

The flowers left thick at nightfall in the wood
This Eastertide call into mind the men,
Now far from home, who, with their sweethearts, should
Have gathered them and will do never again.

HEAD AND BOTTLE

The downs will lose the sun, white alyssum
Lose the bees' hum;

73

But head and bottle tilted back in the cart
Will never part
Till I am cold as midnight and all my hours   5
Are beeless flowers.
He neither sees, nor hears, nor smells, nor thinks,
But only drinks,
Quiet in the yard where tree trunks do not lie
More quietly.   10

HOME

Often I had gone this way before:
But now it seemed I never could be
And never had been anywhere else;
'Twas home; one nationality
We had, I and the birds that sang,   5
One memory.

They welcomed me. I had come back
That eve somehow from somewhere far:
The April mist, the chill, the calm,
Meant the same thing familiar   10
And pleasant to us, and strange too,
Yet with no bar.

The thrush on the oaktop in the lane
Sang his last song, or last but one;
And as he ended, on the elm   15
Another had but just begun
His last; they knew no more than I
The day was done.

Then past his dark white cottage front
A labourer went along, his tread   20

Slow, half with weariness, half with ease;
And, through the silence, from his shed
The sound of sawing rounded all
That silence said.

HEALTH

Four miles at a leap, over the dark hollow land,
To the frosted steep of the down and its junipers black,
Travels my eye with equal ease and delight:
And scarce could my body leap four yards.

This is the best and the worst of it—   5
Never to know,
Yet to imagine gloriously, pure health.

Today, had I suddenly health,
I could not satisfy the desire of my heart
Unless health abated it,   10
So beautiful is the air in its softness and clearness,
        while Spring
Promises all and fails in nothing as yet;
And what blue and what white is I never knew
Before I saw this sky blessing the land.

For had I health I could not ride or run or fly   15
So far or so rapidly over the land
As I desire: I should reach Wiltshire tired;
I should have changed my mind before I could be in
        Wales.
I could not love; I could not command love.
Beauty would still be far off   20
However many hills I climbed over;
Peace would still be farther.

75

Maybe I should not count it anything
To leap these four miles with the eye;
And either I should not be filled almost to bursting
    with desire,   25
Or with my power desire would still keep pace.

Yet I am not satisfied
Even with knowing I never could be satisfied.
With health and all the power that lies
In maiden beauty, poet and warrior,   30
In Caesar, Shakespeare, Alcibiades,
Mazeppa, Leonardo, Michelangelo,
In any maiden whose smile is lovelier
Than sunlight upon dew,
I could not be as the wagtail running up and down   35
The warm tiles of the roof slope, twittering
Happily and sweetly as if the sun itself
Extracted the song
As the hand makes sparks from the fur of a cat:

I could not be as the sun.   40
Nor should I be content to be
As little as the bird or as mighty as the sun.
For the bird knows not of the sun,
And the sun regards not the bird.
But I am almost proud to love both bird and sun,   45
Though scarce this Spring could my body leap four
    yards.

THE HUXTER

He has a hump like an ape on his back;
He has of money a plentiful lack;
And but for a gay coat of double his girth

There is not a plainer thing on the earth
    This fine May morning. 5

But the huxter has a bottle of beer;
He drives a cart and his wife sits near
Who does not heed his lack or his hump;
And they laugh as down the lane they bump
    This fine May morning. 10

SHE DOTES

She dotes on what the wild birds say
Or hint or mock at, night and day,—
Thrush, blackbird, all that sing in May,
    And songless plover,
Hawk, heron, owl, and woodpecker. 5
They never say a word to her
    About her lover.

She laughs at them for childishness,
She cries at them for carelessness
Who see her going loverless 10
    Yet sing and chatter
Just as when he was not a ghost,
Nor ever ask her what she has lost
    Or what is the matter.

Yet she has fancied blackbirds hide 15
A secret, and that thrushes chide
Because she thinks death can divide
    Her from her lover:
And she has slept, trying to translate
The word the cuckoo cries to his mate 20
    Over and over.

SONG

At poet's tears,
Sweeter than any smiles but hers,
She laughs; I sigh;
And yet I could not live if she should die.

And when in June   5
Once more the cuckoo spoils his tune,
She laughs at sighs;
And yet she says she loves me till she dies.

A CAT

She had a name among the children;
But no one loved though someone owned
Her, locked her out of doors at bedtime
And had her kittens duly drowned.

In Spring, nevertheless, this cat   5
Ate blackbirds, thrushes, nightingales,
And birds of bright voice and plume and flight,
As well as scraps from neighbours' pails.

I loathed and hated her for this;
One speckle on a thrush's breast   10
Was worth a million such; and yet
She lived long, till God gave her rest.

MELANCHOLY

The rain and wind, the rain and wind, raved endlessly.
On me the Summer storm, and fever, and melancholy
Wrought magic, so that if I feared the solitude
Far more I feared all company: too sharp, too rude,
Had been the wisest or the dearest human voice.   5
What I desired I knew not, but whate'er my choice
Vain it must be, I knew. Yet naught did my despair
But sweeten the strange sweetness, while through the
    wild air
All day long I heard a distant cuckoo calling
And, soft as dulcimers, sounds of near water falling,   10
And, softer, and remote as if in history,
Rumours of what had touched my friends, my foes, or
    me.

TONIGHT

Harry, you know at night
The larks in Castle Alley
Sing from the attic's height
As if the electric light
Were the true sun above a summer valley: 5
Whistle, don't knock, tonight.

I shall come early, Kate:
And we in Castle Alley
Will sit close out of sight
Alone, and ask no light   10
Of lamp or sun above a summer valley:
Tonight I can stay late.

79

APRIL

The sweetest thing, I thought
At one time, between earth and heaven
Was the first smile
When mist has been forgiven
And the sun has stolen out,   5
Peered, and resolved to shine at seven
On dabbled lengthening grasses,
Thick primroses and early leaves uneven,
When earth's breath, warm and humid, far surpasses
The richest oven's, and loudly rings 'cuckoo'   10
And sharply the nightingale's 'tsoo, tsoo, tsoo, tsoo':
To say 'God bless it' was all that I could do.

But now I know one sweeter
By far since the day Emily
Turned weeping back   15
To me, still happy me,
To ask forgiveness,—
Yet smiled with half a certainty
To be forgiven,—for what
She had never done; I knew not what it might be,   20
Nor could she tell me, having now forgot,
By rapture carried with me past all care
As to an isle in April lovelier
Than April's self. 'God bless you' I said to her.

JULY

Naught moves but clouds, and in the glassy lake
Their doubles and the shadow of my boat.
The boat itself stirs only when I break
This drowse of heat and solitude afloat

To prove if what I see be bird or mote,　　　　　5
Or learn if yet the shore woods be awake.

Long hours since dawn grew,—spread,—and passed on
　　high
And deep below,—I have watched the cool reeds hung
Over images more cool in imaged sky:
Nothing there was worth thinking of so long;　　　10
All that the ring-doves say, far leaves among,
Brims my mind with content thus still to lie.

THE CHALK PIT

'Is this the road that climbs above and bends
Round what was once a chalk pit: now it is
By accident an amphitheatre.
Some ash trees standing ankle-deep in briar
And bramble act the parts, and neither speak　　　5
Nor stir.' 'But see: they have fallen, every one,
And briar and bramble have grown over them.'
'That is the place. As usual no one is here.
Hardly can I imagine the drop of the axe,
And the smack that is like an echo, sounding here.'　　10
'I do not understand.' 'Why, what I mean is
That I have seen the place two or three times
At most, and that its emptiness and silence
And stillness haunt me, as if just before
It was not empty, silent, still, but full　　　15
Of life of some kind, perhaps tragical.
Has anything unusual happened here?'
'Not that I know of. It is called the Dell.
They have not dug chalk here for a century.
That was the ash trees' age. But I will ask.'　　　20
'No. Do not. I prefer to make a tale,

Or better leave it like the end of a play,
Actors and audience and lights all gone;
For so it looks now. In my memory
Again and again I see it, strangely dark,   25
And vacant of a life but just withdrawn.
We have not seen the woodman with the axe.
Some ghost has left it now as we two came.'
'And yet you doubted if this were the road?'
'Well, sometimes I have thought of it and failed   30
To place it. No. And I am not quite sure,
Even now, this is it. For another place,
Real or painted, may have combined with it.
Or I myself a long way back in time . . .'
'Why, as to that, I used to meet a man—   35
I had forgotten,—searching for birds' nests
Along the road and in the chalk pit too.
The wren's hole was an eye that looked at him
For recognition. Every nest he knew.
He got a stiff neck, by looking this side or that,   40
Spring after spring, he told me, with his laugh,—
A sort of laugh. He was a visitor,
A man of forty,—smoked and strolled about.
At orts and crosses Pleasure and Pain had played
On his brown features;—I think both had lost;—   45
Mild and yet wild too. You may know the kind.
And once or twice a woman shared his walks,
A girl of twenty with a brown boy's face,
And hair brown as a thrush or as a nut,
Thick eyebrows, glinting eyes——' 'You have said
    enough.   50
A pair,—free thought, free love,—I know the breed:
I shall not mix my fancies up with them.'
'You please yourself. I should prefer the truth
Or nothing. Here, in fact, is nothing at all
Except a silent place that once rang loud,   55
And trees and us—imperfect friends, we men

82

And trees since time began; and nevertheless
Between us still we breed a mystery.'

FIFTY FAGGOTS

There they stand, on their ends, the fifty faggots
That once were underwood of hazel and ash
In Jenny Pinks's Copse. Now, by the hedge
Close packed, they make a thicket fancy alone
Can creep through with the mouse and wren. Next
    Spring   5
A blackbird or a robin will nest there,
Accustomed to them, thinking they will remain
Whatever is for ever to a bird.
This Spring it is too late; the swift has come.
'Twas a hot day for carrying them up: 10
Better they will never warm me, though they must
Light several Winters' fires. Before they are done
The war will have ended, many other things
Have ended, maybe, that I can no more
Foresee or more control than robin and wren.   15

SEDGE-WARBLERS

This beauty made me dream there was a time
Long past and irrecoverable, a clime
Where any brook so radiant racing clear
Through buttercup and kingcup bright as brass
But gentle, nourishing the meadow grass   5
That leans and scurries in the wind, would bear
Another beauty, divine and feminine,
Child to the sun, a nymph whose soul unstained

83

Could love all day, and never hate or tire,
A lover of mortal or immortal kin.   10

And yet, rid of this dream, ere I had drained
Its poison, quieted was my desire
So that I only looked into the water,
Clearer than any goddess or man's daughter,
And hearkened while it combed the dark green hair 15
And shook the millions of the blossoms white
Of water-crowfoot, and curdled to one sheet
The flowers fallen from the chestnuts in the park
Far off. And sedge-warblers, clinging so light
To willow twigs, sang longer than the lark,   20
Quick, shrill, or grating, a song to match the heat
Of the strong sun, nor less the water's cool,
Gushing through narrows, swirling in the pool.
Their song that lacks all words, all melody,
All sweetness almost, was dearer then to me   25
Than sweetest voice that sings in tune sweet words.
This was the best of May—the small brown birds
Wisely reiterating endlessly
What no man learnt yet, in or out of school.

THE GLORY

The glory of the beauty of the morning,—
The cuckoo crying over the untouched dew;
The blackbird that has found it, and the dove
That tempts me on to something sweeter than love;
White clouds ranged even and fair as new-mown hay; 5
The heat, the stir, the sublime vacancy
Of sky and meadow and forest and my own heart:—
The glory invites me, yet it leaves me scorning
All I can ever do, all I can be,

Beside the lovely of motion, shape, and hue,   10
The happiness I fancy fit to dwell
In beauty's presence. Shall I now this day
Begin to seek as far as heaven, as hell,
Wisdom or strength to match this beauty, start
And tread the pale dust pitted with small dark drops, 15
In hope to find whatever it is I seek,
Hearkening to short-lived happy-seeming things
That we know naught of, in the hazel copse?
Or must I be content with discontent
As larks and swallows are perhaps with wings?   20
And shall I ask at the day's end once more
What beauty is, and what I can have meant
By happiness? And shall I let all go,
Glad, weary, or both? Or shall I perhaps know
That I was happy oft and oft before,   25
Awhile forgetting how I am fast pent,
How dreary-swift, with naught to travel to,
Is Time? I cannot bite the day to the core.

I BUILT MYSELF A HOUSE OF GLASS

> I built myself a house of glass:
> It took me years to make it:
> And I was proud. But now, alas!
> Would God someone would break it.
>
> But it looks too magnificent.   5
> No neighbour casts a stone
> From where he dwells, in tenement
> Or palace of glass, alone.

WORDS

Out of us all
That make rhymes,
Will you choose
Sometimes—
As the winds use   5
A crack in a wall
Or a drain,
Their joy or their pain
To whistle through—
Choose me,   10
You English words?

I know you:
You are light as dreams,
Tough as oak,
Precious as gold,   15
As poppies and corn,
Or an old cloak:
Sweet as our birds
To the ear,
As the burnet rose   20
In the heat
Of Midsummer:
Strange as the races
Of dead and unborn:
Strange and sweet   25
Equally,
And familiar,
To the eye,
As the dearest faces
That a man knows,   30
And as lost homes are:
But though older far
Than oldest yew,—

As our hills are, old,—
Worn new   35
Again and again:
Young as our streams
After rain:
And as dear
As the earth which you prove   40
That we love.

Make me content
With some sweetness
From Wales
Whose nightingales   45
Have no wings,—
From Wiltshire and Kent
And Herefordshire,
And the villages there,—
From the names, and the things   50
No less.

Let me sometimes dance
With you,
Or climb
Or stand perchance   55
In ecstasy,
Fixed and free
In a rhyme,
As poets do.

THE WORD

There are so many things I have forgot,
That once were much to me, or that were not,
All lost, as is a childless woman's child
And its child's children, in the undefiled
Abyss of what will never be again.   5
I have forgot, too, names of the mighty men
That fought and lost or won in the old wars,
Of kings and fiends and gods, and most of the stars.
Some things I have forgot that I forget.
But lesser things there are, remembered yet,   10
Than all the others. One name that I have not—
Though 'tis an empty thingless name—forgot
Never can die because Spring after Spring
Some thrushes learn to say it as they sing.
There is always one at midday saying it clear   15
And tart—the name, only the name I hear.
While perhaps I am thinking of the elder scent
That is like food; or while I am content
With the wild rose scent that is like memory,
This name suddenly is cried out to me   20
From somewhere in the bushes by a bird
Over and over again, a pure thrush word.

UNDER THE WOODS

When these old woods were young
The thrushes' ancestors
As sweetly sung
In the old years.

There was no garden here,   5
Apples nor mistletoe;
No children dear
Ran to and fro.

New then was this thatched cot,
But the keeper was old,   10
And he had not
Much lead or gold.

Most silent beech and yew:
As he went round about
The woods to view   15
Seldom he shot.

But now that he is gone
Out of most memories,
Still lingers on,
A stoat of his,   20

But one, shrivelled and green,
And with no scent at all,
And barely seen
On this shed wall.

HAYMAKING

After night's thunder far away had rolled
The fiery day had a kernel sweet of cold,
And in the perfect blue the clouds uncurled,
Like the first gods before they made the world
And misery, swimming the stormless sea   5
In beauty and in divine gaiety.
The smooth white empty road was lightly strewn

With leaves—the holly's Autumn falls in June—
And fir cones standing up stiff in the heat.
The mill-foot water tumbled white and lit   10
With tossing crystals, happier than any crowd
Of children pouring out of school aloud.
And in the little thickets where a sleeper
For ever might lie lost, the nettle creeper
And garden-warbler sang unceasingly;   15
While over them shrill shrieked in his fierce glee
The swift with wings and tail as sharp and narrow
As if the bow had flown off with the arrow.
Only the scent of woodbine and hay new mown
Travelled the road. In the field sloping down,   20
Park-like, to where its willows showed the brook,
Haymakers rested. The tosser lay forsook
Out in the sun; and the long waggon stood
Without its team: it seemed it never would
Move from the shadow of that single yew.   25
The team, as still, until their task was due,
Beside the labourers enjoyed the shade
That three squat oaks mid-field together made
Upon a circle of grass and weed uncut,
And on the hollow, once a chalk pit, but   30
Now brimmed with nut and elder-flower so clean.
The men leaned on their rakes, about to begin,
But still. And all were silent. All was old,
This morning time, with a great age untold,
Older than Clare and Cobbett, Morland and Crome, 35
Than, at the field's far edge, the farmer's home,
A white house crouched at the foot of a great tree.
Under the heavens that know not what years be
The men, the beasts, the trees, the implements
Uttered even what they will in times far hence—   40
All of us gone out of the reach of change—
Immortal in a picture of an old grange.

A DREAM

Over known fields with an old friend in dream
I walked, but came sudden to a strange stream.
Its dark waters were bursting out most bright
From a great mountain's heart into the light.
They ran a short course under the sun, then back   5
Into a pit they plunged, once more as black
As at their birth; and I stood thinking there
How white, had the day shone on them, they were,
Heaving and coiling. So by the roar and hiss
And by the mighty motion of the abyss   10
I was bemused, that I forgot my friend
And neither saw nor sought him till the end,
When I awoke from waters unto men
Saying: 'I shall be here some day again.'

THE BROOK

Seated once by a brook, watching a child
Chiefly that paddled, I was thus beguiled.
Mellow the blackbird sang and sharp the thrush
Not far off in the oak and hazel brush,
Unseen. There was a scent like honeycomb   5
From mugwort dull. And down upon the dome
Of the stone the cart-horse kicks against so oft
A butterfly alighted. From aloft
He took the heat of the sun, and from below.
On the hot stone he perched contented so,   10
As if never a cart would pass again
That way; as if I were the last of men
And he the first of insects to have earth
And sun together and to know their worth.
I was divided between him and the gleam,   15

The motion, and the voices, of the stream,
The waters running frizzled over gravel,
That never vanish and for ever travel.
A grey flycatcher silent on a fence
And I sat as if we had been there since   20
The horseman and the horse lying beneath
The fir-tree-covered barrow on the heath,
The horseman and the horse with silver shoes,
Galloped the downs last. All that I could lose
I lost. And then the child's voice raised the dead.   25
'No one's been here before' was what she said
And what I felt, yet never should have found
A word for, while I gathered sight and sound.

ASPENS

All day and night, save winter, every weather,
Above the inn, the smithy, and the shop,
The aspens at the cross-roads talk together
Of rain, until their last leaves fall from the top.

Out of the blacksmith's cavern comes the ringing   5
Of hammer, shoe, and anvil; out of the inn
The clink, the hum, the roar, the random singing—
The sounds that for these fifty years have been.

The whisper of the aspens is not drowned,
And over lightless pane and footless road,   10
Empty as sky, with every other sound
Not ceasing, calls their ghosts from their abode,

A silent smithy, a silent inn, nor fails
In the bare moonlight or the thick-furred gloom,
In tempest or the night of nightingales,   15
To turn the cross-roads to a ghostly room.

And it would be the same were no house near.
Over all sorts of weather, men, and times,
Aspens must shake their leaves and men may hear
But need not listen, more than to my rhymes.   20

Whatever wind blows, while they and I have leaves
We cannot other than an aspen be
That ceaselessly, unreasonably grieves,
Or so men think who like a different tree.

THE MILL-WATER

Only the sound remains
Of the old mill;
Gone is the wheel;
On the prone roof and walls the nettle reigns.

Water that toils no more   5
Dangles white locks
And, falling, mocks
The music of the mill-wheel's busy roar.

Pretty to see, by day
Its sound is naught   10
Compared with thought
And talk and noise of labour and of play.

Night makes the difference.
In calm moonlight,
Gloom infinite,   15
The sound comes surging in upon the sense:

Solitude, company,—
When it is night,—

93

Grief or delight
By it must haunted or concluded be.   20

Often the silentness
Has but this one
Companion;
Wherever one creeps in the other is:

Sometimes a thought is drowned   25
By it, sometimes
Out of it climbs;
All thoughts begin or end upon this sound,

Only the idle foam
Of water falling   30
Changelessly calling,
Where once men had a work-place and a home.

FOR THESE

An acre of land between the shore and the hills,
Upon a ledge that shows my kingdoms three,
The lovely visible earth and sky and sea
Where what the curlew needs not, the farmer tills:

A house that shall love me as I love it,   5
Well-hedged, and honoured by a few ash trees
That linnets, greenfinches, and goldfinches
Shall often visit and make love in and flit:

A garden I need never go beyond,
Broken but neat, whose sunflowers every one   10
Are fit to be the sign of the Rising Sun:
A spring, a brook's bend, or at least a pond:

For these I ask not, but, neither too late
Nor yet too early, for what men call content,
And also that something may be sent   15
To be contented with, I ask of Fate.

DIGGING

What matter makes my spade for tears or mirth,
Letting down two clay pipes into the earth?
The one I smoked, the other a soldier
Of Blenheim, Ramillies, and Malplaquet
Perhaps. The dead man's immortality   5
Lies represented lightly with my own,
A yard or two nearer the living air
Than bones of ancients who, amazed to see
Almighty God erect the mastodon,
Once laughed, or wept, in this same light of day.   10

TWO HOUSES

Between a sunny bank and the sun
The farmhouse smiles
On the riverside plat:
No other one
So pleasant to look at   5
And remember, for many miles,
So velvet-hushed and cool under the warm tiles.

Not far from the road it lies, yet caught
Far out of reach
Of the road's dust
And the dusty thought   10
Of passers-by, though each

95

Stops, and turns, and must
Look down at it like a wasp at the muslined peach.

But another house stood there long before: 15
And as if above graves
Still the turf heaves
Above its stones:
Dark hangs the sycamore,
Shadowing kennel and bones   20
And the black dog that shakes his chain and moans.

And when he barks, over the river
Flashing fast,
Dark echoes reply,
And the hollow past   25
Half yields the dead that never
More than half hidden lie:
And out they creep and back again for ever.

COCK-CROW

Out of the wood of thoughts that grows by night
To be cut down by the sharp axe of light,—
Out of the night, two cocks together crow,
Cleaving the darkness with a silver blow:
And bright before my eyes twin trumpeters stand,   5
Heralds of splendour, one at either hand,
Each facing each as in a coat of arms:
The milkers lace their boots up at the farms.

OCTOBER

The green elm with the one great bough of gold
Lets leaves into the grass slip, one by one,—
The short hill grass, the mushrooms small, milk-white,
Harebell and scabious and tormentil,
That blackberry and gorse, in dew and sun,   5
Bow down to; and the wind travels too light
To shake the fallen birch leaves from the fern;
The gossamers wander at their own will.
At heavier steps than birds' the squirrels scold.
The rich scene has grown fresh again and new   10
As Spring and to the touch is not more cool
Than it is warm to the gaze; and now I might
As happy be as earth is beautiful,
Were I some other or with earth could turn
In alternation of violet and rose,   15
Harebell and snowdrop, at their season due,
And gorse that has no time not to be gay.
But if this be not happiness,—who knows?
Some day I shall think this a happy day,
And this mood by the name of melancholy   20
Shall no more blackened and obscured be.

THERE'S NOTHING LIKE THE SUN

There's nothing like the sun as the year dies,
Kind as it can be, this world being made so,
To stones and men and beasts and birds and flies,
To all things that it touches except snow,
Whether on mountain side or street of town.   5
The south wall warms me: November has begun,
Yet never shone the sun as fair as now

While the sweet last-left damsons from the bough
With spangles of the morning's storm drop down
Because the starling shakes it, whistling what   10
Once swallows sang. But I have not forgot
That there is nothing, too, like March's sun,
Like April's, or July's, or June's, or May's,
Or January's, or February's, great days:
August, September, October, and December   15
Have equal days, all different from November.
No day of any month but I have said—
Or, if I could live long enough, should say—
'There's nothing like the sun that shines today.'
There's nothing like the sun till we are dead.   20

LIBERTY

The last light has gone out of the world, except
This moonlight lying on the grass like frost
Beyond the brink of the tall elm's shadow.
It is as if everything else had slept
Many an age, unforgotten and lost—   5
The men that were, the things done, long ago,
All I have thought; and but the moon and I
Live yet and here stand idle over a grave
Where all is buried. Both have liberty
To dream what we could do if we were free   10
To do some thing we had desired long,
The moon and I. There's none less free than who
Does nothing and has nothing else to do,
Being free only for what is not to his mind,
And nothing is to his mind. If every hour   15
Like this one passing that I have spent among
The wiser others when I have forgot
To wonder whether I was free or not,

Were piled before me, and not lost behind,
And I could take and carry them away   20
I should be rich; or if I had the power
To wipe out every one and not again
Regret, I should be rich to be so poor.
And yet I still am half in love with pain,
With what is imperfect, with both tears and mirth, 25
With things that have an end, with life and earth,
And this moon that leaves me dark within the door.

THE THRUSH

When Winter's ahead,
What can you read in November
That you read in April
When Winter's dead?

I hear the thrush, and I see   5
Him alone at the end of the lane
Near the bare poplar's tip,
Singing continuously.

Is it more that you know
Than that, even as in April,   10
So in November,
Winter is gone that must go?

Or is all your lore
Not to call November November,
And April April,   15
And Winter Winter—no more?

But I know the months all,
And their sweet names, April,

99

May and June and October,
As you call and call   20

I must remember
What died in April
And consider what will be born
Of a fair November;

And April I love for what   25
It was born of, and November
For what it will die in,
What they are and what they are not,

While you love what is kind,
What you can sing in   30
And love and forget in
All that's ahead and behind.

THIS IS NO CASE OF PETTY RIGHT
OR WRONG

This is no case of petty right or wrong
That politicians or philosophers
Can judge. I hate not Germans, nor grow hot
With love of Englishmen, to please newspapers.
Beside my hate for one fat patriot   5
My hatred of the Kaiser is love true:—
A kind of god he is, banging a gong.
But I have not to choose between the two,
Or between justice and injustice. Dinned
With war and argument I read no more   10
Than in the storm smoking along the wind
Athwart the wood. Two witches' cauldrons roar.
From one the weather shall rise clear and gay;

Out of the other an England beautiful
And like her mother that died yesterday.   15
Little I know or care if, being dull,
I shall miss something that historians
Can rake out of the ashes when perchance
The phoenix broods serene above their ken.
But with the best and meanest Englishmen   20
I am one in crying, God save England, lest
We lose what never slaves and cattle blessed.
The ages made her that made us from dust:
She is all we know and live by, and we trust
She is good and must endure, loving her so: 25
And as we love ourselves we hate her foe.

RAIN

Rain, midnight rain, nothing but the wild rain
On this bleak hut, and solitude, and me
Remembering again that I shall die
And neither hear the rain nor give it thanks
For washing me cleaner than I have been   5
Since I was born into this solitude.
Blessed are the dead that the rain rains upon:
But here I pray that none whom once I loved
Is dying tonight or lying still awake
Solitary, listening to the rain,   10
Either in pain or thus in sympathy
Helpless among the living and the dead,
Like a cold water among broken reeds,
Myriads of broken reeds all still and stiff,
Like me who have no love which this wild rain   15
Has not dissolved except the love of death,
If love it be for what is perfect and
Cannot, the tempest tells me, disappoint.

AS THE CLOUDS THAT ARE SO LIGHT

As the clouds that are so light,
Beautiful, swift, and bright,
Cast shadows on field and park
Of the earth that is so dark:

Even so now, light one! 5
Beautiful, swift and bright one!
You let fall on a heart that was dark,
Unillumined, a deeper mark.

But clouds would have, without earth
To shadow, far less worth: 10
Away from your shadow on me
Your beauty less would be,

And if it still be treasured
An age hence, it shall be measured
By this small dark spot 15
Without which it were not.

ROADS

I love roads:
The goddesses that dwell
Far along invisible
Are my favourite gods.

Roads go on 5
While we forget, and are
Forgotten like a star
That shoots and is gone.

On this earth 'tis sure
We men have not made   10
Anything that doth fade
So soon, so long endure:

The hill road wet with rain
In the sun would not gleam
Like a winding stream   15
If we trod it not again.

They are lonely
While we sleep, lonelier
For lack of the traveller
Who is now a dream only.   20

From dawn's twilight
And all the clouds like sheep
On the mountains of sleep
They wind into the night.

The next turn may reveal   25
Heaven: upon the crest
The close pine clump, at rest
And black, may Hell conceal.

Often footsore, never
Yet of the road I weary,   30
Though long and steep and dreary,
As it winds on for ever.

Helen of the roads,
The mountain ways of Wales
And the Mabinogion tales   35
Is one of the true gods,

Abiding in the trees,
The threes and fours so wise,
The larger companies,
That by the roadside be,   40

And beneath the rafter
Else uninhabited
Excepting by the dead;
And it is her laughter

At morn and night I hear   45
When the thrush cock sings
Bright irrelevant things,
And when the chanticleer

Calls back to their own night
Troops that make loneliness   50
With their light footsteps' press,
As Helen's own are light.

Now all roads lead to France
And heavy is the tread
Of the living; but the dead   55
Returning lightly dance:

Whatever the road bring
To me or take from me,
They keep me company
With their pattering,   60

Crowding the solitude
Of the loops over the downs,
Hushing the roar of towns
And their brief multitude.

THE ASH GROVE

Half of the grove stood dead, and those that yet lived
    made
Little more than the dead ones made of shade.
If they led to a house, long before they had seen its fall:
But they welcomed me; I was glad without cause and
    delayed.

Scarce a hundred paces under the trees was the interval— 5
Paces each sweeter than sweetest miles—but nothing
    at all,
Not even the spirits of memory and fear with restless
    wing,
Could climb down in to molest me over the wall

That I passed through at either end without noticing.
And now an ash grove far from those hills can bring   10
The same tranquillity in which I wander a ghost
With a ghostly gladness, as if I heard a girl sing

The song of the Ash Grove soft as love uncrossed,
And then in a crowd or in distance it were lost,
But the moment unveiled something unwilling to die   15
And I had what most I desired, without search or desert
    or cost.

FEBRUARY AFTERNOON

Men heard this roar of parleying starlings, saw,
  A thousand years ago even as now,
    Black rooks with white gulls following the plough
So that the first are last until a caw
Commands that last are first again,—a law   5

Which was of old when one, like me, dreamed how
A thousand years might dust lie on his brow
Yet thus would birds do between hedge and shaw.

Time swims before me, making as a day
   A thousand years, while the broad ploughland oak   10
   Roars mill-like and men strike and bear the stroke
   Of war as ever, audacious or resigned,
And God still sits aloft in the array
   That we have wrought him, stone-deaf and stone-
      blind.

THESE THINGS THAT POETS SAID

These things that poets said
Of love seemed true to me
When I loved and I fed
On love and poetry equally.

But now I wish I knew   5
If theirs were love indeed,
Or if mine were the true
And theirs some other lovely weed:

For certainly not thus,
Then or thereafter, I   10
Loved ever. Between us
Decide, good Love, before I die.

Only, that once I loved
By this one argument
Is very plainly proved: 15
I, loving not, am different.

THE UNKNOWN

She is most fair,
And when they see her pass
The poets' ladies
Look no more in the glass
But after her.   5

On a bleak moor
Running under the moon
She lures a poet,
Once proud or happy, soon
Far from his door.   10

Beside a train,
Because they saw her go,
Or failed to see her,
Travellers and watchers know
Another pain.   15

The simple lack
Of her is more to me
Than others' presence,
Whether life splendid be
Or utter black.   20

I have not seen,
I have no news of her;
I can tell only
She is not here, but there
She might have been.   25

She is to be kissed
Only perhaps by me;
She may be seeking
Me and no other; she
May not exist.   30

CELANDINE

Thinking of her had saddened me at first,
Until I saw the sun on the celandines lie
Redoubled, and she stood up like a flame,
A living thing, not what before I nursed,
The shadow I was growing to love almost,   5
The phantom, not the creature with bright eye
That I had thought never to see, once lost.

She found the celandines of February
Always before us all. Her nature and name
Were like those flowers, and now immediately   10
For a short swift eternity back she came,
Beautiful, happy, simply as when she wore
Her brightest bloom among the winter hues
Of all the world; and I was happy too,
Seeing the blossoms and the maiden who   15
Had seen them with me Februarys before,
Bending to them as in and out she trod
And laughed, with locks sweeping the mossy sod.

But this was a dream: the flowers were not true,
Until I stooped to pluck from the grass there   20
One of five petals and I smelt the juice
Which made me sigh, remembering she was no more,
Gone like a never perfectly recalled air.

'HOME'

Fair was the morning, fair our tempers, and
We had seen nothing fairer than that land,
Though strange, and the untrodden snow that made
Wild of the tame, casting out all that was
Not wild and rustic and old; and we were glad.   5

Fair too was afternoon, and first to pass
Were we that league of snow, next the north wind.

There was nothing to return for, except need,
And yet we sang nor ever stopped for speed,
As we did often with the start behind.   10
Faster still strode we when we came in sight
Of the cold roofs where we must spend the night.
Happy we had not been there, nor could be,
Though we had tasted sleep and food and fellowship
Together long.

          'How quick,' to someone's lip   15
The words came, 'will the beaten horse run home!'

The word 'home' raised a smile in us all three,
And one repeated it, smiling just so
That all knew what he meant and none would say.
Between three counties far apart that lay   20
We were divided and looked strangely each
At the other, and we knew we were not friends
But fellows in a union that ends
With the necessity for it, as it ought.

Never a word was spoken, not a thought   25
Was thought, of what the look meant with the word
'Home' as we walked and watched the sunset blurred.
And then to me the word, only the word,
'Homesick,' as it were playfully occurred:
No more.

          If I should ever more admit   30
Than the mere word I could not endure it
For a day longer: this captivity
Must somehow come to an end, else I should be
Another man, as often now I seem,
Or this life be only an evil dream.   35

THAW

Over the land freckled with snow half-thawed
The speculating rooks at their nests cawed
And saw from elm-tops, delicate as flower of grass,
What we below could not see, Winter pass.

IF I SHOULD EVER BY CHANCE

If I should ever by chance grow rich
I'll buy Codham, Cockridden, and Childerditch,
Roses, Pyrgo, and Lapwater,
And let them all to my elder daughter.
The rent I shall ask of her will be only   5
Each year's first violets, white and lonely,
The first primroses and orchises—
She must find them before I do, that is.
But if she finds a blossom on furze
Without rent they shall all for ever be hers,   10
Whenever I am sufficiently rich:
Codham, Cockridden, and Childerditch,
Roses, Pyrgo and Lapwater,—
I shall give them all to my elder daughter.

IF I WERE TO OWN

If I were to own this countryside
As far as a man in a day could ride,
And the Tyes were mine for giving or letting,—
Wingle Tye and Margaretting
Tye,—and Skreens, Gooshays, and Cockerells,   5
Shellow, Rochetts, Bandish, and Pickerells,

Martins, Lambkins, and Lillyputs,
Their copses, ponds, roads, and ruts,
Fields where plough-horses steam and plovers
Fling and whimper, hedges that lovers   10
Love, and orchards, shrubberies, walls
Where the sun untroubled by north wind falls,
And single trees where the thrush sings well
His proverbs untranslatable,
I would give them all to my son   15
If he would let me any one
For a song, a blackbird's song, at dawn.
He should have no more, till on my lawn
Never a one was left, because I
Had shot them to put them into a pie,—   20
His Essex blackbirds, every one,
And I was left old and alone.

Then unless I could pay, for rent, a song
As sweet as a blackbird's, and as long—
No more—he should have the house, not I: 25
Margaretting or Wingle Tye,
Or it might be Skreens, Gooshays, or Cockerells,
Shellow, Rochetts, Bandish, or Pickerells,
Martins, Lambkins, or Lillyputs,
Should be his till the cart tracks had no ruts.   30

WHAT SHALL I GIVE?

What shall I give my daughter the younger
More than will keep her from cold and hunger?
I shall not give her anything.
If she shared South Weald and Havering,
Their acres, the two brooks running between,   5
Paine's Brook and Weald Brook,

With pewit, woodpecker, swan, and rook,
She would be no richer than the queen
Who once on a time sat in Havering Bower
Alone, with the shadows, pleasure and power.   10
She could do no more with Samarcand,
Or the mountains of a mountain land
And its far white house above cottages
Like Venus above the Pleiades.
Her small hands I would not cumber   15
With so many acres and their lumber,
But leave her Steep and her own world
And her spectacled self with hair uncurled,
Wanting a thousand little things
That time without contentment brings.   20

AND YOU, HELEN

And you, Helen, what should I give you?
So many things I would give you
Had I an infinite great store
Offered me and I stood before
To choose. I would give you youth,   5
All kinds of loveliness and truth,
A clear eye as good as mine,
Lands, waters, flowers, wine,
As many children as your heart
Might wish for, a far better art   10
Than mine can be, all you have lost
Upon the travelling waters tossed,
Or given to me. If I could choose
Freely in that great treasure-house
Anything from any shelf,   15
I would give you back yourself,
And power to discriminate

What you want and want it not too late,
Many fair days free from care
And heart to enjoy both foul and fair,   20
And myself, too, if I could find
Where it lay hidden and it proved kind.

LIKE THE TOUCH OF RAIN

Like the touch of rain she was
On a man's flesh and hair and eyes
When the joy of walking thus
Has taken him by surprise:

With the love of the storm he burns,   5
He sings, he laughs, well I know how,
But forgets when he returns
As I shall not forget her 'Go now.'

Those two words shut a door
Between me and the blessed rain   10
That was never shut before
And will not open again.

WHEN WE TWO WALKED

When we two walked in Lent
We imagined that happiness
Was something different
And this was something less.

But happy were we to hide   5
Our happiness, not as they were
Who acted in their pride
Juno and Jupiter:

For the Gods in their jealousy
Murdered that wife and man,   10
And we that were wise live free
To recall our happiness then.

TALL NETTLES

Tall nettles cover up, as they have done
These many springs, the rusty harrow, the plough
Long worn out, and the roller made of stone:
Only the elm butt tops the nettles now.

This corner of the farmyard I like most: 5
As well as any bloom upon a flower
I like the dust on the nettles, never lost
Except to prove the sweetness of a shower.

I NEVER SAW THAT LAND BEFORE

I never saw that land before,
And now can never see it again;
Yet, as if by acquaintance hoar
Endeared, by gladness and by pain,
Great was the affection that I bore   5

To the valley and the river small,
The cattle, the grass, the bare ash trees,
The chickens from the farmsteads, all
Elm-hidden, and the tributaries
Descending at equal interval;   10

The blackthorns down along the brook
With wounds yellow as crocuses
Where yesterday the labourer's hook
Had sliced them cleanly; and the breeze
That hinted all and nothing spoke.   15

I neither expected anything
Nor yet remembered: but some goal
I touched then; and if I could sing
What would not even whisper my soul
As I went on my journeying,   20

I should use, as the trees and birds did,
A language not to be betrayed;
And what was hid should still be hid
Excepting from those like me made
Who answer when such whispers bid.   25

THE CHERRY TREES

The cherry trees bend over and are shedding,
On the old road where all that passed are dead,
Their petals, strewing the grass as for a wedding
This early May morn when there is none to wed.

IT RAINS

It rains, and nothing stirs within the fence
Anywhere through the orchard's untrodden, dense
Forest of parsley. The great diamonds
Of rain on the grassblades there is none to break,
Or the fallen petals further down to shake.   5

And I am nearly as happy as possible
To search the wilderness in vain though well,
To think of two walking, kissing there,
Drenched, yet forgetting the kisses of the rain:
Sad, too, to think that never, never again,   10

Unless alone, so happy shall I walk
In the rain. When I turn away, on its fine stalk
Twilight has fined to naught, the parsley flower
Figures, suspended still and ghostly white,
The past hovering as it revisits the light.   15

SOME EYES CONDEMN

Some eyes condemn the earth they gaze upon:
Some wait patiently till they know far more
Than earth can tell them: some laugh at the whole
As folly of another's making: one
I knew that laughed because he saw, from core   5
To rind, not one thing worth the laugh his soul
Had ready at waking: some eyes have begun
With laughing; some stand startled at the door.

Others, too, I have seen rest, question, roll,
Dance, shoot. And many I have loved watching.
  Some   10

I could not take my eyes from till they turned
And loving died. I had not found my goal.
But thinking of your eyes, dear, I become
Dumb: for they flamed, and it was me they burned.

THE SUN USED TO SHINE

The sun used to shine while we two walked
Slowly together, paused and started
Again, and sometimes mused, sometimes talked
As either pleased, and cheerfully parted

Each night. We never disagreed   5
Which gate to rest on. The to be
And the late past we gave small heed.
We turned from men or poetry

To rumours of the war remote
Only till both stood disinclined   10
For aught but the yellow flavorous coat
Of an apple wasps had undermined;

Or a sentry of dark betonies,
The stateliest of small flowers on earth,
At the forest verge; or crocuses   15
Pale purple as if they had their birth

In sunless Hades fields. The war
Came back to mind with the moonrise
Which soldiers in the east afar
Beheld then. Nevertheless, our eyes   20

Could as well imagine the Crusades
Or Caesar's battles. Everything
To faintness like those rumours fades—
Like the brook's water glittering

Under the moonlight—like those walks   25
Now—like us two that took them, and
The fallen apples, all the talks
And silences—like memory's sand

When the tide covers it late or soon,
And other men through other flowers   30
In those fields under the same moon
Go talking and have easy hours.

NO ONE CARES LESS THAN I

'No one cares less than I,
Nobody knows but God,
Whether I am destined to lie
Under a foreign clod,'
Were the words I made to the bugle call in the morning. 5

But laughing, storming, scorning,
Only the bugles know
What the bugles say in the morning,
And they do not care, when they blow
The call that I heard and made words to early this
    morning.   10

AS THE TEAM'S HEAD-BRASS

As the team's head-brass flashed out on the turn
The lovers disappeared into the wood.
I sat among the boughs of the fallen elm
That strewed an angle of the fallow, and
Watched the plough narrowing a yellow square   5
Of charlock. Every time the horses turned
Instead of treading me down, the ploughman leaned
Upon the handles to say or ask a word,
About the weather, next about the war.
Scraping the share he faced towards the wood,   10
And screwed along the furrow till the brass flashed
Once more.
      The blizzard felled the elm whose crest
I sat in, by a woodpecker's round hole,
The ploughman said. 'When will they take it away?'
'When the war's over.' So the talk began—   15
One minute and an interval of ten,
A minute more and the same interval.
'Have you been out?' 'No.' 'And don't want to,
    perhaps?'
'If I could only come back again, I should.
I could spare an arm. I shouldn't want to lose   20
A leg. If I should lose my head, why, so,
I should want nothing more. . . . Have many gone
From here?' 'Yes.' 'Many lost?' 'Yes, a good few.
Only two teams work on the farm this year.
One of my mates is dead. The second day   25
In France they killed him. It was back in March,
The very night of the blizzard, too. Now if
He had stayed here we should have moved the tree.'
'And I should not have sat here. Everything
Would have been different. For it would have been 30
Another world.' 'Ay, and a better, though
If we could see all all might seem good.' Then

The lovers came out of the wood again:
The horses started and for the last time
I watched the clods crumble and topple over   35
After the ploughshare and the stumbling team.

AFTER YOU SPEAK

After you speak
And what you meant
Is plain,
My eyes
Meet yours that mean,   5
With your cheeks and hair,
Something more wise,
More dark,
And far different.
Even so the lark   10
Loves dust
And nestles in it
The minute
Before he must
Soar in lone flight   15
So far,
Like a black star
He seems—
A mote
Of singing dust   20
Afloat
Above,
That dreams
And sheds no light.
I know your lust   25
Is love.

BRIGHT CLOUDS

Bright clouds of may
Shade half the pond.
Beyond,
All but one bay
Of emerald   5
Tall reeds
Like criss-cross bayonets
Where a bird once called,
Lies bright as the sun.
No one heeds.   10
The light wind frets
And drifts the scum
Of may-blossom.
Till the moorhen calls
Again   15
Naught's to be done
By birds or men.
Still the may falls.

EARLY ONE MORNING

Early one morning in May I set out,
And nobody I knew was about.
    I'm bound away for ever,
    Away somewhere, away for ever.

There was no wind to trouble the weathercocks.   5
I had burnt my letters and darned my socks.

No one knew I was going away,
I thought myself I should come back some day.

I heard the brook through the town gardens run.
O sweet was the mud turned to dust by the sun.   10

A gate banged in a fence and banged in my head.
'A fine morning, sir,' a shepherd said.

I could not return from my liberty,
To my youth and my love and my misery.

The past is the only dead thing that smells sweet,   15
The only sweet thing that is not also fleet.
    I'm bound away for ever,
    Away somewhere, away for ever.

IT WAS UPON

It was upon a July evening.
At a stile I stood, looking along a path
Over the country by a second Spring
Drenched perfect green again. 'The lattermath
Will be a fine one.' So the stranger said,   5
A wandering man. Albeit I stood at rest,
Flushed with desire I was. The earth outspread,
Like meadows of the future, I possessed.

And as an unaccomplished prophecy
The stranger's words, after the interval   10
Of a score years, when those fields are by me
Never to be recrossed, now I recall,
This July eve, and question, wondering,
What of the lattermath to this hoar Spring?

WOMEN HE LIKED

Women he liked, did shovel-bearded Bob,
Old Farmer Hayward of the Heath, but he
Loved horses. He himself was like a cob,
And leather-coloured. Also he loved a tree.

For the life in them he loved most living things,   5
But a tree chiefly. All along the lane
He planted elms where now the stormcock sings
That travellers hear from the slow-climbing train.

Till then the track had never had a name
For all its thicket and the nightingales   10
That should have earned it. No one was to blame.
To name a thing beloved man sometimes fails.

Many years since, Bob Hayward died, and now
None passes there because the mist and the rain
Out of the elms have turned the lane to slough   15
And gloom, the name alone survives, Bob's Lane.

THERE WAS A TIME

There was a time when this poor frame was whole
And I had youth and never another care,
Or none that should have troubled a strong soul.
Yet, except sometimes in a frosty air
When my heels hammered out a melody   5
From pavements of a city left behind,
I never would acknowledge my own glee
Because it was less mighty than my mind
Had dreamed of. Since I could not boast of strength
Great as I wished, weakness was all my boast.   10

I sought yet hated pity till at length
I earned it. Oh, too heavy was the cost!
But now that there is something I could use
My youth and strength for, I deny the age,
The care and weakness that I know—refuse   15
To admit I am unworthy of the wage
Paid to a man who gives up eyes and breath
For what would neither ask nor heed his death.

THE GREEN ROADS

The green roads that end in the forest
Are strewn with white goose feathers this June,

Like marks left behind by someone gone to the forest
To show his track. But he has never come back.

Down each green road a cottage looks at the forest.   5
Round one the nettle towers; two are bathed in flowers.

An old man along the green road to the forest
Strays from one, from another a child alone.

In the thicket bordering the forest,
All day long a thrush twiddles his song.   10

It is old, but the trees are young in the forest,
All but one like a castle keep, in the middle deep.

The oak saw the ages pass in the forest:
They were a host, but their memories are lost,

For the tree is dead: all things forget the forest   15
Excepting perhaps me, when now I see

The old man, the child, the goose feathers at the edge
    of the forest,
And hear all day long the thrush repeat his song.

THE DARK FOREST

Dark is the forest and deep, and overhead
Hang stars like seeds of light
In vain, though not since they were sown was bred
Anything more bright.

And evermore mighty multitudes ride   5
About, nor enter in;
Of the other multitudes that dwell inside
Never yet was one seen.

The forest foxglove is purple, the marguerite
Outside is gold and white,   10
Nor can those that pluck either blossom greet
The others, day or night.

THE GALLOWS

There was a weasel lived in the sun
With all his family,
Till a keeper shot him with his gun
And hung him up on a tree,
Where he swings in the wind and rain,   5
In the sun and in the snow,
Without pleasure, without pain,
On the dead oak tree bough.

There was a crow who was no sleeper,
But a thief and a murderer   10
Till a very late hour; and this keeper
Made him one of the things that were,
To hang and flap in rain and wind,
In the sun and in the snow.
There are no more sins to be sinned   15
On the dead oak tree bough.

There was a magpie, too,
Had a long tongue and a long tail;
He could both talk and do—
But what did that avail?   20
He, too, flaps in the wind and rain
Alongside weasel and crow,
Without pleasure, without pain,
On the dead oak tree bough.

And many other beasts   25
And birds, skin, bone, and feather,
Have been taken from their feasts
And hung up there together,
To swing and have endless leisure
In the sun and in the snow,   30
Without pain, without pleasure,
On the dead oak tree bough.

WHEN HE SHOULD LAUGH

When he should laugh the wise man knows full well:
For he knows what is truly laughable.
But wiser is the man who laughs also,
Or holds his laughter, when the foolish do.

HOW AT ONCE

How at once should I know,
When stretched in the harvest blue
I saw the swift's black bow,
That I would not have that view
Another day   5
Until next May
Again it is due?

The same year after year—
But with the swift alone.
With other things I but fear   10
That they will be over and done
Suddenly
And I only see
Them to know them gone.

GONE, GONE AGAIN

Gone, gone again,
May, June, July,
And August gone,
Again gone by,

Not memorable   5
Save that I saw them go,
As past the empty quays
The rivers flow.

And now again,
In the harvest rain,   10
The Blenheim oranges
Fall grubby from the trees

As when I was young—
And when the lost one was here—
And when the war began   15
To turn young men to dung.

Look at the old house,
Outmoded, dignified,
Dark and untenanted,
With grass growing instead   20

Of the footsteps of life,
The friendliness, the strife;
In its beds have lain
Youth, love, age, and pain:

I am something like that;   25
Only I am not dead,
Still breathing and interested
In the house that is not dark:—

I am something like that:
Not one pane to reflect the sun,   30
For the schoolboys to throw at—
They have broken every one.

THAT GIRL'S CLEAR EYES

(*Handel Street*)

That girl's clear eyes utterly concealed all
Except that there was something to reveal.
And what did mine say in the interval?
No more: no less. They are but as a seal
Not to be broken till after I am dead;   5

And then vainly. Every one of us
This morning at our tasks left nothing said,
In spite of many words. We were sealed thus,
Like tombs. Nor until now could I admit
That all I cared for was the pleasure and pain   10
I tasted in the stony square sunlit,
Or the dark cloisters, or shade of airy plane,
While music blazed and children, line after line,
Marched past, hiding the 'SEVENTEEN THIRTY-
NINE.'

WHAT WILL THEY DO?

What will they do when I am gone? It is plain
That they will do without me as the rain
Can do without the flowers and the grass
That profit by it and must perish without.
I have but seen them in the loud street pass;   5
And I was naught to them. I turned about
To see them disappearing carelessly.
But what if I in them as they in me
Nourished what has great value and no price?
Almost I thought that rain thirsts for a draught   10
Which only in the blossom's chalice lies,
Until that one turned back and lightly laughed.

THE TRUMPET

Rise up, rise up,
And, as the trumpet blowing
Chases the dreams of men,

As the dawn glowing
The stars that left unlit   5
The land and water,
Rise up and scatter
The dew that covers
The print of last night's lovers—
Scatter it, scatter it!   10

While you are listening
To the clear horn,
Forget, men, everything
On this earth new-born,
Except that it is lovelier   15
Than any mysteries.
Open your eyes to the air
That has washed the eyes of the stars
Through all the dewy night:
Up with the light,   20
To the old wars;
Arise, arise!

WHEN FIRST

When first I came here I had hope,
Hope for I knew not what. Fast beat
My heart at sight of the tall slope
Of grass and yews, as if my feet

Only by scaling its steps of chalk   5
Would see something no other hill
Ever disclosed. And now I walk
Down it the last time. Never will

My heart beat so again at sight
Of any hill although as fair   10
And loftier. For infinite
The change, late unperceived, this year,

The twelfth, suddenly, shows me plain.
Hope now,—not health, nor cheerfulness,
Since they can come and go again,   15
As often one brief hour witnesses,—

Just hope has gone for ever. Perhaps
I may love other hills yet more
Than this: the future and the maps
Hide something I was waiting for.   20

One thing I know, that love with chance
And use and time and necessity
Will grow, and louder the heart's dance
At parting than at meeting be.

THE CHILD IN THE ORCHARD

'He rolls in the orchard: he is stained with moss
And with earth, the solitary old white horse.
Where is his father and where is his mother
Among all the brown horses? Has he a brother?
I know the swallow, the hawk, and the hern;   5
But there are two million things for me to learn.

'Who was the lady that rode the white horse
With rings and bells to Banbury Cross?
Was there no other lady in England beside
That a nursery rhyme could take for a ride?   10
The swift, the swallow, the hawk, and the hern.
There are two million things for me to learn.

'Was there a man once who straddled across
The back of the Westbury White Horse
Over there on Salisbury Plain's green wall?   15
Was he bound for Westbury, or had he a fall?
The swift, the swallow, the hawk, and the hern.
There are two million things for me to learn.

'Out of all the white horses I know three,
At the age of six; and it seems to me   20
There is so much to learn, for men,
That I dare not go to bed again.
The swift, the swallow, the hawk, and the hern.
There are millions of things for me to learn.'

LIGHTS OUT

I have come to the borders of sleep,
The unfathomable deep
Forest where all must lose
Their way, however straight,
Or winding, soon or late;   5
They cannot choose.

Many a road and track
That, since the dawn's first crack,
Up to the forest brink,
Deceived the travellers,   10
Suddenly now blurs,
And in they sink.

Here love ends,
Despair, ambition ends;
All pleasure and all trouble,   15
Although most sweet or bitter,
Here ends in sleep that is sweeter
Than tasks most noble.

There is not any book
Or face of dearest look   20
That I would not turn from now
To go into the unknown
I must enter, and leave, alone,
I know not how.

The tall forest towers;   25
Its cloudy foliage lowers
Ahead, shelf above shelf;
Its silence I hear and obey
That I may lose my way
And myself.   30

THE LONG SMALL ROOM

The long small room that showed willows in the west
Narrowed up to the end the fireplace filled,
Although not wide. I liked it. No one guessed
What need or accident made them so build.

Only the moon, the mouse and the sparrow peeped   5
In from the ivy round the casement thick.
Of all they saw and heard there they shall keep
The tale for the old ivy and older brick.

When I look back I am like moon, sparrow, and mouse
That witnessed what they could never understand   10
Or alter or prevent in the dark house.
One thing remains the same—this my right hand

Crawling crab-like over the clean white page,
Resting awhile each morning on the pillow,
Then once more starting to crawl on towards age.   15
The hundred last leaves stream upon the willow.

THE SHEILING

It stands alone
Up in a land of stone
All worn like ancient stairs,
A land of rocks and trees
Nourished on wind and stone.   5

And all within
Long delicate has been;
By arts and kindliness
Coloured, sweetened, and warmed
For many years has been.   10

Safe resting there
Men hear in the travelling air
But music, pictures see
In the same daily land
Painted by the wild air.   15

One maker's mind
Made both, and the house is kind
To the land that gave it peace,
And the stone has taken the house
To its cold heart and is kind.   20

OUT IN THE DARK

Out in the dark over the snow
The fallow fawns invisible go
With the fallow doe;
And the winds blow
Fast as the stars are slow.   5

Stealthily the dark haunts round
And, when the lamp goes, without sound
At a swifter bound
Than the swiftest hound,
Arrives, and all else is drowned;   10

And star and I and wind and deer
Are in the dark together,—near,
Yet far,—and fear
Drums on my ear
In that sage company drear.   15

How weak and little is the light,
All the universe of sight,
Love and delight,
Before the might,
If you love it not, of night.   20

Notes

References

MS. abbreviations and the abbreviation for Thomas's unpublished letters to Robert Frost appear in the note on *MSS., Dating, and Placing of Poems*, p. 145. All other abbreviations are shown in the Bibliography, pp. 420–26.

From Prose to Poetry

Edward Thomas had produced over thirty books of prose, countless reviews, and a number of editions and anthologies before, on 3 December 1914, he wrote his first true poem. Coombes sensibly remarks: 'Speculation as to why Thomas came so late to writing poetry is perhaps no more profitable than speculation as to what he might have gone on to write if war had not ended his life' (p. 181). Yet Coombes himself, like most other critics of Thomas, cannot resist speculating: 'the whole character and temperament included what we call the "poetic sensibility," but included also the reticence and the self-distrust. He was as little the fool that rushes in as a man can be, and his profound regard for the poet's place and function must have added weight to his innate cautiousness' (p. 182). Scannell observes: 'The poetry of young men, except in very special circumstances, is affirmative, ecstatic and optimistic. When it is otherwise, it is obvious that a dramatic persona has been adopted. . . . [Thomas's] poetic personality was not and could not have been that of a young poet: he had to wait for maturity before he was ready to write his poems in their completed form . . .' (pp. 9–10).

Robert Frost has of course been given much of the credit for Thomas's metamorphosis (see Appendix A), although he modestly played down his contribution: 'All he [Thomas] ever got was admiration for the poet in him before he had written a line of poetry' (letter to J. W. Haines, *Selected Letters*, p. 263), or placed the emphasis elsewhere: 'I think [the war] has made some sort of new man and a poet out of Edward Thomas' (letter to Lascelles Abercrombie, p. 193). Cooke believes that the First World War indeed constituted 'the decisive influence' (p. 186): 'So intimately connected are his patriotism and his inspiration that had [Thomas] followed Frost to America he might have stopped writing altogether' (p. 190). Eleanor Farjeon's account features an outside influence (Frost), but her imagery also suggests that what took place was a *natural* development: 'In the autumn of 1914 Edward's own living stream was undammed. The undamming was Robert's doing when, after reading his friend's prose, he told him he had been a poet all his life, and with plain talk for his tools started the water flowing. From October [*sic*] onwards the poetry came down in spate, and produced in Edward's being the enharmonic change that made him, not a different man, but the same man in another key' (E.F., pp. 55–6). This might suggest that the war and Frost were at least as much catalysts as agents; that Thomas's own state of preparedness counted a great deal in the complex chain reaction that occurred.

Thomas's preparedness in 1914 was of two kinds: psychological and imaginative. He had first of all reached the turning point in a mental and spiritual struggle that had racked him for years. The letters to Gordon Bottomley document his

case-history, and there Thomas variously describes his
affliction as 'heavy glum restlessness' (p. 76), 'a devil' (p.
129), 'the damned blues' (p. 144), 'melancholy' (p. 152),
'depression' (p. 188), 'the blacks' (p. 218). Helen Thomas
speaks of 'his demon of melancholy' (W.W.E., p. 91); of
'attacks of gloom and wretchedness' which led at one period
to 'terrible days when I did not know where he was; or, if
he was at home, days of silence and brooding despair' (p. 116).
During this bout he went out one day with a revolver (see
W.W.E., pp. 116–17 and Thomas's story, 'The Attempt,'
L.A.T., pp. 160–73). Thomas experimented with opium,
consulted many doctors, and eventually in 1911 suffered
a nervous breakdown (see *Wind and Mist*, p. 65, and
notes). Part of his malady was the inability to communicate
with others—'social intercourse is only an intense form of
solitude' (L.G.B., p. 53); its greater part failure to come to
terms with himself (see *The Other*, p. 26, and notes): 'I am
always talking about personality & looking for it in others &
envying it in its most varying kinds, & am so conscious of my
own lack of it & so disgusted that daily (I think) I give myself
less & less chance of ever putting forth a little of it' (p. 96).
This double alienation, and the root of his evil, he most frequently characterised as 'self-consciousness.' It resulted in
his 'building himself a house of glass' or hall of mirrors which
conveyed nothing but endless unsatisfactory reflections. 'My
self criticism or rather my studied self contempt is now nearly
a disease' (L.G.B., p. 103).

Thomas's condition was to a considerable extent brought
about by circumstances and the state of his physical health:
'You don't know what it means to make £5 or £6 a week by
reviewing. This week for example, I read review books all
day on Monday & Tuesday, interrupted only by my little

lots of housework, lessons to Merfyn & meals. Then until tonight I have been reading & writing all day with the same interruptions. . . . And now I am so tired that I was amazed that I could merely enjoy some sea tales by John Masefield —also for review—an hour ago. My opinion therefore is worth nothing (except money). I greatly fear I cannot keep up to even my old standard. Original writing I dream about, but never get so far as to get out paper & pen for it. . . . The cuckoo is almost silent. The year has passed; the Spring has done without me; I have not had one good hour of standing still & forgetting time. But I make over £200 a year, or can expect to' (L.G.B., p. 87). 'My great enemy is physical exhaustion which makes my brain so wild that I am almost capable of anything & fear I shall some day prove it' (p. 78). Through overwork, its torture refined by creative frustration, Thomas may have suffered from chronic 'depression,' a type of mental illness that paints the world grey and reduces life to a dreary struggle to keep going: 'I am now uniformly low spirited, listless, almost unable to work, & physically incapable. I have no idea what it means, but I crawl along on the very edge of life, wondering why I don't get over the edge' (p. 160; cf. *Beauty*, p. 46, and see notes).

Thomas never went completely 'over the edge.' Friends, Nature, books, his own writing, provided many alleviations. There was also his obstinate courage, the buried conviction that he could save himself. Thomas seems to have 'felt light' at the end of the tunnel of self-analysis, to have consciously or unconsciously resisted certain forms of outside help because of some inexplicable value attaching to his independent struggle: 'seriously I wonder whether for a person like myself whose most intense moments were those of depression a cure that destroys the depression may not destroy the intensity— a *desperate* remedy?' (L.G.B., p. 163). The disease followed cycles, each of which brought him a tiny stage further (cf. *The Other*). After his breakdown in 1911: 'I am really beginning to see myself. I suppose it is a good thing. Will mystery or the light of common day succeed to the mist that used to seem mystery ?' (p. 216). Two years later, after a relapse: 'I am at last realizing I had better fight my battles instead of sending out lists of the opposing forces' (p. 230). He had by this time met Robert Frost, whose friendship accelerated the healing process and fulfilled a prophecy made in 1906: 'I feel sure that my salvation depends on a person' (p. 129). Frost's recognition of 'the poet in him' and the understanding this implied seems to have released Thomas's personality before it released his poetry. Thomas had been exposed to the world with a poet's extra sensitivity, but without a poet's extra skin, the built-in therapy of complete imaginative expression. His poems explore the same territory as his letters to Gordon Bottomley, but his poetry solves what he could not, and was itself the solution of his life.

Never having undergone the final stages of creative pressure, the bulk of Thomas's prose bears to his poetry the relation of peat to coal, or of coal to diamonds. Coombes's assessment is just: 'I do not think there is any prose work of Edward Thomas of which we can say that the quality is sustained. Inside the covers of a book by him we are likely to get different intentions, approaches, styles. Even a nature book with a definite theme is likely to be a mixture of plain reporting, live description, verbose description, strong or delicate feeling, "literary" feeling, and so on, with uneasy transitions from mood to mood, from subject to subject, from the actual to the "dream" and back again. But many pages, and many essays, have the interest and the beauty of individual writing ...' (pp. 47–8). Cooke, who finds more

dross and less ore, heads his chapter on the prose 'The Road
Not Taken.' But prose was, nevertheless, the road Thomas
took, even if as arduous and frustrating as the road of introversion. Unlike Robert Frost (see general note to *The Signpost*, p. 156) Thomas doggedly persisted down all the roads
open to him, and for more than fifteen years prose was the
only medium of his imagination. '. . . one of the most interesting things about the prose is the way in which it shows something of the writer's struggle through an accumulation of
themes, thoughts, attitudes, stylistic devices, towards sincerity,
the sincerity of vision and expression that the artist has to
win' (Coombes, pp. 19–20).

Thomas's critical prose, like his letters, was always distinguished by clarity of outline, instinctive reference to modern
spoken idiom, and a firm grasp of rhythm. His imaginative
prose, however, took some time to catch up as he sloughed
off the influence of Pater and the Romantic essayists (he
could begin an essay on 'Inns and Books': 'With senses not
averse from the savoursome domesticities of the house . . .'),
habits of perception and diction formed by literature rather
than life: 'I always carry out into the fields a vast baggage of
prejudices from books and strong characters whom I have
met. My going forth, although simple enough to the eye, is
truly as pompous as that of a rajah who goes through the
jungle on a tall and richly encrusted elephant, with a great
retinue, and much ceremony and noise. As he frightens bird
and beast, and tramples on herb and grass, so I scatter from
my path many things which are lying in wait for a discoverer.
There is no elephant more heavy-footed and no rifle more
shattering than the egoism of an imitative brain' (H.E., pp.
153–4). Thomas's real prose master was Richard Jefferies; he
looked back to Borrow, Cobbett and Walton. Thus his
susceptibility to more precious influences and reluctance to

'leave out my "atmosphere" of fancy etc.' (L.G.B., p. 95) may denote, besides youthfulness, the ambition to be more than a 'Nature Writer.' The 'economy and observation' that Cooke admires (p. 105) in the diary notes at the end of *The Woodland Life* (1897) were undoubtedly the most important growth point in Thomas's prose, but the 'Romantic' effort to give pattern and colour to his vision mattered also.

It should be remembered, perhaps, that Thomas's problems of diction and stance were not unique: his struggle was the struggle of the age to liberate itself from the nineteenth century. He might at any point have been able to respond to the rhythmic innovations of Robert Frost (see Appendix A), but his prose develops significantly towards concreteness of style and unity of vision. Thomas achieved the 'leanness' (E.F., p. 51) of his brief, classic autobiography, *The Childhood of Edward Thomas* ('I feel the shape of the sentences & alter continually with some unseen end in view'); the tough, concise fantasy of *Four-and-Twenty Blackbirds*; the documentary sharpness or meditative ripeness of his 'war' essays (see *The Last Sheaf*). Fierce self-criticism made such development inevitable: 'Borrow and Jefferies sans testicles & guts' (of *The Heart of England*, L.G.B., p. 107); 'O Lord, my dipping into 15 closely written note books for solid details to support my soarings & flutterings about the South Country!' (L.G.B., p. 167). Yet he never gave up his talent, as he never gave up himself, but continued to nurture 'my silly little deformed unpromising bantling of originality,' 'the one thing in my life that resembles a hope—a desire, I mean' (L.G.B., p. 85). It was not only his compelled tasks, like *Beautiful Wales*, that frustrated Thomas by their inadequacy. His self-criticism accompanied a restless search for form, upon which he reported to Gordon Bottomley: 'There is no form that suits me, & I doubt if I can make a new form' (L.G.B., p. 57). 'I don't want to write at all, but if I do write, it must be about myself & I had rather do it *apropos* of landscape and imaginary people than popular authors' (p. 82). 'I regret you don't like the landscapes. For landscapes are what I seem to be made for, considering that I have tried for 10 years to do them, & am always trying' (p. 83). 'No other form ever occurs to me, tho I see that I may come to stories of some kind—not plotty cathartics, but episodes ending suddenly & soon; & that a novel is possible, & fine on account of its difficulties' (p. 93).

Thomas's prose shows him experimenting with pure observation and description, more rounded evocation of the countryside, the largely meditative or fanciful essay, 'episodes,' portraits and thinly disguised self-portraits, fantasies, even eventually the novel—*The Happy-Go-Lucky Morgans*. The latter marks one limit which Thomas came up against as a prose-writer: the inability to stop writing 'about himself,' to objectify his feelings as fiction: 'I dislike action and psychology' (L.G.B., p. 93). He had called a typical earlier essay in fictionalised autobiography ('July'), 'one of those crude mixtures of experience & invention which prove me no artist' (L.G.B., p. 206). *The Happy-Go-Lucky Morgans* is based on events in Thomas's London childhood and its best parts have the merit of his autobiography. However, it is certainly composed not of 'plotty cathartics,' or of plot, but of 'episodes ending suddenly & soon,' and derives only a two-dimensional unity from its focus, 'Abercorran House,' home of the magical Morgan family exiled from Wales. The various members and connections of the family, too, comprise a portrait gallery rather than a living nexus. Characters become pegs upon which Thomas hangs meditations—'Mr Stodham speaks for England'—or allegorical fantasies, like Aurelius's story of the 'battle of the green and scarlet' and Ann's of the

'Castle of Leaves.' At the same time there are signs that the various elements in the novel, which concentrates many features of previous books, reflect the different facets of a poetic imagination. One chapter, 'The House under the Hill,' in which Thomas adopts the persona of 'Mr. Torrance,' is crammed with poetic 'sources,' and the book's most powerful creation is wholly symbolic: the 'House of the Days,' 'with a window for every day of the year.' Philip Morgan dreams: 'A tiny figure, as solitary as the first star in the sky, paused at the threshold, to be swallowed up a moment later in darkness. At the same moment Philip awoke with a cry, knowing that the figure was himself' (p. 236).

Each successive Nature book by Thomas involved repetitions yet was differently organised, which suggests a continual effort to combine the same elements in a clinching form. Every attempt signalled some minor advance. In *The Heart of England* and *The South Country* he laid down his imaginative terrain; in *The Icknield Way* and *In Pursuit of Spring* he established his symbolism of the road or journey (and in the latter of the seasons). Again, the dutifully executed *Celtic Stories* and *Norse Tales* helped to nourish the very individual mythology that emerged in *Four-and-Twenty Blackbirds* and *Lob*. Even a loathed pot-boiler like *A Literary Pilgrim in England* gave Thomas the opportunity to relate literature to landscape more continuously than in any of his other books, and by implication to define his own artistic relation to England. In *The Happy-Go-Lucky Morgans* and *The Childhood of Edward Thomas* he probed and shaped his past life more intensively than ever before. The books on Jefferies and Borrow led to himself; while the studies of Pater, Swinburne and Maeterlinck confirmed the toppling of youthful idols in a rite of exorcism. Finally, the very fact that Thomas's poems were 'like quintessences of the best parts of my prose books' (letter to John Freeman, Moore, p. 326) indicates that there was something to distil. Although *The Heart of England, The South Country, The Icknield Way, In Pursuit of Spring* and *The Happy-Go-Lucky Morgans* proved perhaps the main channels of poetry, hardly a book is without some well-spring. The correspondences, the fact that Thomas required no additional apprenticeship (his first poem was a good poem), proclaim that content and imagery were ready to hand when the form was found.

MSS., Dating, and Placing of Poems

The chief MS. sources for Edward Thomas's poems are the British Museum MS. (B.M.), which covers the period 24 December 1914–24 May 1915, and the Bodleian MS. (Bod.), which covers the period 25 June 1915–24 December 1916. Another important source is the MS. held by the Lockwood Memorial Library of the State University of New York at Buffalo (L.M.L.), which contains Thomas's first poems (*Up in the Wind, November, March, Old Man, The Signpost*) and prose sketches which eventually became *Up in the Wind* and *Old Man*. The Berg Collection of the New York Public Library has an exercise book (B.C.) containing MS. drafts of five poems which also appear in B.M. (*The Unknown Bird, The Mill-Pond, Man and Dog, The Gypsy, Ambition*). B.M. and Bod. are notebooks in which Thomas made fair copies of his poems, although they were still subject to later alteration (B.M. exhibits the higher proportion both of redrafting and of divergence from C.P.). L.M.L. and B.C. are more heavily worked over, especially the former, and indicate the full evolution of the poems they contain.

The poems in all these MSS. appear in their order of composition. They are precisely dated by Thomas except in a very few instances. The sequence of poems in this edition follows the MS. chronology, the exact date of each poem's composition being given in the Notes. No MSS. of seven poems could be traced: *Interval, After Rain, The Other, The Mountain Chapel, Birds' Nests, The Glory* and *When First*. Professor R. George Thomas, however, considers there is enough evidence to support the view that Thomas either enclosed typescripts of the first five poems in a letter to Robert Frost dated 15 December 1914, or that he enclosed some of them. All five were certainly written before the end of 1914. These and other typescripts, together with Thomas's letters to Frost (which include some poems copied by hand) are in the possession of the Dartmouth College Library, New Hampshire (D.C.L.). The five poems have accordingly been inserted between *The Signpost* (L.M.L., 7 December 1914) and *The Manor Farm* (B.M., 24 December 1914) in a sequence chosen by the editor. *The Glory* has been placed between the last poem from B.M. and the first poem from Bod. Internal evidence puts *When First* among Thomas's last handful of poems (see note, p. 369).

L.M.L. 4 December 1914.

Thomas's essay, 'Recollections of November' (H.S., pp. 86–202), contains some scattered elements of the poem; as does a passage in *The South Country* (pp. 219–23), which also fathered *Interval* and *After Rain* written at the same period, (see note below).

1. *November's days are thirty.* This echoes the weather-rhyme: 'Thirty days hath September,/April, June and November . . .'

5–6. The imagery of 'dinting' and 'overprinting' reflects Thomas's scrupulous concern to reproduce his observations accurately. His 'eye' not only recorded the surface detail of landscape but penetrated its grain and texture. He proceeds to an almost microscopic analysis of the composition of mud.

21. *after-tempest cloud.* A favourite construction, cf. *Two Pewits* ('after-sunset sky') and in prose: 'At the dying of that windy day the wind is still; there is a bright pale half-moon tangled in the pink whirl of after-sunset cloud' (S.C., p. 21); 'The moon was mounting the clear east, and Venus stood with Orion in the west above a low, horizontal ledge of darkest after-sunset cloud' (I.P.S., p. 74). Another reference occurs in a sequence of thought which parallels 'One imagines a refuge there' etc.: 'Just before night the sky clears. It is littered with small dark clouds upon rose, like rocks on a wild and solitary coast of after-tempest calm, and it is infinitely remote and infinitely alluring. Those clouds are the Islands of the Blest. Even so alluring might be this life itself, this world, if I were out

19 of it' (S.C., pp. 219–20). 'One' in line 28 is thus evidently Thomas's less mature self, the dreamer of some of his prose, who has not fully grasped the complementary functions of 'earth' and 'sky.' The romantically vague language of 'in the pure bright' etc. parodies this past self. 'Another,' who 'sees' with Thomas's full poetic sanction, appreciates 'earth and November' at their true value. It is significant that the word 'earth' occurs five times in the stanza despite its skyward movement. This both reinforces Thomas's point and reveals his characteristic bias.

20

MARCH

L.M.L. 5 December 1914.

March complements *November*: together they initiate the seasonal movement that occurs between and within many of Thomas's poems (see note on lines 18–21 of *The Manor Farm*, p. 174). The poem derives particularly from the first chapter of *In Pursuit of Spring*—and thus perhaps from Robert Frost's advice (see p. 396)—which describes a sequence of March weather:

Snow succeeded, darkening the air, whitening the sky, on the wings of a strong wind from the north of north-west, for a minute only, but again and again, until by five o'clock the sky was all blue except at the horizon, where stood a cluster of white mountains, massive and almost motionless, in the south above the Downs, and round about them some dusty fragments not fit to be used in the composition of such mountains. They looked as if they were going to last for ever. Yet by six o'clock the horizon was dim, and the clouds all but

148

passed away, the Downs clear and extended; the black- **20**
bird singing as if the world were his nest, the wind cold
and light, but dying utterly to make way for a beautiful
evening of one star and many owls hooting.

The next day was the missel-thrush's and the north-
west wind's. The missel-thrush sat well up in a beech
at the wood edge and hailed the rain with his rolling,
brief song; so rapidly and oft was it repeated that it
was almost one long, continuous song. But as the wind
snatched away the notes again and again, or the bird
changed his perch, or another answered him or took his
place, the music was roving like a hunter's. . .
There followed days
of cloudy brightness, brightened cloudiness, rounded
off between half-past five and half-past six by blackbirds singing. The nights were strange children for
such days, nights of frantic wind and rain, threatening
to undo all the sweet work in a swift, howling revolution. Trees were thrown down, branches broken, but
the buds remained . . . With the day came snow, hail,
and rain, each impotent to silence the larks for one
minute after it had ceased. (pp. 26–7)

All the thrushes of England sang at that hour, and
against that background of myriads I heard two or
three singing their frank, clear notes in a mad eagerness
to have all done before dark; for already the blackbirds
were chinking and shifting places along the hedgerows.
(I.P.S., p. 178)

March concentrates, not only several March days into a
quintessential one, but also the whole spirit of *In Pursuit
of Spring* and of many passages in Thomas's prose (cf. his
chapters on 'The End of Winter' and 'Spring' in *The
South Country*, pp. 14–65). Thomas liked to plot the im-

20 perceptible progress of Spring despite continual rebuffs. It takes him nearly three hundred pages of *In Pursuit of Spring* to find 'Winter's grave.' (The symbolic structure of this journey itself anticipates the seasonal metaphors of the poetry.) Thomas's special interest in Spring seems more than conventional. The season of 'thaw,' release, regeneration naturally attracted a depressive temperament, the victim of long frustrations. As man and poet he eventually experienced a 'hoar Spring' (*It Was Upon*). In celebrating Spring's moral victory here, he celebrates his own. And Thomas, like the birds, was 'to pack into that hour/[His] unwilling hoard of song.'

March may have influenced Robert Frost's poem, *Our Singing Strength*.

7–9. *The sun filled earth and heaven . . . tears of joy*. Cooke finds these lines 'unsatisfactory' (p. 130) because they approach too nearly the inflated style of a prose equivalent in *Light and Twilight*; 'Day after day the sun poured out a great light and heat and joy over the earth and the delicately clouded sky . . . So mighty was the sun that the miles of pale new foliage shimmered mistily like snow . . .' (p. 1). Scannell calls the conceit a 'schoolgirl essay image' (p. 29).

21 31. *Stained with all that hour's songs*: 'we feel the silence not only as something enjoyed and as perhaps heralding a near spring but also as the silence which always comes back and which exists at the back of every sound; we note too that for the poet the silence was *stained*, equivocally but not deprecatingly—stain may beautify or mar, or beautify while it mars—"Stained with all that hour's songs" ' (Coombes, pp. 197–8).

L.M.L. 6 December 1914.

See Cooke (pp. 171–2) for the prose sketch, 'Old Man's Beard,' from L.M.L. Sketch and poem were, in fact, based on an actual childhood memory:

> With one of these friends, a girl, I went home once and in her back garden I first saw dark crimson dahlias and smelt bitter crushed stalks in plucking them. As I stood with my back to the house among the tall blossoming bushes I had no sense of any end to the garden between its brown fences: there remains in my mind a greenness, at once lowly and endless. (C.O.E.T., pp. 15–16)

The South Country contains the first stage of artistic evolution:

> Perhaps the happiest childhoods are those which pass completely away and leave whole tracts of years without a memory; those which are remembered are fullest of keen joy as of keen pain, and it is such that we desire for ourselves if we are capable of conceiving such fantastic desires. I confess to remembering little joy, but to much drowsy pleasure in the mere act of memory. I watch the past as I have seen workless, homeless men leaning over a bridge to watch the labours of a titanic crane and strange workers below in the ship running to and fro and feeding the crane ... I recall many scenes: a church and churchyard and black pigs running down from them towards me in a rocky lane—lads-love and tall, crimson, bitter dahlias in a garden—the sweetness of large, moist yellow apples eaten out of doors—children: I do not recall happiness in them, yet the moment that I return to them in fancy I am happy. (p. 133)

21   I once saw a girl of seven or eight years walking alone
down a long grassy path in an old garden. On one hand
rose a peaceful long slope of down; on the other,
beyond the filberts, a high hedge shut out all the pale
blue sky, with white clouds resting on its lower mist
like water-lilies on a still pool . . . For the child there
was no end to the path.

She walked slowly, at first picking a narcissus or two,
or stooping to smell a flower and letting her hair fall
over it to the ground; but soon she was content only
to brush the tips of the flowers with her outstretched
hands, or, rising on tiptoe, to force her head up amongst
the lowest branches of cherry-bloom. Then she did
nothing at all but gravely walk on into the shadow and
into Eternity, dimly foreknowing her life's days. (pp.
144–5)

'Old Man' is a cultivated shrub (clematis) related to
the 'wild clematis' or 'Traveller's-joy,' mentioned in *Lob*,
lines 65–6 and described also in *The Signpost*, lines 5–6.
' "Old man's beard" of the wild clematis flecking the
hedges; like the tail-feathers of a bird of paradise' (T.W.L.,
pp. 201–2). 'It is Old Man's Beard . . . from the long
feathery styles. But observe that the Old Man, as so frequently in English plant names, may also be the Devil'
(*The Englishman's Flora* by Geoffrey Grigson, Phoenix
House, 1958, p. 36). The plant played a continuing part
in Thomas's life: 'The Old Man or Lad's Love you gave
me is now a beautiful great bush at my study door' he
wrote to Gordon Bottomley in 1910 from Wick Green
(L.G.B., p. 201). His garden at Yewtree Cottage, however, provided the poem's immediate setting:

On three sides of the house was the garden in which the
soil was rich, having been cultivated for hundreds of

years. Between it and the garden of the big house next **21**
door was a hedge of tall wild damson trees, and here one
year to our infinite delight a nightingale sang. We soon
had the garden in order—vegetables mostly with a
border of flowers. By the only door into the house we
planted the herbs which [Edward] so loved. Rosemary,
thyme, lavender, bergamot and old man were there, all
direct descendants of our first country garden, which
we had propagated from cuttings each time we moved.
(W.W.E., pp. 144–5)

Old Man is a well-known poem; its reputation may have
been established by F. R. Leavis's praise in his pioneering
appreciation of Thomas (*New Bearings in English Poetry*,
pp. 61–4). Coombes discusses the poem in some detail
(pp. 193–5), as does C. Day Lewis in 'The Poetry of
Edward Thomas' (*Essays by Divers Hands*, XXVIII, 85–7):

On a first reading we might accept the poem at its face
value, as straight description of a homely experience.
We should allow that Thomas's rangy, flexible construction, with its qualifications, hesitations, digres-
sions and repetitions, is well adapted to the kind of
thinking aloud which is going on here; and that the
poem's subject—the attempt to recapture an evasive
memory—is well served by this groping manner of his.
But closer attention discovers, behind the properties
of the poem—the herb, the child, the garden—a
moralizing element none the less tenacious for being
subdued to the material in which it is working. "Old
Man, or Lad's-Love,—in the name there's nothing To
one that knows not Lad's-love, or Old Man"; he is
playing possum here, at the start: whether we know
the herb or not, we must be struck by the way its two
names contradict each other; and this paradox (*Old*

21 Man—*Lad's*-love) emblematically and obliquely introduces the first theme—the theme of age trying to recall
something out of its youth. Another hint follows immediately: "Growing with rosemary and lavender" brings
up the association of "rosemary for remembrance."
Then the poet admits that "Even to one that knows it
well, the names Half decorate, *half perplex*, the thing
it is": there is some enigma behind the herb and its
names; and indeed, behind his response to them. "And
yet I like the names," he says; then moves on to another
paradox, "The herb itself I like not, but for certain I
love it."

Old Man inaugurates the exploration of memory which
occupies so much of Thomas's poetry. It analyses the
very nature of the process before he goes on to pursue
individual memories in such poems as *Adlestrop*, *Over
the Hills*, *The Cuckoo* and *The Mill-Pond*. Mnemo-
syne (Memory) is the mother of Thomas's Muse in a
particularly significant sense. The poetry of a late starter
has inevitably a retrospective tendency: Thomas was
transmuting the experience of twenty years, and his habits
of mind and imagination compelled him to inspect
minutely the elusive 'meaning' of that experience. He
dealt with personal crisis by mining his own past, just as
he dealt with the external crisis of war by mining the
past of England. Thomas's later poems look forward
rather than back, but *Old Man*, like other early poems of
comparable scope (*The Signpost*, *The Other*), seems to
anticipate the whole cycle or circuit of his poetry. Its
'avenue' leads to 'darkness,' perhaps 'up to the forest
brink' of *Lights Out* (p. 132, see notes). In Thomas's
vision life emerges from the 'unknown' only to pass back
into it.

8. *And yet I like the names.* See notes on *If I Should Ever* **21** *by Chance*, lines 2–3 (p. 331) and *Lob*, lines 77–8 (p. 245) for the importance of 'names' to Thomas. *Old Man* is partly a poem about poetry. Thomas begins by investigating the resonance and suggestion of words themselves and the relation of 'name' to 'thing.' He then takes in actual experience and the long-term emotional results of experience in child and poet. The poem finally passes beyond language, experience, and conscious emotion to face what ultimately challenges all poetry: the unknown, unnamed layers of human personality and existence.

21–4. *Of garden rows . . . Forbidding her to pick.* In these **22** lines syntax and rhythm dramatise more emphatically than elsewhere the 'bent path' of memory. The technique is repeated in lines 36–9 to endow the negative, nonexistent 'path' with a ghostly tangibility.

39. *Only an avenue, dark, nameless, without end.* C. Day Lewis comments: 'as in so many of [Thomas's] poems, we are made gradually aware that the offered mystery—the Old Man or Lad's-love, and what it signifies, for example—is only a tributary, leading on to and swelling the mysterious river of existence itself. "Only an avenue, dark, nameless, without end": it is a sombre line: an avenue, by definition, must be leading to something: but an avenue without end—what is that leading to? So the poem closes on the greatest of its paradoxes, the darkest mystery of all' (op. cit., pp. 86–7). Nevertheless, despite the poem's overt statements, it has itself explored and illuminated as much of the avenue as is humanly and imaginatively possible. There may be reassurance, too, in the fact that Thomas has supervised the making of the child's memory.

THE SIGNPOST

23 L.M.L. 7 December 1914.

The Signpost resembles Robert Frost's famous poem
The Road Not Taken:

> Two roads diverged in a yellow wood,
> And sorry I could not travel both
> And be one traveller, long I stood
> And looked down one as far as I could
> To where it bent in the undergrowth; ...

> I shall be telling this with a sigh
> Somewhere ages and ages hence:
> Two roads diverged in a wood, and I—
> I took the one less travelled by,
> And that has made all the difference.

Frost indeed conceived *The Road Not Taken* as a parody
of Thomas, consciously assuming his friend's more
hesitant personality. In letters he teased Thomas for
failing to recognise its derivation. Lawrance Thompson
sums up Frost's account of the poem's genesis: 'While
living in Gloucestershire in 1914, Frost frequently took
long walks with Thomas through the countryside. Re-
peatedly Thomas would choose a route which might
enable him to show his American friend a rare plant or a
special vista; but it often happened that before the end of
such a walk Thomas would regret the choice he had made
and would sigh over what he might have shown Frost if
they had taken a "better" direction' (*Selected Letters of
Robert Frost*, introduction, p. xiv). Cooke, however,
questions Frost's story as an 'attempt to veil [the] "secret
places" of his mind from the over-curious,' using the two

poems (pp. 205–8) to illustrate the temperamental and **23** imaginative *differences* between the poets as they confront a similar situation. Nevertheless Frost knew his Thomas even if he did not know himself: 'I could not decide. If I went on foot, I could do as I liked on the plain. There are green roads leading from everywhere to everywhere. But, on the other hand, it might be necessary at that time of year to keep walking all day, which would mean at least thirty miles a day, which was more than I was inclined for' (I.P.S., p. 16). 'I looked at my maps. Should I go through Swindon, or Andover, or Winchester, or Southampton? I had a mind to compass all four; but the objection was that the kinks thus to be made would destroy any feeling of advance in the journey' (I.P.S. pp. 26–7). Moral choices, too, exacted obsessive deliberation or retrospection. At bad periods Thomas would 'spend hours, when I ought to be reading or enjoying the interlacing flight of 3 kestrels, in thinking out my motives for this or that act or word in the past until I long for sleep' (L.G.B., p. 129). In fact, the capacity for infinitely scrupulous discrimination became one of the strengths of his poetry. Frost was more impatient, and in his poem accepts half-wistfully the limitation of possibility consequent on decisive choice.

The Signpost appropriately marks the start of Thomas's poetic journey into himself. *The Other* also dramatises two tendencies of his nature and regards life as a pilgrimage of discovery. The 'journey,' perhaps Thomas's favourite metaphor, also defines his characteristic method: all his poems are stages in a quest, or a question, with *The Signpost* standing as question-mark. The ultimate 'goal' of the traveller is doubtful and rarely attained (see note on lines 17–18 of *I Never Saw that Land*

23 *Before*, p. 342). The situation presented in *The Signpost* resembles traditional folk-parables of choice, and Thomas exploits this archetypal dimension in his language and rhythms. For an extended analysis of the poem see C. B. Cox and A. E. Dyson, *Modern Poetry: Studies in Practical Criticism*, Arnold, 1963, pp. 48–51.

8–10. *A voice says ... never been born.* The first 'voice' corresponds to the absolutism of youth in requiring an immediate and unqualified decision. The second 'voice' is evidently older and wiser, and takes over (line 14 ff.) to analyse maturely the real complexity of life and choice.

11. *One hazel lost a leaf of gold.* The shortness of this line and a flattening out of stress in its first three syllables suggest the hazel's loss. A general rhythmic contrast with line 12 points up the relation between subtle flexibility and heavy emphasis in the overall rhythm of the poem. Thomas's descriptive matter moves through delicate variations of stress. When the second 'voice' moralises, however, stressed and unstressed syllables become more sharply distinguished to produce a gnomic jogtrot effect ('Whatever happens, it must befall' etc.), which is further enhanced by resounding rhymes. 'Be' (significantly) is rhymed three times and two couplets (lines 15–16, 19–20) receive a full feminine rhyme.

13. *what 'twould be.* Countrymen's expressions form a constant element in Thomas's poetic language—he had tried to make his later prose 'as near akin as possible to the talk of a Surrey peasant' (Julian Thomas, preface, C.O.E.T., p. 8)—but may be additionally exploited for special purposes. ''Twould' and ''twill' underline the traditional element in the situation. So, too, do phrases like 'it must befall,' 'between death and birth,' framed to evoke formulas of fairy tale and folk lore. (See general

note to *Lob*, p. 238, for Thomas's use of proverbial **23** speech.)

21–9. *and your wish . . . out in the air.* 'The life of Tirnanoge was all beautiful, being of a kind that men have always refused to think possible, because it was active and full of variety yet never brought death or decay, weariness or regret. This cannot easily be imagined by earthly men. They say that perfect happiness would be dull if it were possible. If they could imagine it, they would not love it so utterly when they possessed it like Ossian; many would refuse it because it wipes out the desire and the conscious memory of earth' (*Celtic Stories*, p. 78 and P.E.T., p. 152). Thomas was very much an 'earthly man,' fond of quoting (or misquoting) Wordsworth's affirmation that 'the very world' ('earth' in Thomas's versions) is 'the place where in the end/We find our happiness, or not at all' (1804 poem on the *French Revolution* and see *Prelude*, 1805, x, 726–8). Thus the homesickness predicted by the 'voice' also embraces the essential materials of his poetry: weather, day and night, land and sea, the seasons. The centrality and inclusiveness of this 'catalogue' (see note, p. 332) indicates that in *The Signpost* Thomas discovers his proper poetic focus and direction, his true 'voice'— that of a man 'standing upright out in the air/Wondering . . .'

30. *Wondering where he shall journey, O where?* The poem clearly comes full circle at this point. But although it may appear to end as it began, with a question-mark, the second voice has implied that earthly existence, with all its uncertainties, may be preferable to a 'heaven' where every question is answered. To be is a question.

No MS. of this poem or of *After Rain*, with which it
seems closely linked, survives (see p. 146). The poems
are mentioned together in a letter to Eleanor Farjeon
dated 10 January 1915 (E.F., p. 110). Lines 8–9 of *After
Rain* ('all that has/Been left by November of leaves')
point to a dating in early December. A passage in *The
South Country* anticipates both poems:

In the morning the ground is beautiful with blue light
from one white-clouded pane of sky that will not be
hidden by the tumultuous rain ... Beyond is forest
again. First, scattered cottages and little yellow apples
beaming pale on crooked trees; then solitudes of
heather and bracken, traversed and lighted by blue
waters, ponds and streams among flats of rushes; and
beyond, at either hand, woods on low and high land
endlessly changing from brightness to gloom under
windy clouds. The roads are yellow, and oaks and
beeches hang over them in whispering companies. The
wind reigns, in the high magnificent onset of the
clouds, in the surging trees, in the wings of rooks and
daws, in bowing sedges and cotton grass, in quivering
heather and grass, in rippling water, in wildly flying
linen; yet in the open there is a strange silence because
the roar in my ears as I walk deafens me to all sound ...

... And yet once more the road pierces the dense
woodland roar, form and colour buried as it were in
sound, except where a space of smoothest turf expands
from the road, and out of the crimson berries of an old
thorn comes the voice of a robin singing persistently;
and past that, inevitably, is a cottage among the beeches.
(pp. 220–2)

Scannell observes that 'all Edward Thomas's poems **24**
show a deliberate and fruitful opposing of contrasting
moods and attitudes and a counterpoising and reconciling
of the language in which these attitudes are embodied.
They reflect the ceaseless inner conflict and the struggle
for peace which never seemed to give him respite.' He
goes on to make the illuminating comment that *Interval*
'shows clearly the way in which Thomas used opposites
to create associative tensions which move gradually
towards the final reconciliation of "This roaring peace,"
the calm which is actually a suspended violence, the only
tranquillity which the poet had experienced' (see pp.
17–18).

3. *makes way*. 'I mean in "Interval" that the night did
postpone her coming a bit for the twilight. Night might
have been expected to come down on the end of day
and didn't. "Held off" would have been stricter' (E.F.,
p. 110). Stricter, but less powerfully ambiguous. 'Makes
way,' which suggests that night relinquishes a position
already gained, links a generous yielding in Nature with
the sense of release in Thomas himself.

24. '. . . "under storm's wing" was not just for the metre'
(E.F., p. 110).

AFTER RAIN   **25**

See note on MS. of previous poem.

Thomas employs the same 'limping' couplet form in
Head and Bottle.

'An interesting "rain" anthology could be compiled
from Thomas's writings' (Coombes, p. 89).

At all times I love rain, the early momentous thunder-

25   drops, the perpendicular cataract shining, or at night
the little showers, the spongy mists, the tempestuous
mountain rain. I like to see it possessing the whole
earth at evening, smothering civilization, taking away
from me myself everything except the power to walk
under the dark trees and to enjoy as humbly as the
hissing grass, while some twinkling house-light or
song sung by a lonely man gives a foil to the immense
dark force. I like to see the rain making the streets, the
railway station, a pure desert, whether bright with
lamps or not. It foams off the roofs and trees and
bubbles into the water-butts. It gives the grey rivers
a demonic majesty. It scours the roads, sets the flints
moving, and exposes the glossy chalk in the tracks
through the woods. It does work that will last as long
as the earth. It is about eternal business. In its noise
and myriad aspects I feel the mortal beauty of immortal things. (S.C., p. 281 and P.E.T., p. 120)

In Thomas's prose and poetry there is an image from the
'myriad aspects' of rain to match every facet and nuance
of feeling. It can represent an alien 'immense dark force'
(in *Rain*), or sympathise with human emotion or solitude:
'Half a kiss, half a tear' (*Sowing*). In *After Rain* it is 'both
dark and bright': a destroyer that has ravaged the scene,
and a creator, an artist, that has added new beauties.

17–18. *like little black fish, inlaid,/As if they played*. In
Thomas's fantasy 'The Castle of Leaves' (H.G.L.M., pp.
207–19) children watch, when the castle falls, 'the dead
leaves swim by like fishes, crimson and emerald and
gold' (p. 214). Thomas maintained a polite argument with
Eleanor Farjeon over these lines: ' "As if they played" I
was anxious to have in. It describes the patterns of the fish
but it comes awkwardly perhaps after inlaid.' Six days

later: 'I wonder whether I can do anything with "inlaid" **25**
and "played." The inlaid, too, is at any rate perfectly
precise as I saw the black leaves 2 years ago up at the top
of the hill, so that neither is a rhyme word only' (E.F.,
pp. 110–11). 'Inlaid' is an inlaid word.

24–5. *Uncountable/Crystals*. Thomas breaks the formal
mould of the poem just as it and the rainless lull ends.
The one-word line, enjambement and off-rhyme add up
to a more decisive departure from the norm than occurs
elsewhere; and, together with the liquid sounds, suggest
the brimming potential of the rain.

THE OTHER   26

The Other, Thomas's most sustained symbolic structure,
was among the first poems he wrote. No MS. survives
(see p. 146).

The poem is a prophetic microcosm of Thomas's whole
scope and development as a poet. Its allegorical landscape comprises the 'forest' of his last poems as well as
'the sum/Of what's not forest.' There are many premoni-
tions of subsequent poems. Thomas outlines the main
features of his imagery as well as a major symbolism, that
of the road or journey (see general note to *Roads*, p.
315). The conflicts of his inner life are thus acted out on a
universal stage. He had written to a friend in 1911: 'I hope
it [vegetarianism] will cure my head, which is almost
always wrong now—a sort of conspiracy going on in it
which leaves me only a joint tenancy and a perpetual
scare of the other tenant and wonder what he will do'
(Moore, p. 172).

Thomas's conception of 'the Other' or *alter ego* owes

26 something to the German legend of the 'doppelgänger,'
a sinister double who dogs one's footsteps. He first
sketched the idea in *In Pursuit of Spring*, a book which
has also fertilised the poem in subsidiary details. Throughout his journey 'from London to the Quantock Hills'
Thomas is intermittently haunted by a figure he dubs
the 'Other Man.' First sighted freeing a caged chaffinch,
then sketching a weather-vane, the 'Other Man' eventually appears before Thomas at an 'inn':

> At first I did not grasp the connection between this
> dripping, indubitably real man and the wraith of the
> day before. But he was absurdly pleased to recognize
> me, bowing with a sort of uncomfortable graciousness
> and a trace of a cockney accent. His expression changed
> in those few moments from a melancholy and too
> yielding smile to a pale, thin-lipped rigidity. I did not
> know whether to be pleased or not with the reincarna-
> tion, when he departed to change his clothes. (p. 119)

On a subsequent occasion Thomas reacts to a rhapsody
from the 'Other Man' about Nature:

> "I suppose you write books," said I. "I do," said he.
> "What sort of books do you write?" "I wrote one all
> about this valley of the Frome ... But no one knows
> that it was the Frome I meant. You look surprised.
> Nevertheless, I got fifty pounds for it." "That is a
> lot of money for such a book!" "So my publisher
> thought." "And you are lucky to get money for doing
> what you like." "What I like!" he muttered, pushing
> his bicycle back uphill, past the goats by the ruin, and
> up the steps between walls that were lovely with humid
> moneywort, and saxifrage like filigree, and ivy-leaved
> toadflax. Apparently the effort loosened his tongue. He
> rambled on and on about himself, his past, his writing,

his digestion; his main point being that he did not like **26**
writing. He had been attempting the impossible task
of reducing undigested notes about all sorts of details
to a grammatical, continuous narrative. He abused
notebooks violently. (pp. 219–20)

The 'Other Man' is Thomas's most sustained prose self-
portrait and self-parody, exaggerating his literary pre-
dilections and problems, his love of Nature and traditional things, his melancholy introversion. It is interesting
that in the poem the roles are reversed. The narrator
becomes this pest, the greater 'bore'; while 'the Other'
generally exemplifies the deeper, more elusive areas of the
poet's nature. The quest for 'the Other' is a quest for
self-knowledge; complementary aspects of Thomas move
towards integration. But the points at which they converge
are blurred: the whole action of the poem, in fact, takes
place inside one head. As with the 'goal' (see note, p.
342), the pursuit itself constitutes discovery.

2–4. *To feel the light ... the sweet mint.* A concentrated
sequence of sense impressions. '*Feel* the light' boldly
fuses different kinds of physical response, cf. '*tasted*
sunlight,' line 15. Thomas seems to evoke the first consciousness of childhood as well as the uncomplicated
reaction of youth or happiness to Nature.

17–20. *What to do ... until myself I knew.* Cooke comments: 'Even the syntax makes him the pursuer of
himself' (p. 204). Coombes makes the same point in his
discussion of the poem (pp. 217–20). The elliptical 'When
caught' could apply equally to the narrator and to 'the
Other', the knowing and the unknown self.

21. *the inns.* 'An impulse as sick and as profound as the
fatigue du nord, or as that which drove Richard Jefferies
from inland meadows to the sea, goads some of us to the

26 life of inns. Something, we may think, that overpowers the delicious sense of home, bids us exchange that for an abode that is a truer symbol of our inconstant lodging on the earth.' (H.S., p. 39)

29–30. *never-foamless shores/Make better friends than those dull boors*. A similar declaration to that in Shakespeare's song: 'Blow, blow, thou winter wind,/Thou art not so unkind/As man's ingratitude . . .' (*As You Like It*, II, vii). The 'boors' represent the insensitivity that hurt or repelled Thomas throughout his life.

27 32. *the unseen moving goal*: see note, p. 342.

37. *Desire of desire*. The narrator has rejected the facile 'remedies' which are substitutes for 'wholeness' and self-knowledge. He wants no antidote or anodyne for pain and longing: the conditions of life.

40. *I quite forgot I could forget*. The possibility of escape is no longer significant, let alone attractive. This advance in health subsequently opens a new door.

61–80. *I sought then in solitude . . . An old inhabitant of earth*. The setting of these stanzas owes something to Thomas's climactic portrayals of Salisbury Plain in *In Pursuit of Spring*: 'I emerged into the glory and the peace of the Plain, of the unbounded Plain and the unbounded sky, and the marriage of sun and wind that was being celebrated upon them' (p. 172). '. . . over the wall of [the Plain] rounded clouds, pure white and sunlit, were heaving up. Rain threatened again, but did no more. The late afternoon grew more and more quiet and still, and in the warmth I mistook a distant dog's bark, and again a cock's crowing, for the call of a cuckoo, mixed with the blackbird's singing' (p. 177). 'Solitude' is accepted as organic to the process of self-discovery: in life Thomas resolved his mental crises without the help of doctors, and his condition throughout his poetry is also 'solitary' (see **27** general note to *A Gentleman*, p. 229). This courage pays off. The poet strikes a balance between the different sides of himself, expressed by harmony with and within nature. His integration is ratified by the reconciliation of characteristic images: 'earth and sky,' light and darkness, become inextricably mingled. Thomas may in fact be celebrating the poise and release he found in poetry itself. 'The Other' is significantly absent from these stanzas, in which the two are one.

67. *crocketed*. Crockets are Gothic architectural orna- **28** ments in the form of buds or curled leaves. In *In Pursuit of Spring* Thomas describes Steeple Ashton church as 'bristling with coarse crockets all over, and knobby with coarse gargoyles' (p. 176).

80. *An old inhabitant of earth.* In 'The First Cuckoo' Thomas analyses our pleasure in recurrent seasonal events: 'I am not forgetting how much of the thrill may be due to the feeling of a fresh start, combined with that of being an old inhabitant of the earth' (L.S., p. 60).

81–7. *Once the name . . . Moments of everlastingness.* 'When . . . bowers' is a self-contained clause in which Thomas suggests an alternative description (to 'melancholy') of his state: 'happiness and powers/Coming . . ./And weaknesses quitting . . .' An understood 'I' is the subject of 'Smiled and enjoyed.' The odd syntax prolongs the poet's self-analysis, establishing a kind of past continuous tense which resembles a 'moment of everlastingness.' The 'melancholy'/'happiness' relation anticipates lines 18–21 of *October* (p. 97, see note).

87. *Moments of everlastingness.* Cf. Henry Vaughan, *The Retreate*: 'But felt through all this fleshly dresse/Bright *shootes* of everlastingnesse.' This echo suggests that

28 Thomas has arrived at the nearest he gets to a religious affirmation. *The Other* may also invoke another Metaphysical and religious poet, George Herbert. Coombes points out that 'the poem curiously recalls in one or two places *The Pilgrimage* of George Herbert ...: in that poem we have "A long it was and weary way," and "A wasted place, but sometimes rich"' (p. 217). On his spiritual journey Herbert passes through 'Fancies medow,' 'Cares cops' and 'the wilde of Passion' to reach 'the gladsome hill.' Like Thomas's 'goal,' Herbert's 'hill' is always 'further.' In his introduction to *The Temple* and *A Priest to the Temple* Thomas bestows on Herbert the accolade of a favourite quotation from Wordsworth's *Lark*: 'Type of the wise who soar, but never roam;/True to the kindred points of Heaven and Home!' He clearly appreciates the Englishness of Herbert's Anglicanism, but betrays no recognition that, despite his faith, Herbert's agonised self-questioning curiously resembles Thomas's own. Herbert's poetry explores a similar despair: 'Nothing performs the task of life' (*Affliction IV*), and a similar recovery: 'And now in age I bud again,/After so many deaths I live and write;/I once more smell the dew and rain,/And relish versing ...' (*The Flower*). In *Home* (p. 54, see general note) and *The Other*, however, the agnostic does seem to maintain an implicit dialogue with the Christian. Herbert plays a part, too, in *In Pursuit of Spring*. On a Sunday near Bemerton, once Herbert's parish, Thomas repeats two stanzas from *Sunday* and recalls Izaak Walton's *Life of Mr George Herbert*: 'The bells, the sunshine after storm, the elm trees, and the memory of that pious poet, put me into what was perhaps an unconscious imitation of a religious humour ... The Other Man, however, overtook me, and upset the humour' (p. 140). The 'Other Man' does so by quoting **28** 'with unction exaggerated to an incredibly ridiculous degree' one of Herbert's sonnets, and by launching into an agnostic tirade.

89–90. *While what I sought, nevertheless,*/*That I was seeking, I did not guess*: although I did not realise the true object of my search ('While, nevertheless, I did not guess that I was seeking what I sought'). Cf. lines 17–20. This syntax exactly reproduces the poet's psychological mystery tour. The direction and conclusion of the sentence itself are hard to 'guess.'

91. *That time was brief.* It is impossible to maintain this kind of balance indefinitely: that it has been achieved at all is what counts. In a sense the poem has already reached its climax and solution.

93–103. *Till once amid a tap-room's din . . . his laughter.* Coombes comments: 'when the other in the taproom complains that he lives "under a ban" because of the pursuer's relentlessness, he is stating a condition which is precisely central to the pursuer himself, and which we have been made strongly to feel through all the vicissitudes of the journey' (p. 219). A *ban* means a curse—and traditionally it is death to meet one's doppelgänger face to face. The impulse on both sides to evade, the reason why the narrator 'slips away,' may have its counterpart in a reaction which showed itself in Thomas's youth:

I fancied myself at walking . . . and I started at scratch with a dozen boys in front of me. All of them were behind in a quarter of a mile or so, except one, and him I was just passing. His five yards' start had all along seemed to me unfair. However, he was done with; so was the boy who notoriously ran. But their footsteps and their panting sounded close behind. I had enjoyed

28   catching up and walking through the others. Still more
I hated being pursued. Soon after George began to run
beside me, and when I was within a hundred yards of
the tape, I began to believe that the running boy was
gaining on me. I could not stand it. Turning off the
track I threw myself down on the grass on the pretext
that I had a stitch. (C.O.E.T., pp. 114–15)

Direct confrontation of 'the Other'—perhaps because it
involves the dreaded 'self-consciousness'—yields less than
the posture of strategic receptivity adopted in lines 61–80
and defined in lines 89–90.

29 104–8. *I steal out of the wood . . . like ducks.* 'I awoke to
hear ducklings squeaking, and a starling in the pine tree
imitating the curlew and the owl hunting' (I.P.S., p. 216).
The poem in a sense comes full circle at this point,
returning to some of the language and imagery of its first
stanza. However, there is strangeness as well as fami-
liarity. The image of the imitative starlings disturbs in the
same way as the exchange of characteristics between
birds, fish and human beings in *The Hollow Wood* (see
note, p. 182)—it may parody the narrator's abortive
consummation with 'the Other.' This new dimension
indicates that progress has not been entirely circular.
Further stages and cycles of the journey are anticipated.

29   THE MOUNTAIN CHAPEL

No MS. of this poem survives (see p. 146).

    The chapel is a Welsh one, 'Siloh,'
    standing bravely,—at night, it often seems perilously,
    —at the end of a road, beyond which rise immense
    mountains and impassable, and, in my memory, always

the night and a little, high, lonely moon, haunted for **29**
ever by a pale grey circle, looking like a frail creature
which one of the peaks had made to sail for his pleasure
across the terrible deeps of the sky. But Siloh stands
firm, and ventures once a week to send up a thin music
that avails nothing against the wind; although close to
it, threatening it, laughing at it, able to overwhelm it,
should the laugh become cruel, is a company of elder
trees, which, seen at twilight, are sentinels embossed
upon the sky—sentinels of the invisible, patient, un-
conquerable powers: or (if one is lighter-hearted) they
seem the empty homes of what the mines and chapels
think they have routed; and at midnight they are not
empty, and they love the mountain rain, and at times
they summon it and talk with it, while the preacher
thunders and the windows of the chapel gleam. (B.W.,
pp. 25–6)

The poem may also recall a chapel by the sea:

a little desolate white church and white-walled grave-
yard, which on December evenings will shine and seem
to be the only things at one with the foamy water and
the dim sky, before the storm; and when the storm
comes the church is gathered up into its breast and is a
part of it, so that he who walks in the churchyard is
certain that the gods—the gods that grow old and
feeble and die—are there still ... (B.W., p. 199 and
P.E.T., p. 59)

The passage ends: '... while an ancient wind is ceaselessly remembering ancient things.'

4–5. *The loss of the brook's voice/Falls like a shadow.* This
image not only evokes accurately what happens as you go
round a mountain fold, but also brilliantly fuses 'sound
and view' in the tension between 'voice' and 'shadow.' It

29 is equally bold of Thomas to compare a 'loss' to something that can be seen.

30 34–42. *Or one of the gods . . . This wind was old. The Mountain Chapel* is the poem in which Thomas most directly expresses his anti-religion or religion of Nature: it may be a preliminary definition of terms. The whole scene comprises the only chapel where an agnostic can worship (see note on lines 13–14 of *February Afternoon*, p. 311). The poet looks beyond hymn-singing in a Welsh chapel, beyond the more pagan gods its setting conjures up, to invoke the wind as the primary source of religious awe. All mythologies are ultimately cut down to size by the *natural* forces that really maintain the earth.

30   BIRDS' NESTS

No MS. of this poem can be traced (see p. 146).

'In the dense green coverts of the summer hedgerows nests were difficult to find, but now they show at every turn. The cunning basket-work of the lesser whitethroat, so frail as to seem incapable of holding the smallest egg, is filled with rotting black leaves and haws that have dropped thus early.' (T.W.L., p. 91)

31 15. *Once a dormouse dined there on hazel-nuts*: Thomas would have been able to tell this from the shells, as dormice, wood mice and squirrels all have their own characteristic way of breaking open a nut.

B.M. 24 December 1914.

Thomas included *Haymaking* (p. 89, see notes) and
The Manor Farm in his anthology *This England* (see
general note to *Lob*, p. 29) under his pseudonym 'Edward
Eastaway.' The poems are numbered I and II and appear
at the end of the section 'Her Sweet Three Corners' (pp.
111–12). Even without this context their related significance is apparent. They possess and express the quintes-
sentially English quality Thomas wished his anthology to
distil. In both poems he strips off a series of historical
layers to suggest the timeless mystery that is England.
The complementary scenes of Winter and midsummer
become 'unchangeable' or 'immortal,' achieve an archetypal finality. On a personal level *The Manor Farm*, like
Tears (p. 39, see note on line 1), seems to trace the process of emotional and imaginative thaw. It may be that
in this early poem Thomas is discovering an important
source of his poetic vision.

1–2. *The rock-like mud unfroze a little . . . road.* Thaw is
dramatised by the sounds in these lines (cf. *Thaw*, p. 110).
The hard consonants and heavy stresses of 'rock-like
mud' unfreeze in 'unfroze' and give way to a succession
of tripping liquids. Thomas had previously attempted the
same effect in prose: 'Down each side of every white
road runs a stream that sings and glitters in ripples like
innumerable crystal flowers. Water drips and trickles and
leaps and gushes and oozes everywhere, and extracts the
fragrance of earth and green and flowers under the heat
that hastens to undo the work of the snow.' (S.C., p. 45)
4. *spite of the sun.* By removing the 'in' of 'in spite of'
Thomas restores to 'spite' its original power and makes

NOTES

31 the earth's obstinacy both human and active. This usage or archaism is typical of the quiet liberties he takes with language; cf. 'silentness' (which means something different from 'silence') and 'a pretty February thing.'

9–10. *The church and yew/And farmhouse.* The run-on repetition of 'and' contributes to the effect of stillness, of life slowed down and suspended. Cf. in *Tears* 'stirring and sweet/And warm.'

17. *Against a fly, a solitary fly.* The repetition, besides following the swish of the horses' tails, slows down the movement of this section to a dead stop.

32 18–21. *The Winter's cheek flushed ... a season of bliss unchangeable.* Such a bold fusion of all the seasons only carries further a phenomenon evident throughout Thomas's poetry. Many poems resemble *The Manor Farm* in having as their focus the point at which seasons meet and mesh. In *October* (p. 97) 'The rich scene has grown fresh again and new/As Spring.' *But These Things Also* (p. 58) ends with the declaration 'Spring's here, Winter's not gone.' Both within and between poems Thomas himself observes a kind of seasonal cycle. The consciousness of 'Spring' offsets that of 'Winter' and vice versa: 'Spring and summer and autumn had come— flowing into one another with that secrecy which, as in the periods of our life, spares us the pain of the irretraceable step ...' (H.E., p. 157 and P.E.T., p. 76). His moods are never final, but evolve like the seasons. Thomas's Nature prose also contains many observations of the way one season anticipates or recalls another. *The Woodland Life*, prophetic as first books often are, constitutes an organic account of the year's cycle in the countryside given unity by this kind of interlocking. One essay, 'A Touch of Winter,' includes some of the bones of *The*

Manor Farm. Having described a scene of snow combined **32** with omens of Spring Thomas comes upon an oasis in Winter: 'Where this sheltered hollow ends, almost at a farmhouse door, a great yew-tree leans over... On the ancient bricks so dull and brown the yellow blossoms of the jasmine are studded thick, and they creep on to the tiled roof, weather-stained to browns and dingy reds. ... Passing the farmyard and the pied pigeons fluttering among the horses' feet, the road itself is worn deep through sand and chalk.' (pp. 114–15)

23–4. *for ages since/This England, Old already, was called Merry.* As well as conveying a sense of historical layers (Old England—Merry England—This England) Thomas connects two layers of literary reference. He presumably took over 'This England,' and his anthology title, from John of Gaunt's celebration in *Richard II* (II.i.31ff.) of 'this blessed plot, this earth, this realm, this England.' He remarks in his essay 'England': 'Already, before Langland, a Gloucester man, Robert of Gloucester, had called England "merry" in his chronicle:—

"England is a right merry land, of all on earth it is best,
    Set in the end of the world, as here, all in the west."
It was the Merry England of the English people, "full of mirth and of game, and men oft-times able to mirth and game, free men of heart and with tongue" ' (L.S., pp. 101–2). The epigraph to the 'Merry England' section of *This England* is a slightly different version of Robert of Gloucester's lines.

B.M. 25 December 1914.

Professor R. George Thomas remarks in a note on *The Pocket Book of Poems and Songs for the Open Air* that '[Thomas's] informed interest in folk-music ... has almost passed unnoticed by critics of his poetry' (L.G.B., p. 127). With some expert help Thomas sought out the most authentic words and airs for his anthology, which supplies musical notation for every song. His division of the book into sections (The Invitation, The Start in the Morning, Wayside Rest, Village and Inn, The Footpath, Evening) makes it an embryonic *This England* cast in the form of a journey. Thomas's love of folk songs went very deep: 'I prefer any country church or chapel to Winchester or Chichester or Canterbury Cathedral, just as I prefer "All round my hat," or "Somer is icumen in," to Beethoven' (S.C., p. 4). Such songs seemed to him the culminating expression, the poetry, of a traditional way of life:

> And of all music, the old ballads and folk songs and their airs are richest in the plain, immortal symbols. The best of them seem to be written in a language that should be universal, if only simplicity were truly simple to mankind. Their alphabet is small; their combinations are as the sunlight or the storm, and their words also are symbols. Seldom have they any direct relation to life as the realist believes it to be. They are poor in such detail as reveals a past age or a country not our own. They are in themselves epitomes of whole generations, of a whole countryside. They are the quintessence of many lives and passions made into a sweet cup for posterity ... The words, in league

with a fair melody, lend themselves to infinite inter- **32**
pretations, according to the listener's heart. What
great literature by known authors enables us to interpret
thus by virtue of its subtlety, ballads and their music
force us to do by their simplicity. The melody and
the story or the song move us suddenly and launch us
into an unknown. They are not art, they come to us
imploring a new lease of life on the sweet earth, and so
we come to give them something which the dull eye
sees not in the words and notes themselves, out of our
own hearts, as we do when we find a black hearthstone
among the nettles . . . (H.E., pp. 226–7)

Thomas felt that all this had implications for contemporary poetry:

I cannot help wondering whether the great work done
in the last century and a half towards the recovery of
old ballads in their integrity will have any effect beyond
the entertainment of a few scientific men and lovers of
what is ancient, now that the first effects upon Wordsworth and his contemporaries have died away. Can it
possibly give a vigorous impulse to a new school of
poetry that shall treat the life of our time and what in
past times has most meaning for us as freshly as those
ballads did the life of their time? (S.C., p. 246)

The fact that *The Lincolnshire Poacher* and *A-Rovin'*
provided him with early inspiration suggests that Thomas
himself received such a 'vigorous impulse.' The two
'Old Songs' signpost its pervasive, more unobtrusive
workings in his poetry. The freshness of songs and
ballads was a touchstone which helped Thomas to go
back, like Frost, 'through the paraphernalia of poetry into
poetry again.' In January 1915 he wrote two further
poems, *The Penny Whistle* and *The Gypsy*, which affirm

32 the archetypal pull of folk music. Each 'Old Song'
significantly turns into a celebration of Thomas's own
new song; allows him to express his pleasure in the act
of 'singing': 'It is a strange kind of delight to sing or
whistle just,' 'And all I did was to repeat.'

Thomas selected *The Lincolnshire Poacher* for two
anthologies, *The Pocket Book of Poems and Songs for the
Open Air* and *This England* (the 'Vital Commoners'
section):

> When I was bound apprentice, in famous Lincolnshire,
> Full well I served my master for more than seven year,
> Till I took up to poaching, as you shall quickly hear;
> Oh, 'tis my delight of a shiny night, in the season of
> the year. . . .

This folk song governs Thomas's inspiration more completely than does *A-Rovin'* in his next poem. He assumes
its language and climate with an ease which suggests that
the song met him more than half way. The poaching
career of the 'apprentice,' with its rich nocturnal com-
pensations, must have seemed a natural analogue of
Thomas's secret spiritual and imaginative life during his
years of hackwork. (Richard Jefferies' *The Amateur
Poacher* had been a formative book, see Biographical
Extracts, p. 382.) He uses the refrain as a song within a
song to affirm the necessary consummation of all his
experience in words.

4. *But 'tis my delight of a shiny night in the season of the
year*. This refrain line chances to combine two of Thomas's
most characteristic image-groups: the opposition of light
and darkness, the sense of seasonal evolution.

33 19. *to sing or whistle just*. A different version of this phrase
evidently appeared in a draft of the poem Thomas sent
to Eleanor Farjeon (or it may be a mis-transcription).

His answer to her criticism is well known: 'As to "sing **33** and whistle first," I don't think "to whistle and to sing" which is formally correct is as good. If I am consciously doing anything I am trying to get rid of the last rags of rhetoric and formality which left my prose so often with a dead rhythm only. If I can be honest and am still bad in rhythm it will be because I am bad in rhythm.' (E.F., p. 110)

AN OLD SONG 33

B.M. 26 December 1914.

See general note to previous poem. Thomas is drawing on a sea shanty, best known as *A-Rovin'*, but also called *Amsterdam* or *The Maid of Amsterdam*. Stanza five gives its first verse and full chorus (which includes 'Mark well what I do say').

3–6. *The one small wave . . . The vacant sand.* Possibly an image of Thomas's spiritual sterility being irrigated by his new inspiration. Cf. 'this flat grey shore which surprises the tide by being inaccessible to it' (E.F., p. 13).

13. *my bridge.* The 'light' is a bridge leading to life, and **34** 'the sailors' song' a bridge similarly beckoning towards poetry. The poem as a whole has a bridge-like structure, and thus contrasts with the homogeneousness of Thomas's first *Old Song*. It establishes connections between tradition and personal utterance, and between landscape and art, which are 'mixed sweet.'

B.M. 30 December 1914.

> When a hot sun has dried the woods the wind beats a
> cloud of pollen like grey smoke from the yews on the
> beechen coombes which are characteristic of Hamp-
> shire. They are steep-sided bays, running and narrow-
> ing far into and up the sides of the chalk hills, and
> especially of those hills with which the high flinty
> plateau breaks down to the greensand and the plain.
> These steep sides are clothed with beeches, thousands
> of beeches interrupted by the black yews that resemble
> caverns among the paler trees . . . (S.C., pp. 30–1)

The Combe is a forerunner of *The Chalk Pit* (p. 81, see
notes), and its location resembles the 'dells' described in
Thomas's essay on 'Chalk Pits' (L.S., pp. 27–37): 'Once
I met a small bear in one of the tangled dells in this
neighbourhood. He was curled up in the sun between
bushes of gorse, and his master's head was buried in his
fur. If the bear had been alone it might have been a scene
in Britain before Caesar's time, but though it was 1904
the bear looked indigenous. This dell is one of those which
may be natural or artificial, or perhaps partly both, a
small natural coombe having been convenient for excavation in the chalk . . . The dell is a long narrow chamber
with a floor rising towards the beginning of [a] steep
slope. The sides of it are worn by the rabbits and support
little but gaunt elder bushes' (pp. 36–7). 'Cross over to
[the dells], and they are seen to be more like ponds [than
islands] full of everything but water . . . One is so broken
up by the uneven diggings, the roots of trees, and the riot
of brambles that a badger is safe in it with a whole pack
of children' (pp. 31–2). Thomas was attracted by the

'mystery' (*The Chalk Pit*, line 58) inherent in such over- 35
grown hollows with their entanglements of living and
dead matter, eerie suggestion of human and non-human
presences.

1–6. *The Combe . . . rabbit holes for steps.* Entry into the
Combe is dramatised by techniques like those employed
throughout *The Path* (p. 63, see note on lines 1–3). A
jerky, 'scrambling' progress over footholds of nouns
makes it imaginatively, if not actually ('no one'), accessible.

12. *That most ancient Briton of English beasts.* The layers
of suggestion in this line are even more powerfully
compressed than in the last line of *The Manor Farm* (p.
31, see note). Thomas brings his repetition of 'ancient'
to a brilliantly specific conclusion, while opening up
further perspectives of time through the play between
'Briton' and 'English.' The whole poem, indeed, seems
to complement *The Manor Farm*, written six days before.
It corrects anything that may have been over-idealised in
Thomas's earlier vision. In place of eternal English sunlight and 'bliss' he discovers an indigenous darkness and
death. By killing the badger man has both violated his
bond with Nature and revived an older, more savage link
between them (the Combe was already 'dark'). Such
slaughter strikes at the roots of *civilised* England ('That
most ancient Briton') and may connect with Thomas's
awareness of the bloodshed in France.

THE HOLLOW WOOD   35

B.M. 31 December 1914.
    Thomas's essay, 'The Maiden's Wood' (R.U., pp.

35 145–63), anticipates in details of its setting this early 'forest' poem (cf. *The Dark Forest*, p. 125, and see general note). *The Hollow Wood* is discussed by Coombes (pp. 191–3) and by C. Day Lewis in 'The Poetry of Edward Thomas':

> From outside, we see [the poem] as a precise, factual description of a decaying wood. But, if we venture nearer the heart of this hollow wood, we find it a very disquieting place: the contrast between the goldfinch in the sun outside and the goings-on within is sinister: there is something wrong with a wood "Where birds swim like fish—Fish that laugh and shriek," and where dead or dying trees are kept evergreen by lichen, ivy, and moss—the hosts given a semblance, a mockery of life, by their parasites. The way he talks about them— "*half-flayed* and dying," "the dead trees *on their knees*" —they might almost be people. What makes this little poem so disturbing is that, from its description of natural processes, there arises a sense of something *against* nature. No doubt, if we were flying above that wood, like the goldfinch, the birds within it might seem to be moving in a different element, swimming like fish: and birds do "laugh and shriek." But, by a telescoping of the two facts, the natural is made un-natural—"Where birds swim like fish—*Fish* that laugh and shriek." Similarly, in the second stanza an image of dying trees is warped by giving an ironic twist to the meaning of "evergreen" and by showing them to us "*on their knees* In dog's-mercury and moss." (*Essays by Divers Hands*, XXVIII, 87–8)

1–7. *Out in the sun ... pale hollow wood.* The counter-pointing of quick, thin 'i' sounds and hollow 'o' sounds helps to establish the contrast and eerie connection be-

tween bird and wood. 'The hollow wood,' primarily a
wood in a hollow (which the sun cannot penetrate), also
suggests a wood consisting of hollow or dead trees, and a
ghost-wood emptied of life.

2. *flits and twits*. '. . . five or six goldfinches twitter as they
flit round the heads of rigid teazels on the waste' ('Flowers
of Frost,' P.E.T., p. 88).

8–9. *Lichen, ivy, and moss/Keep evergreen the trees.* 'Never
was ivy more luxuriant under the beeches, nor moss so
powerful as where it arrays them from crown to pedestal.
The lichens, fine grey-green bushy lichens on the thorns,
are as dense as if a tide full of them had swept through the
coombe' (S.C., p. 32). '. . . the many dead and mossy
stems of trees already decayed' (R.U., p. 147).

12. *dog's-mercury*: a 'gloomy crop-plant of damp woods
and leaf mould and dead twigs' (*The Englishman's Flora*
by Geoffrey Grigson, Phoenix House, 1958, p. 226).
Grigson lists other more sinister names of this poisonous
plant, e.g. 'boggart-flower' and 'snakeweed.' '. . . the
foliage of dog's mercury, everywhere of equal height,
gloomy and cool and tinged with a lemon hue, almost
closed over the narrow grassless ribbons of brown earth
and dead leaves' (R.U., p. 146).

THE NEW YEAR   36

B.M. 1 January 1915.

Some of Thomas's early poems describe meetings in
lonely places with solitary old men after the manner of
Wordsworth (cf. *Man and Dog*, p. 45 and *House and
Man*, p. 49). Like Wordsworth's 'solitaries' these figures
convey some basic human essence inextricably bound up

36 with Nature. But already in *Man and Dog* Thomas is working towards *Lob*, evolving a more social and sociable archetype. Throughout most of his poetry he assumes himself the role of the 'solitary.'

2. *New Year's morning*. The conception of the poem may owe something to traditional portraits of the dying year as an ancient man.

3–14. *I could not tell . . . like a tortoise's*. Thomas identifies his old man with both animals and inanimate objects. Cf. Wordsworth's 'Leech-gatherer' in *Resolution and Independence* who is said to resemble 'a huge stone,' itself 'like a sea-beast crawled forth':

> Such seemed this Man, not all alive nor dead,
> Nor all asleep—in his extreme old age:
> His body was bent double, feet and head
> Coming together in life's pilgrimage . . .

12. *Fly-the-garter*. A memory from the time when Thomas was 'sent to a day school . . . in Battersea':

The playground was asphalt; again there were no organized games, but a dozen groups playing leap frog, fly the garter, or tops, or chasing one another, or simply messing about. "Fly the garter"—if that is its right name—was a grand game to see played by a dozen of the biggest boys. I forget how it came about, but by degrees at length there were four or five boys bent double, forming a continuous line of backs. Each grasped the one in front of him and the first of them had his head, protected by his hands, against the playground wall. From half-way across the playground a big boy ran at a gallop, his ironshod heels pounding the asphalt, towards this line of boys who could see him approaching between their legs. Reaching the line and putting his hands upon the first back to help him leap

he leaped forward into the air. A brilliant leaper would **36**
use only one hand for the take off: the other gave a
sonorous smack on the right place in passing. With legs
outspread he flew along the line of backs, and alighted
upon the fourth or fifth of them. The lighter his weight,
the more fortunate was the steed thus accidentally
mounted: the heavier, the greater was the chance that
both together crashed to the ground. Then, I think, the
leaper added another to the line of backs and set the
next leaper an impossible task. The last stayer had a
good double row of admirers, silent during the run
and the leap, uproarious at the alighting. (C.O.E.T.,
pp. 79–80)

THE SOURCE   36

B.M. 4 January 1915.
9–12. *Till forth the dumb source . . . The triumph of earth.* **37**
The source of the river, formerly inaudible, has now
become so augmented by the rain that it 'breaks forth'
in flood. The 'dumb source' may also be Thomas himself
and 'the triumph of earth' the triumph of poetry and
sanity over violent psychological forces (cf. *Wind and
Mist*). The alliteration and assonance of robust consonantal sounds in lines 11–12 effectively 'drowns' any
reverberation of 'rain and wind' to confirm earth's
'triumph.'

THE PENNY WHISTLE   37

B.M. 5 January 1915.
3. *ghylls*: deep rocky clefts, usually wooded, and follow-

37 ing the course of a stream. The word was originally 'gill' until Wordsworth romanticised its spelling in several poems.

11. *charcoal-burners*: burners of wood in a slow fire to make charcoal. For a detailed description of English charcoal-burners see Arthur Ransome, *Swallows and Amazons* (1930), ch. XIII. By 1915 they could, like gipsies (see note, p. 200), be seen as links with an older way of life now vanishing. Cf. Walter de la Mare, *The Pigs and the Charcoal-Burner*, in *Peacock Pie* (1913)— a book Thomas knew and loved. *The Penny Whistle* resembles de la Mare's poem in stanza-form and rhyme-scheme.

16. *that crescent fine*: 'the new moon'; c . *The Gypsy*, line 28 (p. 48).

17-20. *And her brother . . . than I am saying.* A concentrated anticipation of *The Gypsy*, lines 15 ff.

38 A PRIVATE

B.M. 6–7 January 1915.
4. *Mrs. Greenland's Hawthorn Bush*: a catch, which is part of the ploughman's joke—at first it seems to be an inn. Although the joke is eventually on the ploughman, Thomas's irony also characteristically connects peacetime and wartime experience, sleep and death.

38 SNOW

B.M. 7 January 1915.
Thomas uses this vivid image in the first chapter of *In Pursuit of Spring*: 'If snow fell, there was no more of it

in the valleys than if a white bird had been plucked by a **38**
sparrow-hawk . . .' (p. 23). The idea is traditional, e.g.
in the riddle of the snow and the sun:

> White bird featherless
> Flew from Paradise,
> Pitched on the castle wall;
> Along came Lord Landless,
> Took it up handless,

And rode away horseless to the King's white hall.
The 'December:Christmass' section of John Clare's *The
Shepherds' Calendar* contains the following picture of
children:

> And some to view the winter weathers
> Climb up the window seat wi glee
> Likening the snow to falling feathers
> In fancys infant extacy
> Laughing wi superstitious love
> Oer visions wild that youth supplyes
> Of people pulling geese above
> And keeping christmass in the skyes

ADLESTROP   38

B.M. 8 January 1915.

A passage in *The South Country* has contributed to both
Adlestrop and *Haymaking* (p. 89, see general note):
'Follow one of these roads past straight avenues of elms
leading up to a farm (built square of stone, under a
roof of thatch or stone slate, and lying well back from the
road across a level meadow with some willows in the
midst, elms round about, willow herb waving rosy by the
stream at the border), or merely to a cluster of ricks; and

38 presently the hedges open wide apart and the level white road cools itself under the many trees of a green . . . and, behind [the farmhouse is], the bended line of hills a league away, wedding the lowly meadows, the house and the trees to the large heavens and their white procession of clouds out of the south and the sea' (pp. 11–12). The poem, one of Thomas's most anthologised pieces, also owes something to his fine prose sketch 'A Third-Class Carriage' (L.S., pp. 45–50 and P.E.T., pp. 213–15), in which the humanity and imagination of the people in the carriage are tested during a moment when 'the train stopped at the edge of a wood where a thrush was singing, calling out very loud, clear things in his language over and over again' (p. 49).

8. *only the name*. A trigger-phrase which acts as the pivot of the poem, releasing the swifter, ampler movement of the last two stanzas. From this point syntax and rhythm expand to match the spiralling, widening perspectives they present.

39   TEARS

B.M. 8 January 1915.

Tears follows up the achievement of *The Manor Farm* (p. 31, see notes) in capturing a timeless, peculiarly English essence. The arrested scenes in this case, however, are less tranquil: they communicate a sense of vitality and power straining at the leash. Cooke pinpoints the disturbing element in the poem: 'despite their superficial splendour, both hounds and soldiers also suggest a less attractive reality. The hounds are out to kill ("upon the scent") and merge into one menacing animal—"a

great dragon", the troops have lost some of their indi- **39**
viduality by being "in line" and "in white tunics," while
it is a martial air that "pierces" the silence. The profound
ambiguity of the poem's basic emotion is caught in that
astonishing paradox "rage of gladness". (p. 222)

1. *It seems I have no tears left.* The poet is numb, visited
only by the 'ghosts' of tears. Yet as he goes on to recount
the two experiences which summoned up those 'ghosts,'
recollection becomes so intense (it becomes reliving) that
some power of feeling is, by implication, restored. Like
The Manor Farm, the poem explores the process of
emotional and imaginative thaw. This process naturally
combines painful elements with a predominantly joyful
intensity of response ('truths,' 'beauty'). The rhythm of
the poem, too, 'warms up' after Thomas's flat opening
statement and the clogging monosyllables of line 2 with
its awkward double parenthesis. Language and imagery
become progressively more vivid.

6. *Blooming Meadow.* From May 1904 to September 1906
the Thomases lived at Elses Farm in the Weald of Kent
near Sevenoaks, an experience which also may have
influenced *Haymaking* (p. 89): 'I tried my hand at
brewing, wine-making, hop-picking and even reaping.
Of course hay-making on the lovely slope of Blooming
meadow was a festival for us all at the farm, and we learnt
how the ricks that rose like a town in the rick-yard were
shaped so symmetrically, and thatched as carefully as a
house' (W.W.E., p. 107). The name seems to distil all
the colour and life that the poem depicts.

10. *Strange solitude was there and silence.* 'Silence' is
common to Thomas's evocations of the timeless in *Tears*,
The Manor Farm ('a Sunday silentness') and *Haymaking*
('And all were silent'). The observer is also 'solitary' in

39 *The Manor Farm* and the word occurs in the poem. 'Solitude' and 'silence' (and sun) are often linked in Thomas's prose, e.g.: 'two lovers of sixteen years old gathering nuts in the warm sun, the silence, the solitude' (S.C., p. 227).

15. '*The British Grenadiers.*' 'I don't think I could alter "Tears" to make it marketable. I feel that the correction you want made is only essential if the whole point is in the British Grenadiers as might be expected in these times.' (Letter to Edward Garnett, quoted in Garnett's introduction to *Selected Poems*, 1927, p. viii.)

40 OVER THE HILLS

B.M. 9 January 1915.

... a mountain stream, which many stones tore to ribbons, was with me for miles, and to the left and to the right many paths over the hills ran with alluring courses for half a mile, like happy thoughts or lively fancies, and ended suddenly. The mountains increased in height as the sun sank, and their sides began to give a home to enormous, still shadows and to rich, inaccessible groves among the clefts. And in the end of the afternoon I came to a village I knew, which grew round an irregular lawn.

From the inn, I could see the whole village ... Six bells that rang three miles off and some white downs of cloud on the horizon were in harmony. It was a time when the whole universe strove to speak a universal speech ... But, as it seemed, owing to my fault, the effort was unsuccessful, and I rose hurriedly and left the village behind. ('August,' B.W., pp. 176–7)

Scannell uses the poem to illustrate the modernity of **40** Thomas's technique: 'Thomas uses rhyme and, in line four, half-rhyme, very much in the way that a poet of the fifties or sixties like Philip Larkin uses it: that is to say, not in conformity with a strict, preconceived pattern, but at intervals so spaced that the chime of vowel and consonant occurs faintly, uninsistently until the poem draws towards its end, when the rhymes are closer together, more emphatic before the finality of the terminating couplet.' (p. 31)

14–19. *Recall . . . rush and stone.* A number of Thomas's earliest poems (*Adlestrop, Tears, The Cuckoo*) are concerned with memory; but *Over the Hills*, like *Old Man* (p. 21, see notes), directly traces the process. Thomas brilliantly abstracts an image from the mountain scene to serve as a bridge back to it. The dramatic sense of progression at the end of the poem, whereby words not technically active *sound* so ('rests . . . stirs . . . rush'), effectively completes a 'recall' which is as total as possible.

THE LOFTY SKY 40

B.M. 10 January 1915.

The Lofty Sky dramatises Thomas's skyward urge, or desire for spiritual liberation, more effectively than other poems because it is defined in terms of an impatience with the earth. Spiralling couplets follow upwards the movement of his eye and the floating of the tench. The poet seeks renewal in temporarily rejecting his usually preferred context; cf. Robert Frost: 'I'd like to get away from earth awhile/And then come back to it and begin over' (*Birches*). He may, further, be registering the

40 exhilaration of his new poetic element. Thomas's imagery, vocabulary and rhythm of aspiration sometimes carry traces of his admiration for Shelley, e.g. the lark-simile in *After You Speak* (p. 120). The lines: 'They are no more/ Than weeds upon this floor/Of the river of air' in *The Lofty Sky*, like the phrase 'dark surge' in *Two Pewits* (p. 61), recall Shelley's *Ode to the West Wind*.

More specifically, the poem echoes Walter de la Mare's *Nobody Knows* (*Peacock Pie*, 1913) which celebrates the power and freedom of the wind ('Just a great wave of the air,/Tossing the leaves in its sea') in contrast with man's situation:

> And so we live under deep water,
>> All of us, beasts and men,
> And our bodies are buried down under the sand,
>> When we go again . . .

41 19–34. *I am like a fish . . . where the lilies are.* In an essay called 'A Winter Morning' Thomas looks out of the window after reading Keats: 'outside, the trees and barns and shed were quiet and dim, and as much submerged and hidden from the air in which I had been living as the green streets of motionless lily and weed at the bottom of some lonely pool where carp and tench go slowly' (H.E., p. 161). Man on earth is in the position of a fish at the bottom of a pool. 'Where the lilies are' accordingly represents the sky or heaven. Thomas's shift of perspective surprises us into a recognition that man's element has its own restricting density.

26

THE CUCKOO

B.M. 15 January 1915.

Thomas refers in 'An Old Farm' to 'the palpitating, groaning shout of the shepherd, *Ho ! ho ! ho ! ho ! ho !*' (H.E., p. 72). The same passage fed *Haymaking* (see p. 284) and *Cock-Crow* (see p. 296).

SWEDES

B.M. 15 January 1915.

Thomas wrote to Gordon Bottomley: 'I wonder if I can touch "Swedes." It is one of the least like myself I fancy' (L.G.B., p. 247). This is probably the reaction of most readers to the poem's exotic quality. But verbal and actual colour is not so uncommon in Thomas's poetry as it might appear. We are surprised in *Health* by a Yeatsian litany of resonant names; in *Cock-Crow* by 'Heralds of splendour'; in *The Path* by tints of moss, 'gold, olive, and emerald.' Thomas's palette is by no means restricted to the predominant greens and browns of the countryside or of prosaic utterance. The very reserve of his poetry can unleash a special kind of rhetoric and intensity. It is like a fine tweed which in close-up reveals brilliant flecks of colour. *Swedes* itself certainly achieves in an overwhelming fashion Wordsworth's objective in the *Lyrical Ballads*: 'to choose incidents and situations from common life . . . and . . . to throw over them a certain colouring of imagination, whereby ordinary things should be presented to the mind in an unusual way.'

1–4. *They have taken the gable . . . Unsunned.* Thomas notes the unexpected dazzle of swedes in a prose descrip-

42 tion of Spring's arrival: 'A cart goes by all a-gleam with a load of crimson-sprouting swedes and yellow-sprouting mangolds that seem to be burning through the net of snow above them' (S.C., pp. 44–5).

4. *more tender-gorgeous.* More naturally, movingly magnificent. Thomas undeniably takes a risk with this shot-gun compound. It might be adduced as evidence of imaginative strain or schizophrenia in the poem, yet the hyphen opens an effective channel between the vibrantly familiar and the coldly exotic. Any shock is partially absorbed by the gradual way in which the whole comparison is introduced.

6. *the Valley of the Tombs of Kings*: a valley in Thebes containing the tombs of pharaohs of the 18th, 19th and 20th dynasties.

7–10. *A boy crawls down . . . Blue pottery, alabaster, and gold.* Thomas concludes 'Leaving Town' (H.E., pp. 1–18) by describing his entry into a 'shadowed wood' at dawn and discovery of the rich colours it conceals:

> Suddenly my mind went back to the high dark cliffs of Westminster Abbey, the blank doors and windows of endless streets, the devouring river, the cold gloom before dawn, and then with a shudder forgot them and saw the flowers and heard the birds with such a joy as when the ships from Tarshish, after three blank years, again unloaded apes and peacocks and ivory, and men upon the quay looked on; or as, when a man has mined in the dead desert for many days, he suddenly enters an old tomb, and making a light, sees before him vases of alabaster, furniture adorned with gold and blue enamel and the figures of gods, a chariot of gold, and a silence perfected through many ages in the company of death and of the desire of immortality. (p. 18)

194

The items in line 10 refer back to 'the white and gold and **42**
purple of curled fronds.' 'Alabaster' in particular implies
their contrasting coldness, artifice, and lack of animation.
11. *Amen-hotep.* Amenhotep II, a pharaoh of the
eighteenth dynasty who reigned from c.1450 B.C. to
c.1425 B.C., has a well-preserved tomb in the Valley of
the Tombs of Kings. He was proud of his physical
prowess and of his reputation as a horseman and
charioteer.
11–12. *But dreamless . . . sweet as Spring.* In his final
couplet Thomas more explicitly contrasts the unchanging
panoply of the dead Pharaoh with the swedes, in whose
warm colour Spring seems to be hibernating, to be at once
recalled and promised. Winter, unlike death, can 'dream.'
The poem as a whole illustrates Thomas's tendency to
look to natural things, rather than to God or organised
religion, for emblems of hope and renewal.

THE UNKNOWN BIRD **43**

B.M. and B.C. 17 January 1915.
   In *The Happy-Go-Lucky Morgans* 'Mr. Torrance'
remembers such a bird:
   "Only one bird sang in [the cypress tree], and that was
   a small, sad bird which I do not know the name of. It
   sang there every month of the year, it might be early or
   it might be late, on the topmost point of the plume. It
   never sang for long, but frequently, and always suddenly. It was black against the sky, and I saw it nowhere else. The song was monotonous and dispirited,
   so that I fancied it wanted us to go, because it did not
   like the cheerful garden, and my father's loud laugh,

43   and my mother's tripping step: I fancied it was up there watching the clouds and very distant things in hope of a change; but nothing came, and it sang again, and waited, ever in vain. I laughed at it, and was not at all sorry to see it there, for it had stood on that perch in all the happy days before, and so long as it remained the days would be happy. My father did not like the bird, but he was often looking at it, and noted its absence as I did. The day after my sister died he threw a stone at it—the one time I saw him angry—and killed it. But a week later came another, and when he heard it he burst into tears, and after that he never spoke of it but just looked up to see if it was there when he went in or out of the porch." (pp. 146–7)

21   *that La-la-la ! was bodiless sweet.* Unfettered by name or body, the bird's song concentrates the mystery which all birds hold for Thomas. It may also represent the summons of his imagination.

22–5.   *Sad more than joyful . . . taste it.* An early, clumsier version of Thomas's matured speculations in *October* (p. 97) or *Liberty* (p. 98) about the ambiguous connection between joy and sadness (see notes). The syntactical maze, and 'if I must say/That it was one or other,' make the passage a classic instance of his reluctance to draw any clear-cut distinction that might falsify the shades of his perception.

29–30.   *Happy sometimes . . . heavy heart.* The verbal and structural repetition in these lines, their 'heavy' emphasis, contrasts with the broken-up quality of line 31 and 'wandering' stresses of line 32.

THE MILL-POND

44

B.M. and B.C. 18 January 1915.

Thomas's prose includes several descriptions of mill-ponds, of which these are perhaps closest to the poem: 'The stream going helpless and fast between high banks is gloomy until it is turned to bright, airy foam and hanging crystal by the mill; over the restless pool below hangs a hawthorn all white and fragrant and murmurous with bloom ... Over the green grass walks the farmer's daughter in a white dress ... She is a Lady May, careless, proud, at ease' (H.E., pp. 181–4 and see P.E.T., pp. 78–9). In *In Pursuit of Spring* Thomas passes 'a ruined flock-mill' near a weir: 'we could see its white wall of foam half a mile higher up the river, which was concealed by alders beyond' (p. 219).

MAN AND DOG

45

B.M. and B.C. 20 January 1915.

Man and Dog draws on Thomas's account of 'An Umbrella Man' (S.C., pp. 194–200) who 'was returning— if the grave was not too near at the age of seventy-seven— to a primeval wildness and simplicity.' Both prose and poem contributed to the evolution of 'Lob' (see p. 233). 6. *Straight but lame.* 'He was of middle height and build, the crookedest of men, yet upright, like a branch of oak which comes straight with all its twistings' (S.C., p. 194). 'He had lost his youth in battle, for a bullet went through his knee ...' (p. 195).
7. *flag-basket*: a basket made of reeds.

45 8. *Alton*: a town in east Hampshire.

9. *Chilgrove*: a village near Chichester in west Sussex.

10. '*a money-box*': some savings to tide him over for a few days.

12. *flint-picking*: picking stones out of the field (after the sheep had cropped it) to leave it clear for cultivation. 'The old mothers whose usefulness is more or less past . . . go into the field to work picking up stones at a shilling a day. I saw three of them at it in the rain, they gathered the flints (size of a fist or two) and carried them clear off the field in their aprons without the help of horse or cart.' (*Selected Letters of Robert Frost*, p. 118)

15. *on dock and line*: on the docks and railways.

17–19. *In 'seventy-four . . . corn and couch will grow*. 'He was a labourer's son, and he had already had a long life of hoeing and reaping and fagging when he enlisted at Chatham. He had kept his musket bright, slept hard and wet, and starved on thirteenpence a day, moving from camp to camp every two years.' (S.C., p. 195)

couch: couch-grass which, with its creeping root-stalks has to be weeded out from among the crops.

28. *He kept sheep in Wales*. 'He' is the 'foxy Welsh grandfather' of 'the small brown bitch.' This imaginative pedigree adds to the historical and geographical dimensions of the poem. Like the man, his dog is closely identified with the countryside which she also works for love rather than profit.

46 38. *that bedfellow*: the bitch, regarded by farmers as a danger to their poultry and sheep.

39–40. *Many a man sleeps worse . . . 'In the trenches.'* Thomas's apparently casual interpolations of the war into the consciousness of this poem anticipate the technique and theme of *As the Team's Head-Brass* (p. 119, see **46** notes).

46–8. *They passed . . . the twilight of the wood.* 'The man for good' has an ominous ring, cf. 'The day Jack Noman disappeared' at the end of *May the Twenty-third*.

All Thomas's 'Lob' figures tend to vanish up lanes or to become absorbed into landscape. His prose portrait concludes: 'The old man smacked his lips as he drained the salty broth, tried three times to light his empty pipe and then knocked out the ashes and spat vigorously, and took a turn up the lane alone in the scent of the bracken' (S.C., p. 200).

BEAUTY **46**

B.M. 21 January 1915.

Thomas wrote to Gordon Bottomley on 30 March 1908:

> An east wind or a wind from underground has swept over everything. Friends, Nature, books are like London pavements when an east wind has made them dry and harsh & pitiless. There is no joy in them. They are more dead than if they were in a Museum correctly labelled. And this is true not only this morning, but every morning, every afternoon & every night. I am now uniformly low spirited, listless, almost unable to work, & physically incapable. I have no idea what it means, but I crawl along on the very edge of life, wondering why I don't get over the edge. (L.G.B., p. 160)

Seven years later in the poem Thomas could recognise the residual spark of life and imagination which enabled

46 him to survive, and to become a poet ('Beauty is there').
10. *Cross breezes cut the surface to a file*: i.e. they cut it
into a mesh of fine lines like the criss-cross pattern on a
file's blade. This metaphor of torment carries connotations of the file's coldness and hardness.

47   THE GYPSY

B.M. and B.C. 22 January 1915.

In a fine prose description of a fair (S.C., pp. 271–7)
Thomas captures the same vitality and tawdriness. He
regretted the passing of the gipsy as he regretted the
passing of the true 'countryman': 'Before it is too late, I
hope that the Zoological Society will receive a few pairs
at their Gardens. With them, or in neighbouring paddocks
(or whatever, for the sake of human dignity, they are
called), should be some Gypsies' (*The Country*, p. 22).
'... against the hedge a gipsy family pretend to shelter
from the windy rain; the man stands moody, holding the
pony, the women crouch with chins upon knees, the
children laugh and will not be still. They belong to the
little roads that are dying out: they hate the sword-like
shelterless road, the booming cars that go straight to the
city in the vale below' (S.C., p. 219). '[The gypsies]
connect Borrow with what is strange, with what is simple,
and with what is free ... Their mystery is the mystery
of nature and life. They keep their language and their
tents against the mass of civilization and length of time.
They are foreigners but as native as the birds' (*George
Borrow*, p. 237). In the poem Thomas prefers a rough
gipsy music to more conventional Christmas harmonies.
Its spirit is caught by the lively jogtrot of his own hexa-
meter couplets.

5–6. '*Give a penny* . . . '*Indeed I have not any.* Cf. the **47** nursery rhyme, 'Simple Simon.' In the general context of Christmas 'the Gypsy' and her baby just hint at the Nativity.

17. *While his mouth-organ changed to a rascally Bacchanal dance.* Bacchanal is an adjective or noun deriving from Bacchus, Roman name for Dionysus, the Greek god associated with fertility, civilisation, and wine. His devotees have traditionally been given to wild dancing and revelry. The poem, too, changes its tune or pitch at this point as Thomas works up, through his catalogue of the fair, to a climax of extreme intensity and abandon.

18. '*Over the hills and far away.*' 'Tom, he was a piper's son,/He learnt to play when he was young,/And all the tune that he could play/Was, "Over the hills and far away".' 'The refrain "Over the hills and far away" has been used by poets and song writers on numerous occasions' (*Oxford Dictionary of Nursery Rhymes*, p. 409).

20. *Cheap-jack*: a pedlar who sells cheap trifles.

21. *Christmas corpses.* A sardonic oxymoron. Thomas's 'fair' suggests not just the commercialisation of Christmas but also the whole 'Vanity Fair' of the world into which Christ was—or was not—born.

22. *the kneeling ox.* Evocation of the Nativity becomes more explicit. Thomas Hardy's poem *The Oxen*, written in the same year as *The Gypsy*, contains the lines: ' "Come; see the oxen kneel//In the lonely barton by yonder coomb . . .",' and exhibits a similar relaxation of scepticism.

26–8. *but for the spark* . . . *a crescent moon.* The agnostic **48** Thomas has mocked Christmas by celebrating it as a pagan festival ('Bacchanal,' 'underworld') through the medium of 'the Gypsy boy,' who 'redeems' the fair and

48 the darkness by purely human (and artistic) means. Nevertheless the imagery of light at this point offers a formal parallel with the Star in the East.

48   AMBITION

B.M. and B.C. 23 January 1915.

Another day, a wide and windy day, is the jackdaw's, and he goes straight and swift and high like a joyous rider crying aloud on an endless savannah . . . Towards the end of March there are six nights of frost giving birth to still mornings of weak sunlight, of an opaque yet not definitely misty air. The sky is of a milky, uncertain pale blue without one cloud. Eastward the hooded sun is warming the slope fields and melting the sparkling frost. In many trees the woodpeckers laugh so often that their cry is a song . . .

It is not spring yet. Spring is being dreamed, and the dream is more wonderful and more blessed than ever was spring. What the hour of waking will bring forth is not known. Catch at the dreams as they hover in the warm thick air. Up against the grey tiers of beech stems and the mist of the buds and fallen leaves rise two columns of blue smoke from two white cottages among trees; they rise perfectly straight and then expand into a balanced cloud, and thus make and unmake continually two trees of smoke. No sound comes from the cottages. The dreams are over them . . . With inward voices of persuasion those dreams hover and say that all is to be made new, that all is yet before us, and the lots are not yet drawn out of the urn. (S.C., pp. 20–3)

An essay, 'The Pride of the Morning,' in *The Heart of England* linked more closely with *Health* (p. 75, see

general note) may also look forward to *Ambition*. The **48**
setting of both poems is an early Spring early morning
and they belong to Thomas's intensive exploration of
Spring in Nature and man. The prose source of *March*
includes the following: 'The half-moon at the zenith of
a serene, frosty night led in a morning of mist that filled
up all the hollows of the valley as with snow: each current
of smoke from locomotive or cottage lay in solid and
enduring vertebrae above the mist . . .' (I.P.S., pp. 27–8).
Ambition seems related to *The Glory* (p. 84, see notes),
where the poet's attitude in a similar situation is more
equivocal. This has structural consequences: the greater
part of *Ambition* is devoted to Thomas's acceptance of the
intoxicating 'invitation' approached so cautiously in *The
Glory*.

4–7. *Jackdaws began to shout and float and soar . . . wide
sky*. Thomas also introduces these symbols of liberation
into an essay called 'January Sunshine' (which ends on the
imperative 'Be beautiful and enjoy and live!'): 'In the
immense crystal spaces of fine windy air . . . the jackdaws
play. They soar, they float, they dance, and they dive and
carve sudden magnificent precipices in the air, crying all
the time with sharp, joyous cries that are in harmony with
the great heights and the dashing wind.' (H.E., p. 156)

23. *fell like a bell:* onomatopoeiac internal rhyme. Cooke
points out (p. 191) the resemblance to the last stanza of
Keats's *Ode to a Nightingale*: 'Forlorn! the very word is
like a bell/To toll me back from thee to my sole self!'
Ambition belongs in vocabulary ('astir,' 'plumes of pearly
smoke,' 'Elysium,' 'bower,' 'prime,' ''twixt,' 'rime') and
in its use of 'the suspended moment' to the 'Keatsian'
group of Thomas's poems, e.g. *The Glory, October,
Liberty* etc.

B.M. 3, 4 February 1915.

See general note to *The New Year*, p. 36. *House and Man* derives from Thomas's prose portrayal of 'Norgett' and his dwelling 'Oldhurst':

> a thatched house built of flints in the middle of oak woods not far off—ancient woods where the leaves of many Autumns whirled and rustled even in June. It was three miles from the hard road, and it used to seem that I had travelled three centuries when at last I emerged from the oaks and came in sight of that little humped gray house and within sound of the pines that shadowed it. It had a face like an owl; it was looking at me. Norgett must have heard me coming from somewhere among the trees, for, as I stepped into the clearing at one side, he was at the other. I thought of Herne the Hunter on catching sight of him. He was a long, lean, gray man with a beard like dead gorse, buried gray eyes, and a step that listened. He hardly talked at all, and only after questions that he could answer quite simply. Speech was an interruption of his thoughts, and never sprang from them; as soon as he ceased talking they were resumed with much low murmuring and whistling—like that of the pine trees— to himself, which seemed the sound of their probings in the vast of himself and Nature. His was a positive, an active silence. (I.P.S., pp. 100–1)

The man in the poem has still further, and more alarmingly, become assimilated to his environment; losing both house and identity to the forest. Thomas thus suggests the vulnerability of human civilisation and personality before natural or perhaps unconscious forces.

The forest has taken on life ('the trees looked') in **49** proportion as the man has been denuded of it ('half/ Ghost-like') and reduced to a thing ('half like a beggar's rag'). Even memory 'dims' rather than clarifies him.

1. *One hour.* It is only an hour since the poet has seen the man (who may be in part an ironic self-portrait).

20. *A magpie like a weathercock in doubt.* Reminiscent of a line in William Morris's *The Message of the March Wind,* a poem which Thomas admired and included in his *Pocket Book of Poems and Songs for the Open Air*: 'And the vane on the spire-top is swinging in doubt.'

PARTING   50

B.M. 11 February 1915.

The 'parting' was probably from Thomas's son Mervyn, who left on that day to go to America with the Frosts and with whom Thomas had rather unhappy relations.

1–12. *The Past is a strange land ... sadden the sad.* Thomas might have been expected to envy 'the perished self' who no longer suffers, but there is an implicit recoil from 'the Past' as equivalent to death: 'That lacks all blood and nerve and wit.' At the end of the poem the poet more openly prefers the present, life, which can be 'stirred or strained,' to the levelling out of all emotion. Cf. *Home*, p. 54 and see notes.

17–24. *Not as what had been remedied ... like this.* Cf. Philip Larkin, *Lines on a Young Lady's Photograph Album* (*The Less Deceived*, The Marvell Press, 1955, p. 14):

> ... in the end, surely, we cry

50   Not only at exclusion, but because
It leaves us free to cry. We know *what was*
Won't call on us to justify
Our grief, however hard we yowl across

The gap from eye to page.

Thomas does not simply regret his failure to put things right. Like Larkin he laments the intervening vacuum that seals off 'the Past' from contact with our present lives. 22. *spiritualized*: disembodied, unreal, a ghost of its former self. Thomas does not attach to the word its usual value.

51   FIRST KNOWN WHEN LOST

B.M. 11 February 1915.
4. *bill*: bill-hook, a hooked knife used for pruning.

51   MAY THE TWENTY-THIRD

B.M. 15 February 1915.
1–10. *There never was a finer day . . . luck to endure.* While alert to the special quality of every month and season Thomas was particularly versed in the gradations of Spring from February to May. Here Spring seems on the point of becoming Summer ("'Twas the first day that the midges bit,' line 39), but is still 'pursued by tempests overpast.' Similar contraries are reconciled to establish another 'perfect' day in *Haymaking* (p. 89). Thomas's essay 'The Artist' (L.A.T., pp. 130–9), which anticipates the setting of *May the Twenty-third*, also supplied details for *Haymaking* (see notes):

This, said Adams to himself, staring strangely at the **51**
dry brushes and blank paper before him, this was the
fairest day of the whole year, the youngest child of a
long family of days, each fairer than its elder. First,
there were two days following suddenly, hot and
cloudless, upon weeks of storm, of sullenness, and of
restless wind and rain vexing the new leaves and
scattering the blossoms; and at the end of the second
a thunderstorm out of the east ascended lightly and
travelled rapidly away without silencing the birds.
. . . Adams found himself waiting day after day for the
end and crown of this energy and change.

There came a lustrous morning early assailed from
all quarters of the sky in turn, as if the heavens were
besieging the earth, by thunder and after long, brooding
intervals, thunder again and again, now with cannonad-
ing and now one boom or blast followed by no sound
except its echo and the challenge of the pheasants.
The lark in the sky, the blackbird in the isolated
meadow elms, the nightingale in the hazel and bluebell
thickets, sang on; and before the last of the assault
Adams set out, inwardly confident in the day's future.

He walked steadily, but more and more slowly, into
the broadening and deepening beauty of the great
day. So hot was it that the heat alone would have
made him happy, and yet the east wind urged him to
go on and on. . . (pp. 130-2)

12–27. *Old Jack Noman . . . cress in his basket.* Helen **52**
Thomas told Robin Skelton that Jack Noman's original
was 'a tramp who used to call asking for left-off clothes
and selling watercress. He used to disappear for long
periods, and then appear again as jaunty as ever. We
thought his disappearances were spent in prison, for we

52 knew he stole. But we liked him, and if Edward had a
particularly warm but outworn garment—especially one
he really had liked—he saved it until Jack came again'
(*Selected Poems*, Hutchinson, 1962, note, p. 112). In his
prose Thomas draws several portraits of this tramp or
'watercress-man' under such names as Jackalone, Jack
Runaway and Jack Horseman: '. . . close by stood the tall
old watercress-man, Jack Horseman, patiently waiting for
the right moment to touch his hat. His Indian complexion
had come back to the old soldier, he was slightly tipsy,
and he had a bunch of cowslips in his hat' (H.G.L.M.,
p. 176). 'What dreams are there for that aged child who
goes tottering and reeling up the lane at mid-day? He
carries a basket of watercress on his back. He has sold
two-pennyworth, and he is tipsy, grinning through the
bruises of a tipsy fall, and shifting his cold pipe from one
side of his mouth to the other. Though hardly sixty he is
very old, worn and thin and wrinkled, and bent sideways
and forward at the waist and the shoulders. Yet he is
very young. He is just what he was forty years ago when
the thatcher found him lying on his back in the sun instead
of combing out the straw and sprinkling it with water for
his use. He laid no plans as a youth; he had only a few
transparent tricks and easy lies. Never has he thought of
the day after to-morrow' (S.C., p. 25). At the beginning of
The Heart of England the same figure becomes harbinger
of romance and the countryside to a boy in a suburban
street—Thomas himself perhaps (pp. 2–3; and see pp.
11–15 and P.E.T., pp. 63–7).

Jack arrives in the poem like the spirit of May. He
materialises, like Autolycus in *The Winter's Tale* (IV.iii),
after the ground has been prepared for him, combining
in his appearance the freshness and heat of the season.

28–38. 'Where did they come from . . . Wheatham hill. **52**
Jack is related to Lob by his names, his proverbial
wisdom, and the mixture of roguery and generosity in
his make-up. He seems to represent, however, a more
purely pagan vitality—as opposed to a spirit which has
evolved through history. Some primary or primal quality
attaches to him.

36. roll-walk-run. An audacious compound whose elements function as verbs rather than as nouns. Its head-
long stresses and full-blooded sounds capture Jack's
jauntiness.

39–44. 'Twas the first day . . . like hops. These lines consummate the unusually intense happiness of the poem,
which survives the shadow, mysterious rather than
mournful, cast into the sunlight by its final couplet. All
life's abundance—midges, dust, bluebells—acquires an
equal sensuous value. It is rarely that Spring, or any other
season, can 'do nothing to make [Thomas] sad.'

THE BARN   **53**

B.M. 22 February 1915.

In *The Icknield Way* Thomas becomes fascinated by
the strange case of 'Lone Barn' where a man and his
family had squatted for some time in miserable conditions
(pp. 236–48). Huge barns were a feature of the Wiltshire
downs, but 'Lone Barn,' 'this black barn,' seems to have
made a special contribution to both this poem and *The
Barn and the Down* (p. 59): '. . . [it] lies unexpectedly in a
small hollow at one of the highest points of the downs,
three miles from the nearest hamlet. It had long been
deserted. The farm-house was ruinous, and a fox taking

53 refuge there could not be dislodged from the fallen
masonry and elder and yew tree roots ... I knew the
farm-house and had often wondered about the man who
built it in that solitude somewhere in the eighteenth
century ... An old plum tree, planted when barn and
house were built, and now dead and barkless, stood against
one end, and up it had climbed a thick ivy stem that
linked barn and tree inseparably with a profusion of
foliage, emerald and white. The last of its doors lay just
outside in the dead embers of the tramps' fire. Thus open
on both sides to the snow-light and the air the barn
looked the work rather of nature than of man. The old
thatch was grooved, riddled, and gapped, and resembled
a grassy bank that has been under a flood the winter
through; covered now in snow it had the outlines in
miniature of the hill on which it was built' (pp. 237–40).
In 'Earth Children' an old countryman and his wife
inhabit 'part of a farmhouse, the rest having fallen to ruin,
and from human hands to the starlings, the sparrows,
and the rats' (H.E., p. 141).

18. *Making a spiky beard.* A characteristically brilliant
piece of bird-observation: the feathers under a starling's
beak stick out when its breast is inflated in song. This
exuberant portrait proves that there is life in the poet
and perhaps the barn yet, confirming a jaunty tone in the
whole poem despite its derelict subject.

54 HOME

B.M. 23 February 1915.

This is the first, the most generalised and most symbolic
of Thomas's three 'Home' poems (see p. 74, p. 108 and

notes). 'You know I am no traveller. I am always wanting **54**
to settle down like a tree for ever' (L.G.B., p. 52). 'But
it is hard to make anything like a truce between these two
incompatible desires, the one for going on and on over
the earth, the other that would settle for ever, in one place
as in a grave and have nothing to do with change ...
The two desires will often painfully alternate. Even on
these harvest days there is a temptation to take root forever
in some corner of a field or on some hill from which the
world and the clouds can be seen at a distance.' (S.C.,
p. 186)

Cooke suggests (p. 228) that Thomas's 'title is taken
from a poem by George Herbert called "Home" in which
he longs to quit "this world of wo",' and contrasts the attitude of agnostic and Christian to death. He relates the
third and fourth stanzas to Hamlet's 'To be or not to be'
soliloquy. Earlier, Cooke challenges D. W. Harding's
citing of the poem as an instance of Thomas's 'pervasive
nostalgia' (in 'A Note on Nostalgia,' *Scrutiny* I, 1932,
8–19). Harding's criteria for nostalgia include the 'crav-
ing for an adequate social group,' and the regressive
desire for an ideal state or a state free from difficulty.
These he finds in Thomas:

> It would be a mistake to complain because Edward
> Thomas refused to account for his moods and label
> them. But it is a defect that, through a failure to probe
> his unhappiness, he implied that its causes were re-
> moter, less tangible and more inevitable than in fact
> they were. He seems to do this, for instance, in a charac-
> teristic poem called *Home.* The poem almost certainly
> springs from nostalgic feelings, but Edward Thomas
> gives them a much larger significance, larger than they
> deserve. [First two stanzas quoted.] One may even

54   detect, what Thomas rarely betrays, the nostalgic's
lack of genuine humility: "all that they mean I know."
But he goes on to confess, not to nostalgia, but to the
much more overwhelming doubt whether any life,
once known, could satisfy him. It is well to remember
that these, after all, are criticisms of what might have
been only one phase of Edward Thomas's poetry . . .
But of his existing body of poetry one may say that,
though he does not avow it, there are signs everywhere
of the predicament encountered by those who are
isolated without being self-sufficient. (p. 19)

Cooke argues that in *Home* there is adequate 'resistance'
(Harding's own requirement) to 'nostalgia' (pp. 225–9).

1–8. Cf. the first two stanzas of Thomas Hardy's poem,
To Life.

1. *Not the end: but there's nothing more*. This elliptical
opening succinctly dramatises the poet's sense of inhabiting a limbo between here and the hereafter. 'But
there's nothing more' with its 'finite' verb undercuts the
latent potential of 'Not the end.' Life is not over, but has
nothing more to offer.

13–16. *And could I . . . things that were*. Cf. *The Signpost*,
lines 21–9 (p. 23) and *Liberty*, lines 24–7 (p. 99), and
see notes.

17–20. *Remembering ills . . . what was well*. Cf. *Parting*,
line 15 ff. (p. 50) and see notes. *Parting* was written twelve
days before *Home* and similarly consists of six quatrains.
The two poems, each of which mythologises a 'land,' seem
to be complementary and to form a progression. 'Home'
is related to the sterile 'Past' repudiated in *Parting* for the
sake of the complex living moment. It also comprehends
death, or any possible future, rejected on similar grounds.
Despite discontent, or the more subtle feeling that he has

fully experienced both the pleasures and pains of life 54
and assimilated their meaning (if this is neurotic it is
depressive not regressive). Thomas will not yield to his
strong recurrent urge to 'go back' or forward (see note
on his 'love of death,' p. 313). Nevertheless, he mounts
his 'resistance' with greater difficulty than is usual in
the poetry of this period. The poem concludes stoically,
rather than with an affirmation of life.

24. *blink at*: try to ignore and endure.

THE OWL   55

B.M. 24 February 1915.

This poem seems to have been constructed with
particular conscientiousness. Thomas heavily underlines
in the first two stanzas the essentials of comfort—'food,
fire, and rest'—and his syntax is carefully discriminating
throughout: 'hungry, and yet not starved,' etc. Such care
and unusually overt qualification match the clear moral
distinctions drawn in the poem. Thomas is telling us and
himself 'plain,' and the feelings aroused here, his sense of
'what I escaped/And others could not,' coincide with
those that formed the basis of his decision to join up (see
general note to *This is No Case of Petty Right or Wrong*,
p. 308). James Reeves analyses the poem in *The Critical
Sense* (Heinemann, 1956, pp. 79–82).

10. *No merry note*. Reeves points out that Thomas is
referring to 'When icicles hang by the wall,' the song at
the end of *Love's Labour's Lost*: 'Then nightly sings the
staring owl,/Tu-whit;/Tu-who, a merry note,/While
greasy Joan doth keel the pot.'

13. *salted*. 'It is the repeated word, *salted*, which is at

55 once ambiguous yet absolutely right for [Thomas's] purposes. The owl grieves, lonely in the cold night, and the poet pities those who don't share the warmth and comfort that he is privileged to enjoy; but he is too honest to deny that, while his sympathy for the "soldiers and poor" is authentic, his awareness of their privation adds to his own pleasure and contentment while at the same time it awakens the sense of guilt. So when he says, "And salted was my food, and my repose," the word *salted* certainly means *flavoured* or *spiced*, but at the same time less comfortable connotations are invoked: the harshness of salt, the salt in the wound, the taste of bitterness, and of tears.' (Scannell, pp. 19–20)

55   THE CHILD ON THE CLIFFS

B.M. 11 March 1915.

The sea figures little in Thomas's poetry, although it contributed to his sense of England:

Westward, for men of this island, lies the sea; westward are the great hills. In a mere map the west of Britain is fascinating. The great features of that map, which make it something more than a picture to be imperfectly copied by laborious childish pens, are the great promontories of Caernarvon, of Pembroke, of Gower and of Cornwall, jutting out into the western sea, like the features of a grim large face, such a face as is carved on a ship's prow. These protruding features, even on a small-scale map, thrill the mind with a sense of purpose and spirit. They yearn, they peer out ever to the sea, as if using eyes and nostrils to savour the utmost scent of it, as if themselves

calling back to the call of the waves. (S.C., pp. 8–9)   **55**
Like Lob Thomas was actually and imaginatively 'sea-
blue-eyed,' yet presents more conspicuously his 'land
face.' In prose he writes of the sea as a foreign element,
'unearthly,' untouched by human history.

Thomas told Eleanor Farjeon: 'I like the Child on the
Cliff. It is a memory between one of my young brothers
and myself which he reminded me of lately. He was
most of the child and I have been truthful. I think I can
expect some allowances for the "strangeness" of the
day' (E.F., pp. 127–8). Despite the allowances we also
make for the fancifulness and innocent morbidity of the
child's eye view, Thomas's reproduction of his perceptions and language seems a little forced. *The Child in the
Orchard* (p. 131) is toughened by its nursery rhyme/folk
element. Nevertheless, Thomas's sea child and his land
child are complementary (as the formal parallel between
the poems might suggest).

13–16. *Fishes and gulls ring no bells ... up in heaven.* **56**
Thomas may be referring to legendary drowned cities
and lands off the south-western coast of Britain (e.g.
Lyonesse between Land's End and the Scilly Isles)
whose church bells can sometimes be heard. 'Outside, by
the window, is the village idiot, with a smile like the sound
of bells ascending from a city buried in the sea' (B.W.,
p. 98).

B.M. 12 March 1915.

The symbolism of the poem is anticipated by a passage
in *Beautiful Wales*:

> Next day I crossed the river. At first, the water seemed
> as calm and still as ice. The boats at anchor, and
> doubled by shadow, were as if by miracle suspended
> in the water. No ripple was to be seen, though now
> and then one emitted a sudden transitory flame,
> reflected from the sun, which dreamed half-way up
> the sky in a cocoon of cloud. No motion of the tide
> was visible, though the shadows of the bridge that
> cleared the river in three long leaps, trembled and
> were ever about to pass away. The end of the last
> leap was unseen, for the further shore was lost in mist,
> and a solitary gull spoke for the mist. (pp. 110–11 and
> P.E.T., p. 54)

Thomas's rhyming appropriately suggests both progress
and a state of suspension. The internal rhymes in the
first and third lines of each stanza maintain a forward
impetus which is retarded by the similar ending of the
last two lines. The latter creates a curious effect of stasis
or hiatus, as if the poem refuses to move on to a full
rhyme or any kind of further conclusion but remains
itself a 'bridge.'

B.M. 16 March 1915.

Thomas was brought up in the London streets and
suburbs, but the whole direction of his life and art led

away from them: both *The Heart of England* and *In* **57**
Pursuit of Spring begin with a blessed departure from the
city. Yet in *Good-Night*, in *The Childhood of Edward
Thomas* and other autobiographical writings, he salutes
his origins: 'the Common . . . was large enough to provide
us with many surprises and discoveries for years'
(C.O.E.T., p. 39); 'The streets were a playground almost
equal to the Common' (p. 41). Town and country touch
in *Good-Night*, as in one prose original:

> Several times two or three children passed beneath the
> window and chattered in loud, shrill voices, but they
> were unseen. Far from disturbing the tranquillity, the
> sounds were steeped in it; the silence and stillness of
> the twilight saturated and embalmed them. But pleasant
> as in themselves they were entirely, they were far more
> so by reason of what they suggested.
>
> These voices and this tranquillity spoke of Spring.
> They told me what an evening it was at home. I knew
> how the first blackbird was whistling in the broad oak,
> and, farther away—some very far away—many thrushes
> were singing in the chill, under the pale light fitly
> reflected by the faces of earliest primroses. (I.P.S.,
> pp. 19-20)

Another seminal passage reveals more positively Thomas's
fascination with the puzzle of 'people living in no ancient
way' (H.E., p. 7). (In a sense it was for such people, for
his past self, that he wrote his Nature books and poems.)

> . . . these streets are the strangest thing in the world.
> They have never been discovered. They cannot be
> classified. There is no tradition about them. Poets have
> not shown how we are to regard them. They are to us
> as mountains were in the Middle Ages, sublime, diffi-
> cult, immense; and yet so new that we have inherited

57 no certain attitude towards them, of liking or dislike.
They suggest so much that they mean nothing at all.
... They propose themselves as a problem to the mind,
only a little less so at night when their surfaces hand
the mind on to the analogies of sea waves or large
woods ... Once [in a new suburb] I came upon a line
of willows above dead reeds that used to stand out by
a pond as the first notice to one walking out of London
that he was in the country at last; they were unchanged;
they welcomed and encouraged once more. The lighted
windows in the mist had each a greeting; they were as
the windows we strain our eyes for as we descend to
them from the hills of Wales or Kent; like those, they
had the art of seeming a magical encampment among
the trees, brave, cheerful lights which men and women
kept going amidst the dense and powerful darkness.
The thin, incompleted walls learned a venerable
utterance. (H.E., pp. 4–6)

4. *the noise of man, beast, and machine prevails*. 'Somewhere far off I could hear an angry murmur broken by
frantic metallic clashings. No one sound out of the
devilish babble could I disentangle, still less, explain.
A myriad noises were violently mixed in one muddy,
struggling mass of rumbling and jangling ... Above
all, the babble was angry and it was inhuman ... As I
realised that it was the mutter of London, I sighed, being
a child, with relief, but could not help listening still for
every moment of that roar as of interlaced immortal
dragons fighting eternally in a pit.' (H.G.L.M., pp. 226–7)

5–8. *But the call ... seem a king*. Thomas's reconciliation
or 'unfamiliar' or 'strange' with 'familiar' relates *Good-
Night* to *Home* (p. 74) and other poems where he experiences unexpected peace or fulfilment (cf. *The Bridge*).

218

9–10. *the ghost/That in the echo lives and with the echo* 57
dies: Thomas as a child.

16. *All Friends' Night*: a coinage on the principle of 'All
Souls' Day/Night.'

BUT THESE THINGS ALSO 58

B.M. 18 March 1915.

5–8. *The shell of a little snail . . . purest white.* Like lines
4–16 of *November* (p. 19), this stanza impressively displays both the microscopic accuracy of Thomas's eye
and the care which rescues from oblivion 'all that men
scorn' or fail to take into account. The 'minutiae' of the
grass (little, chip, mite, small) are kept distinct in two
ways, partly by the itemizing syntax and partly by consonantal clashes where individual words meet: 'snail
bleached,' 'chip of flint.'

16. *And Spring's here, Winter's not gone*: a classic Thomas
observation.

THE NEW HOUSE 58

B.M. 19 March 1915.

The new house was at Wick Green (see general notes
to *Wind and Mist*, p. 225 and *When First*, p. 370). This
short lyric doubly anticipates Thomas's more extended
treatment of the same subject in *Wind and Mist*, since it
puts prophetically what that poem examines retro-
spectively. 'The new house' also looks forward to 'the
dark house' of the later poetry.

15. *how the wind would sound.* This understated sug- 59
gestion gives off an infinitely ominous reverberation.

59

B.M. 22-3 March 1915.

See general note to *The Barn*, p. 209.

9–12. *Then the great down . . . black of night.* The move-ment of this stanza dramatises the poet's altering per-spective and rising sense of menace: 'great' prepares for the heavier stress on 'grew,' 'barn' for 'black.' Lines 13–14 conversely trace a decline, through a bathetic repetition of 'barn' and the throwaway short line, in which 'less' is the only conspicuous word.

60 24. *So the barn was avenged.* Because the poet's pride in his 'cautiousness' has gone before a fall: what he 'dis-dained' as the barn has proved to be the down. Despite Thomas's light touch *The Barn and the Down* may explore issues of emotional perspective and balance, the human tendency to make mountains out of molehills and the reverse.

60 SOWING

B.M. 23 March 1915.

A perfect lyric about perfection in which a series of apparently simple statements adds up to an evocation of poised tranquillity rare in Thomas's poetry. He has dramatised this poise by making sentence and stanza co-extensive, so that any enjambement is finally contained.

15. *Half a kiss, half a tear.* This precisely descriptive, infinitely suggestive line epitomises the balance of the poem's mood and movement.

B.M. 23 March 1915.

A joyous sequel to *March* (p. 20, see notes). Thomas was born on 3 March 1878.

8. *this unnamed, unmarked godsend* It is rare for Thomas to praise something 'unnamed,' but the wonder of the event lies in its unpredictable, gratuitous quality. In any case he (or she) effectively 'marks' and 'names' it himself, 'this singing day.' Like *March*, *March the Third* may have prompted Robert Frost to a poem: *The Valley's Singing Day.*

10–12. *How it may shift . . . this singing day?* In both *The South Country* and *In Pursuit of Spring* Thomas charts the rising and falling of the overture to Spring until it reaches its culmination:

At the lower margin of the wood the overhanging branches form blue caves, and out of these emerge the songs of many hidden birds. I know that there are bland melodious blackbirds of easy musing voices, robins whose earnest song, though full of passion, is but a fragment that has burst through a more passionate silence, hedge-sparrows of liquid confiding monotone, brisk acid wrens, chaffinches and yellowhammers saying always the same thing (a dear but courtly praise of the coming season), larks building spires above spires into the sky, thrushes of infinite variety that talk and talk of a thousand things, never thinking, always talking of the moment, exclaiming, scolding, cheering, flattering, coaxing, challenging, with merry-hearted, bold voices that must have been the same in the morning of the world when the forest trees lay, or leaned, or hung, where they fell. Yet I can distinguish neither

61 blackbird, nor robin, nor hedge-sparrow, nor any one voice. All are blent into one seething stream of song. It is one song, not many. It is one spirit that sings. (S.C., pp. 21–2)

61 TWO PEWITS

B.M. 24 March 1915. Revised version on 4 May.

According to Thomas, *Two Pewits* 'had to be as clear as glass' (E.F., p. 134). This clarity, and its apparent simplicity of language and form, should not blind us to the fact that the poem is a display of technical virtuosity matching the freewheeling expertise of the birds. Thomas's fascination with the aerial ballet of pewits emerged as early as his first book, *The Woodland Life*:

> It is a beautiful sight to watch their facile turns of flight as each strives to surmount his rival. Now a couple seem as one bird, and again they part to soar and twist in opposite directions. As they race the sun gleams on their crests and greenish bars, and the peewit swings in the air with his prowess of flight. In a straight steady motion, rare indeed with a peewit, their wings are soundless, but in the whirling dashes from side to side in combat or amorous display a strange wind-like rush is made as if their joints were stiff. Under a strong sun, when it is dazzling to look up, this rushing sound betrays the bird as it passes overhead. (p. 16)

Pewits eventually became, perhaps, an image of personal and poetic liberation which also concentrates certain features of Thomas's aesthetic. John Danby calls the poem 'an exemplary instance of Thomas's polarised world ... The birds sporting and crying midway between the moonlit sky and darkened earth intensify the light **61** and darkness they reflect. In them, as if by their closer juxtaposition, the opposites are raised to a higher tension—a vivid, troubled, chequered activity against the discrete rest that sky or earth separately represent.' ('Edward Thomas,' *Critical Quarterly*, I, 1959, 309)

WILL YOU COME?   **62**

B.M. 25 March 1915.

See note on Thomas's love poems, p. 324. *Will You Come?* has technical and thematic affinities with *Two Pewits*.

THE PATH   **63**

B.M. 26 March 1915.

In Chapter IX of *The South Country* Thomas proposes 'a history of England written from the point of view of one parish, or town, or great house' in which he will include 'the histories of roads': 'Every traveller in Hampshire remembers the road that sways with airy motion and bird-like curves down from the high land of clay and flint through the chalk to the sand and the river. It doubles round the head of a coombe, and the whole descent is through beech woods uninterrupted and all but impenetrable to the eye above or below except where once or twice it looks through a narrow slit to the blue vale and the castled promontory of Chanctonbury twenty miles south-east. As the road is a mere ledge on the side

63 of a very steep hill the woods below it hurry down to a precipitous pit full of the glimmering, trembling and murmuring of innumerable leaves and no sight or sound of men. It is said to have been made more than half a century ago to take the place of the rash straight coach road which now enters it near its base.' (pp. 153–4)

This 'road' poem (see general note to *Roads*, p. 315) itself constitutes a 'path' or series of paths. The winding, exploratory quality of Thomas's syntax becomes heightened, as it does in all cases where he excavates some memory, origin, or essence. The path here symbolises on a smaller scale a process of discovery or recovery like that dramatised in *Old Man* (p. 21, see notes). It stands, perhaps, for the path taken by Thomas's imagination—'to some legendary/Or fancied place.' Its situation corresponds to his mental tightrope, poise between normality ('the level road') and nightmare ('the precipitous wood below').

1–3. *Running along a bank* . . . *there is a path.* The syntactical and rhythmical construction of these lines is repeated with variations throughout the poem, each instance a microcosm of its overall movement. Thomas delays or underplays his main verbs, while participial phrases and subordinate clauses lead us down the path. Smooth, 'running' movements are interrupted by emphatic stresses: 'checks the sight,' 'but in vain,' 'it ends where the wood ends.' Such 'checks' frustrate and tantalise the reader.

17–22. *To see a child* . . . *the wood ends.* Sustained enjambement attaches a heightened drama to the last stages of the path and the poem. Characteristic twists or forks of meaning also ramify the mystery: 'overhangs'/'underyawns,' 'As if,' 'Or,' 'sudden.' Although the poem may

have literally reached a dead end we are not wholly **63**
cheated. Thomas has opened up possibilities of imaginative adventure which still reverberate. The real issue,
typically, runs counter to his overt statement.

THE WASP TRAP   **64**

B.M. 27 March 1915.
   A wasp trap is a jam jar, emptied but still sticky, with
water at the bottom of it to drown the wasps.
13–16. *For wasps meant . . . So glistening.* There may be
just a hint here that the beautiful surface of the poem,
like that of the moonlight, is deceptive: the wasp trap is
a death trap. 'From the dead apple-bough' looks forward
to the refrain line at the end of each stanza of *The Gallows*
(p. 125).

A TALE   **64**

B.M. 28 March 1915.
3–4. *The periwinkle crawls . . . into the wood.* A periwinkle
is spreading into the wood from the garden of the ruined
cottage, possibly the lesser Periwinkle which 'crawls'
over the ground on freely rooting stems.

WIND AND MIST   **65**

B.M. 1 April 1915.
   Cf. *The New House* (p. 58). At the end of 1909 the
Thomases moved into a house built specially for them

65 by Geoffrey Lupton at Wick Green (see general note to *When First*, p. 370). 'I am back again with the intolerable swishing of the trees in rain & wind which I have had ever since I came here last Christmas' (L.G.B., p. 206). Helen Thomas vividly portrays their unease in this house where, in 1911, Thomas suffered a nervous breakdown.

> . . . somehow we could not love the house. The heavy oak was raw and new, and seemed to resent its servitude in beam and door, and with loud cracks would try to wrench itself free. There was nothing in that exposed position to protect us from the wind, which roared and shrieked in the wide chimneys, nor have I ever heard such furious rain as dashed vindictively against our windows. The fire of logs burning in the hearth seemed not to respond so much to our fostering care as to the wind which drew it up in great leaping flames and sent sheaves of sparks into the roaring darkness. Often a thick mist enveloped us, and the house seemed to be standing on the edge of the world, with an infinity of white rolling vapour below us. There was no kindness or warmth or welcome about that house. (W.W.E., p. 133)

Like *Up in the Wind* (C.P., p. 96), *Wind and Mist* has affinities with the blank-verse dialogues of Robert Frost (see Appendix A). The physical and psychological territory of both poems belongs to the poets' common ground, though in *Wind and Mist* Thomas has made the situation more personal, the symbolism more pervasive than is usual with Frost. All the same, his colloquialism of diction and rhythm has a faint New England accent ('No offence,' 'on a cliff's edge almost'). Thomas imitates Frost's dovetailing of two speakers' remarks, dynamic counterpointing of different attitudes to make a whole, and perhaps the framework of a place or its atmosphere

being explained to a stranger by someone familiar with it. **65**
⎛The poem may be intimately linked with Thomas's
⎝breakdown, for the actual 'wind and mist' which tor-
mented him at Wick Green have come to represent two
related though contrasting psychological assaults. 'Mist'
or 'cloud' denotes remoteness from reality, 'wind' a
possession by violent forces. The protagonist is describ-⎞
ing a state of dissociation and of extreme vulnerability⎠
His unduly sensitive perceptions are opposed to the
'sanity,' which at times approaches banality, of his in-
terrogator and of 'the house-agent's young man' (line 69).
7. *To play upon this board.* The patchwork of fields suggests an image from chess.
25. *a castle in Spain.* Not just a romantic image but also
the proverbial phrase synonymous with 'castle in the air,'
a day-dream or fantasy of wish-fulfilment. The term
doubly suggests the deceptive, mirage-like quality of the
house. Thomas may have recollected a drawing by his
friend James Guthrie: 'Look again at his "Castle in
Spain"; how it is perched up above that might of forest
like a child that has climbed whence it cannot descend'
(Thomas's preface to *A Second Book of Drawings* by
James Guthrie, T. N. Foulis, 1908).
26-8. *I have thought . . . lived there then.*' Thomas wrote
to Bottomley of Berryfield Cottage in November 1906:
'We are now become people of whom passers by stop to
think: How fortunate are they within those walls. I know
it. I have thought the same as I came to the house &
forgot it was my own.' (L.G.B., p. 126)
46. *The clay first broke my heart, and then my back.* 'The **66**
garden improves but the clay breaks first the back & then
the heart' (letter of 1911, L.G.B., p. 211).
48-9. *a child/Was born*: Myfanwy, Thomas's 'daughter the

66 younger.' The birth was difficult, and some time later the baby was stricken by a mysterious illness. Although she recovered, the period of anxiety 'more than ever increased our growing dislike of [the house]' (W.W.E., p. 135).

54. *cloud-castle*. Thomas's essay *Cloud Castle* is included in the posthumous collection, *Cloud Castle and Other Papers*. Two friends walking home at night see a huge hill which 'seemed a mountain forest ... Round upon round it rose up, nodding but secure, until its summit overhung the rocky base and on this ledge was the likeness of a wall and turret in ruins. Such a castle it might have been as a child draws with its eyes out of nothing, when it reads for the first time of the Castle Perilous or Joyous Gard, set far above the farms and churches and factories of this world ... And this mount, this mountain forest and overhanging brow, this incredibly romantic ruin upon the shelf of it, were built out of cloud in the violet western sky' (pp. 3–4). 'Cloud-castle' not only suggests a castle in the clouds and one made of cloud: it has the same overtones as 'a castle in Spain' (see note above).

54–68. *I had forgot the wind ... wind and mist*. The word 'wind' is repeated nine times in this passage, five times at the end of a line. 'Wind and mist' concludes successive lines. Such obsessional reiteration powerfully conveys the protagonist's neurosis ('Pray do not let me get on to the wind'), his feelings of persecution.

56. *You would not understand about the wind*. Coombes compares Frost's 'You don't know what I mean about the flowers' (*The Self-Seeker*)—the line is preceded by 'He thinks you ought to pay me for my flowers.' Cf. also his 'But what would interest you about the brook' (*The Mountain*).

59 *unreal* ironical, since the whole sequence underlines **66**
the speaker's schizoid distance from life and other people >
('You are all like that'). However, a further irony is provided by the implication that in some ultimate sense his
'reality' is truer and deeper than the everyday one.

71–3. *But one word . . . being young again.*' This curiosity **67**
and courage indicates that, while the protagonist has
more or less 'returned to normal,' he values the testing
his spirit has undergone in the 'cloud-castle' of madness. >

A GENTLEMAN   67

B.M. 2 April 1915.

An uncharacteristic poem—it seems closer to Thomas
Hardy than to Edward Thomas—apart from the whip-
lash scorn of 'one/With crimes yet undiscovered or
undone,' and the subtler irony playing through the
Gipsy's account of the 'gentleman.' The prose origin of
the poem, a memory of 'Mr. Torrance's' in *The Happy-
Go-Lucky Morgans*, helps us to interpret the irony. Here
the Gipsy is the inn-keeper's wife, 'a little mousy woman
with mousy eyes': 'The Gypsy was a most Christian
body. She used to treat with unmistakeable kindness,
whenever he called at the inn, a gentleman who was
notoriously an atheist and teetotaler. When asked up-
braidingly why, she said: "He seems a nice gentleman,
and as he is going to a place where there won't be many
comforts, I think we ought to do our best to make this
world as happy as possible for him".' (p. 132)

The poem appears uncharacteristic because of the unusual detail of its social portraiture. Unlike Robert Frost,
Thomas generally presents himself as a lone figure in an

67 unpopulated landscape. He wrote self-critically to Gordon
Bottomley in 1905: 'What will you say of my 25,000
words of landscape, nearly all of it without humanity
except what it may owe to a lanky shadow of myself—I
stretch over big landscapes just as my shadow does at
dawn, right over long fields & hedges into the woods &
away!' (L.G.B., p. 80). At the same time it *was* usual for
Thomas to be a note-taker, an eavesdropper, at inns.
Although always essentially an outsider, he valued the
undemanding social contact they provided.

68   LOB

B.M. 3, 4 April 1915.

Lob was 'very close to [Edward's] heart' (E.F., p. 173),
and perhaps the best received of Thomas's earlier poetic
ventures by his immediate circle. Robert Frost liked it:
'The goodness is in Lob. You are a poet or you are
nothing . . . I like the first half of Lob best: it offers
something more like action with the different people
coming in and giving the tones of speech. But the long
paragraph is a feat. I never saw anything like you for
English' (*Selected Letters*, p. 164). Gordon Bottomley
liked it (L.G.B., p. 248); and Thomas wrote to Eleanor
Farjeon: '[Bottomley] agrees with everyone about "Lob" '
(E.F., p. 147). The poem met, however, with some
incomprehension. It was rejected by *Blackwood's Magazine*
even though Thomas had thoughtfully altered 'Mother
Dunch's Buttocks' to 'Happersnapper Hanger' in case of
objections to 'the disgusting line' (E.F., p. 145). Edward
Garnett found it 'a little breathless or rough' on the first
reading, but Thomas confidently defended his methods:

'I am doubtful about the chiselling you advise. It would **68**
be the easiest thing in the world to clean it all up and
trim it and have every line straightforward in sound and
sense, but it would not really improve it. I think you read
too much with the eye perhaps. If you *say* a couplet like
> "If they had mowed (*sic*) their dandelions and sold
>
> Them fairly they could have afforded gold."

I believe it is no longer awkward. Then "because" at the
end of a line looks awkward if one is accustomed to an
exaggerated stress on the rhyme word which I don't think
necessary' (quoted in Garnett's introduction to *Selected
Poems*, 1927, p. xi). *Lob* was eventually published, together with *Words*, in *Form*, a periodical edited by Austin
O. Spare and Francis Marsden (I, i, April 1916).

Lob is undoubtedly one of Thomas's finest achieve-
ments, standing in the same central relation to his 'English'
poems as *The Other* to his poems of the inner road. It is
unequalled as a poem based upon English mythological
material. Despite the interest taken in myth by poets of
the Romantic revival, surprisingly few sought out English
legends and folk tales as opposed to Classical or Celtic
ones. Two latter-day Romantics who did, William Morris
(1834–1896) and Charles M. Doughty (1843–1926),
Thomas held in perhaps excessively high esteem.
Doughty almost parodies Thomas in his historical sense
of English culture; his admiration of 'robust old authors'
and 'ideal endeavour to continue the older tradition of
Chaucer and Spenser.' He deliberately employed archaic
vocabulary both in poetry and in his famous prose work
Arabia Deserta. Thomas imitated Doughty neither in this
nor in his jingoistic patriotism; but the latter's massive
epic poem *The Dawn in Britain* touched some chord.
Thomas reviewed enthusiastically every section of the

68 poem that appeared and declared to Gordon Bottomley:
'Doughty is great. I see his men & women whenever I
see noble beeches, as in Savernake forest, or tumuli or
old encampments, or the line of the Downs like the backs
of a train of elephants, or a few firs on a hilltop' (L.G.B.,
p. 135). There were occasional reservations, Thomas
admitting that 'positively Doughty is an antiquarian'
(L.G.B., pp. 118–19). Nevertheless, he gave Doughty
fuller representation than any other living author in his
anthology *This England*. And perhaps Thomas realises
implicitly in *Lob* what Doughty too self-consciously
attempted. The poem crystallises an accumulated sense
of English landscape, history, character, lore, literature
and language in narrative couplets of Chaucerian robust-
ness.

In setting *Lob* is a microcosm of England, or more
narrowly of Thomas's 'South Country.' 'In a sense this
country is all "carved out of the carver's brain" and has
not a name. This is not the South Country which measures
about two hundred miles from east to west and fifty from
north to south. In some ways it is incomparably larger
than any country that was ever mapped, since upon
nothing less than the infinite can the spirit disport itself.
In other ways it is far smaller—as when a mountain with
tracts of sky and cloud and the full moon glass themselves
in a pond, a little pond' (S.C., p. 10). The 'South Country'
can expand to include the Celtic fringes of Wales and
Cornwall (see note on *Words*, lines 43–4, p. 280), so its
heart and epitome is Wiltshire rather than the Home
Counties. Thomas spent childhood holidays at Swindon
and returned to Wiltshire while writing a book on his
earliest and deepest influence (see Biographical Extracts,
p. 382), the 'Wiltshireman' Richard Jefferies, who was one

of Lob's incarnations: 'the genius, the human expression, **68**
of this country, emerging from it, not to be detached from
it any more than the curves of some statues from their
maternal stone' (R.J., p. 1). The first chapter of *Richard
Jefferies* is taken up with a minute topographical description of the county, 'the genial reticence of its fat leazes,
its double hedges like copses, its broad cornfields, its oaks
and elms and beeches, its unloquacious men, its immense
maternal downs' (p. 20). The geography of Wiltshire
includes its history: 'tumuli and earthworks that make
the earth look old, like the top bar of a stile, carved by
saunterers, bored by wasps, grooved and scratched and
polished again, or like a schoolboy's desk that has blunted
a hundred ingenious knives' (p. 5). For Thomas, Wiltshire was a rich imaginative seam concentrating every
stratum of civilisation in England.

Scattered through Thomas's prose books are many types
and prototypes of Lob himself. He turns up first as 'A
Wiltshire Molecatcher': 'It may be that he carries secrets
which shall die with him; so, at least, his morose reserve
suggests ... Seated in the mound, between high double
hedges, at noon over his "dinner," luxuriously pillowed
among lush grass and golden pilewort, with his back
leaning against an elm, he will converse intelligently on
subjects that might have been deemed beyond his care,
with a sharpness of sense and economy of words that
bespeak a healthy mind cleansed by the pure hillside air'
(T.W.L., pp. 49–50). He becomes 'An Umbrella Man'
(cf. *Man and Dog*, p. 45 and see notes): 'Labourer, soldier,
labourer, tinker, umbrella man, he had always wandered,
and knew the South Country between Fordingbridge
and Dover as a man knows his garden. Every village,
almost every farm-house, especially if there were hops

68 on the land, he knew, and could see with his blue eyes as he remembered them and spoke their names. I never met a man who knew England as he did' (S.C., p. 198). He is the old man remembered by an exile from the countryside: 'You may be sure there were hundreds like him in Shakespeare's time and in Wordsworth's, and if there aren't a good sprinkling of them, generation after generation, I do not know what we shall come to, but I have my fears. I warrant, every man who was ever any good had a little apple-faced man or woman like this somewhere not very far back in his pedigree. Where else will he get his endurance, his knowledge of the earth, his feeling for life and for what that old man called God ? When a poet writes, I believe he is often only putting into words what such another old man puzzled out among the sheep in a long lifetime.' (*The Country*, p. 9 and P.E.T., p. 137)

An original source for such portraits and for *Lob* must have been the salty old countryman, David Uzzell, whom Thomas met in Wiltshire when he was fourteen and kept in touch with till his own death: 'I called [him] Dad, in the Wiltshire style, almost from the first day. I remember him first as a stiff straight man, broad-shouldered and bushy bearded, holding his rod out and watching his float very intently. . . He knew the names of most birds and could imitate their cries: his imitations of the jack-daw calling his name, and of the young rook crying and swallowing a worm at the same time, were wonderful. The flowers, too, he knew, both the common pretty flowers and those whose virtues he had read of in Culpeper's *Herbal*. With dried and powdered dock root and with extracts of leaves, flowers or bark, he composed dark medicinal-looking draughts' (C.O.E.T., pp. 129–31).

'Old-fashioned Times' (H.E., pp. 85–90) draws on **68** Uzzell's life.

⟮ A literary source for Lob may have been *The Bettes-worth Book* (1901) by 'George Bourne' (George Sturt), and its sequel, *Memoirs of a Surrey Labourer* (1907). Bettesworth was a real man whose conversation Sturt simply transcribed and edited. Reviewing *The Bettesworth Book* Thomas praised it as 'a near approach to perfection,' and maintained this note when discussing it together with its sequel in *In Pursuit of Spring* (pp. 83–8): 'a volume which ought to go on to the most select shelf of country books, even beside those of White, Cobbett, Jefferies, Hudson, and Burroughs.' Thomas's description of Bettesworth clearly relates to the prose passages quoted above: 'Bettesworth had fought in the Crimea, and during sixty years had been active unceasingly over a broad space of English country—Surrey, Sussex, and Hampshire—always out of doors. His memory was good, his eye for men and trades a vivid one, and his gift of speech unusual, "with swift realistic touch, convincingly true"; so that a picture of rural England during the latter half of the nineteenth century, by one born in the earlier half and really belonging to it, is the result. The portrait of an unlettered pagan English peasant is fascinating.' Julian Thomas comments on his brother's desire to make his prose 'as near akin as possible to the talk of a Surrey peasant': 'He was thinking, no doubt, of George Sturt's Bettesworth' (C.O.E.T., preface, p. 8).

Thomas was compiling *This England: An Anthology from her Writers* during the first months of 1915, the period of his early poetry. The anthology contains the following sections: This England, Merry England, Her Sweet Three Corners, London, Abroad and Home Again,

68 Great Ones, The Vital Commoners. Although Thomas firmly disclaimed a patriotic motive (see below), it is likely that his profounder awareness of a threat to all he most valued made the task precious and urgent (see general note to *This is No Case of Petty Right or Wrong*, p. 305). This awareness simultaneously triggered off his poetic recall of England, which the material he was assembling undoubtedly fed (see notes below). Thomas introduced his anthology as follows: 'This is an anthology from the work of English writers rather strictly so called. Building round a few most English poems like "When icicles hang by the wall,"—excluding professedly patriotic writing because it is generally bad and because indirect praise is sweeter and more profound,—never aiming at what a committee from Great Britain and Ireland might call complete,—I wished to make a book as full of English character and country as an egg is of meat. If I have reminded others, as I did myself continually, of some of the echoes called up by the name of England, I am satisfied.'

This England was thus both a source-book for *Lob* and a preliminary embodiment of Thomas's objectives in the poem. All his favourite authors are represented—Chaucer, Shakespeare, Browne, Walton, Cobbett, Wordsworth, Keats, Clare, Borrow, Morris, Jefferies, Hardy, W. H. Hudson, Doughty—and 'Edward Eastaway' takes his rightful place among them with *Haymaking* and *The Manor Farm*. In his essay 'England' Thomas glosses a passage he might have added to his three choices from *The Compleat Angler*: 'Since the war began I have not met so English a book, a book that filled me so with a sense of England, as this, though I have handled scores of deliberately patriotic works ... In Walton's book I

touched the antiquity and sweetness of England—English **68**
fields, English people, English poetry, all together.
You have them all in one sentence, where the Milkwoman,
mother of Maudlin the milkmaid, is speaking to Piscator
and Venator: "If you will but speak the word, I will
make you a good syllabub of new verjuice: and then you
may sit down in a haycock, and eat it; and Maudlin shall
sit by and sing you the good old song of the 'Hunting in
Chevy Chase,' or some other good ballad, for she hath
store of them ..." ' (L.S., p. 109). Most of Thomas's
allusions in *Lob* fuse 'English fields, English people,
English poetry' after the manner of the Milkwoman's
sentence.

A final element which Thomas brought to the making of
Lob was his interest in folk lore and fairy tales. He had
collected traditional songs (see general note to *An Old
Song*, p. 176), and compiled *Celtic Stories* (1911) and
Norse Tales (1912). Closer to *Lob*, however, (and to
Thomas's heart) was a more original work, *Four-and-
Twenty Blackbirds* (conceived in 1913 but not published
until 1915). 'I wish I had gone on where the Proverbs
left off. Probably I never shall, unless "Lob" is the
beginning' (E.F., p. 172). 'They [my proverb stories] are
rather English, I fancy' (letter to Edward Garnett, introduction to *Selected Poems*, 1927, p. xii). In *Four-and-
Twenty Blackbirds*, ostensibly a children's book, Thomas
invents absurd origins for proverbs like 'It's all my eye
and Betty Martin,' 'One swallow doesn't make a summer'
etc. He cavalierly mixes his materials to produce a
personal mythology of England. For example, inside a
'horse of willow' at the siege of 'Troy Town' in Dorset
('Never look a gift horse in the mouth') lies 'a band of
strong men from Devon, Bill Brewer, Jan Stewer, Peter

68 Gurney, Peter Davy, Daniel Whiddon, Harry Hawke,
and Tom Cobleigh, who was uncle by marriage to all the
rest' (p. 48). The book covers a wide geographical area
from Land's End to Scotland. It is full of cherished place
names and of such personal names as Giles Harkaway,
Henry Smallpiece, 'old Jack Eastaway,' 'Bob Dumpling
of Dumpling Green in Norfolk.' *Four-and-Twenty
Blackbirds*, like *Lob*, celebrates not only English lore but
its manifestation in 'English words.' Proverbs mate the
collective wisdom of a people with the genius of their
language. The poem, the squire's son, and Lob all employ
proverbial expressions in the spirit of Lydia Fairweather,
a gipsy who speaks solely in proverbs, and is wiser than
those who laugh at her: 'You do no harm, though: you
leap like a cock at a blackberry. Your wit's as long in
coming as Cotswold barley, and without it you might as
well live on Tewksbury mustard. Were you born at
Wotton under Weaver where God came never?' (pp.
109–10)

Lob is a name (perhaps commoner in the north of
England) of the hobgoblin (Hob) or Robin Goodfellow.
The Fairy in *A Midsummer Night's Dream* addresses
Puck as 'thou lob of spirits' (II.i) and goes on to describe
the typical activities of this 'shrewd and knavish sprite':

> . . . are you not he
> That frights the maidens of the villagery;
> Skim milk, and sometimes labour in the quern,
> And bootless make the breathless housewife churn;
> And sometime make the drink to bear no barm;
> Mislead night-wanderers, laughing at their harm?
> Those that Hobgoblin call you, and sweet Puck,
> You do their work, and they shall have good luck:
> Are you not he?

Thomas may have remembered Rudyard Kipling's **68**
Puck of Pook's Hill (1906), a work he knew, where Puck,
'the oldest Old Thing in England,' represents continuity
and the genius of the country. The name 'Lob' has been
connected with Milton's 'Lubbar Fend' in *L'Allegro*, who
lies down after threshing corn all night, 'And stretch'd
out all the Chimney's length,/Basks at the fire his hairy
strength.' Thomas included a poem, *Lubber Breeze*, by
his friend T. Sturge Moore in *The Pocket Book of Poems
and Songs for the Open Air*, which describes how 'the
lubber' arrests a windmill: 'The breeze in the great
flour-bin/Is snug tucked in;/The lubber, while rats
thieve,/Laughs in his sleeve' (p. 183). Katharine M.
Briggs points out that the attribution of 'Lob' to a spirit
suggests that he is not a small fairy but 'of full mortal
size' (*The Anatomy of Puck*, Routledge, 1959, p. 24).
It seems to be agreed that the term 'Lob,' like the term
'lubber,' conveys some suggestion of heaviness or dull-
ness, but the etymology and real significance of the word
are uncertain. Thomas has certainly extended its scope
beyond any previous usage. Nevertheless, such associations give Lob his magical dimension; while further
archetypal but earthier qualities are suggested by references
to the 'Jack' cycle of fairy tales (see notes below).

All this, together with his basic representation as a
countryman, comprehensively equips Lob as a mythological figure able to sum up the English character and
the character of England as they have evolved through
time, in landscape, and in language. There are really
three Lobs in the poem: the historical portrait, the
squire's son, and Thomas himself who receives a kind
of laying on of hands from the latter. *Lob* is ultimately a
portrait of the artist and Thomas takes on here and else-

68 where Lob's function of naming and thus continuing
things that matter, of 'keeping clear old paths that no-
one uses.' Accordingly the poem itself (and all Thomas's
poetry) is a guarantee that Lob 'lives yet.' It is a Noah's
ark, transmitting to the future an essential cultural continuity and exemplifying, like its subject, a sanity and
imagination, not simply English but human, which is
always in danger of being lost.

2. *In search of something chance would never bring.* The
poet's symbolic journey or quest is to have a more
positively successful issue than usual: perhaps because he
is exploring cultural as opposed to personal identity.

3–5. *An old man's face . . . sea-blue-eyed.* The colours and
contours of the face reflect those of Wiltshire and England
(see general note to *The Child on the Cliffs*, p. 214). 'Sweet
as any [a] nut' is a proverbial phrase slightly adapted by
Thomas for metrical and other reasons, cf. 'Jack of
every trade' (line 134). He may have remembered W. H.
Davies, *The Child and the Mariner*: 'An old seafaring
man was he; a rough/Old man, but kind; and hairy, like
the nut/Full of sweet milk.'

9. *the barrows.* There is a barrow (grave-mound) called
'Adam's grave' within the bounds of Alton Priors.

10. *scaring sparrows.* Birds used to be 'scared' away from
seeds with wooden clappers, songs and shouts. This was
proverbially a child's first employment; cf. a passage from
Cobbett's autobiography which Thomas included in *This
England*: 'My first occupation was, driving the small birds
from the turnip seed, and the rooks from the pease'
(T.E., p. 163).

12. *couldn't find it, by digging.* Thomas ironically juxta-
poses the old man's knowledge of 'the way' with the
excavation's failure. This omen ensures that the poem's

imaginative 'digging' into England will yield more than **68** can a purely scientific approach. Thomas could be scornful of specialists, like archaeologists, who interpret man's relation to his environment more narrowly and crudely than the artist: '. . . of these many folds in our nature the face of the earth reminds us, and perhaps, even where there are no more marks visible upon the land than there were in Eden, we are aware of the passing of time in ways too difficult and strange for the explanation of historian and zoologist and philosopher' (S.C., p. 157).

14–17. *three Manningfords . . . Alton Barnes and Alton Priors.* All these villages belong to the same area in Wiltshire, south-east and east of Devizes. The obsessive quality of the poet's search, the importance of precision, is communicated by his brooding repetition of the place names (cf. lines 1–2 of *Old Man*, p. 21) and scrupulous syntax. A sense of mystery, a confusion or fusion of real and imagined landscapes, is later enhanced by the situation of the villages: 'Lurking to one side' etc. Lob is typically 'glimpsed' up 'paths and lanes.'

26–30. *shot the weathercock . . . afforded gold.* Thomas's characterisation of the local people is not wholly idealised. Shooting the weathercock is a traditional act of folly resembling the feats of the men of Gotham (see note below), and there are implications of trickery and inefficiency.

38. *the White Horse.* A horse cut out in the chalk of the **69** downs, (cf. 'the Westbury White Horse,' *The Child in the Orchard*, line 14, p. 132). Thomas refers in *In Pursuit of Spring* to 'that very tame White Horse above Alton Priors' (p. 15). Such horses constitute a particularly dramatic link with the past.

40–2. *A girl proposed . . . Marked on the maps.'* Thomas

69 (and the girl) has evidently conjured 'Adam Walker' out of local place names to suggest the interweaving of man's life with his surroundings. 'You will find "Welsh Ways" all over England. Walkers or Workaway Hill, where the Ridgeway descends southward from Wansdyke to the Pewsey Valley [the region of the villages], is said to be a corruption of Weala-wege, and to have been called Walcway (or Welshway) by a shepherd not long ago.' (I.W., p. 22)

44–6. *Who loved wild bird . . . loved the earth.* The only blood sport ever practised by Thomas himself was fishing; but he understood 'the sportsman's tenuous emotion of loving the hare that he has killed' (R.J., p. 38) and the paradox inherent in any native countryman's love of the earth: 'Where men and children are at close grips with nature, and have to wrest a living from the soil or the sea, there is apt to hide, like an imprisoned toad, at the very roots of their philosophy, if it does not flap like a crow in the topmost branches, a feeling that all the life that is not with them—as horse and sheep and cow and sheep-dog are—is against them. . . [Jefferies] arose out of the earth, and he had its cruelty.' (p. 34)

56–7. *Lob-lie-by-the-fire/Came in my books.* The best known literary reference to this figure 'comes in' Beaumont and Fletcher's *The Knight of the Burning Pestle* (III. 423-6), where the Citizen's wife informs her husband: 'there's a pretty tale of a Witch, that had the divels marke about her, God blesse us, that had a Giant to her sonne, that was cal'd *Lob-lie-by-the-fire*, didst never here it *George* ?' (The name bears out or brings out the connotations of laziness in the word 'lob,' see note above.) It seems more likely however that the squire's son (and Thomas) first encountered Lob-lie-by-

the-fire in some children's book such as *Jackanapes*, etc. **69**
by Juliana Horatia Ewing (S.P.C.K., 1892), which includes the tale of 'Lob-lie-by-the-Fire or the Luck of
Lingborough' with the gloss: 'Lob-lie-by-the-fire ... is a
rough kind of Brownie or House Elf, supposed to haunt
some north-country homesteads, where he does the work
of the farm-labourers ...' Cf. also the poem *Lob Lie by
the Fire* in Walter de la Mare's *A Child's Day* (1912).

58–78. *He has been in England ... he might say.* A beautiful sequence which richly defines the immemorial interaction between man and Nature as well as the role of
language in cementing the union. Thus proclaimed as
sensitive namer of flowers, birds and hills, Lob becomes
more openly a portrait of the artist. Representing 'nat-
uralised' man, he bestows in turn names that humanise
Nature: 'Bridget-in-her-bravery,' 'Mother Dunch's Buttocks,' and link animate and inanimate: 'the Hog's Back.'

61. *as I guess.* An echo of Chaucer with whom this
phrase (= as I suppose, judge) was a stock construction and line-ending, e.g. 'But Venus is it soothly, as I
gesse' (*Knight's Tale*, 1102).

65–6. *old herbal Gerard*: John Gerard (1545–1612), who **70**
wrote a celebrated *Herball* (1597) or botanical work from
which Thomas took the following extract for *This
England*:

> The Traveller's Joy is found in the borders of fields
> among thorns and briers, almost in every hedge, as you
> go from Gravesend to Canterbury in Kent; in many
> places of Essex, and in most of these southerly parts
> about London, but not in the north of England that I
> can hear of ... The flowers come forth in July; the
> beauty thereof appeareth in November and December.

70 It is called commonly *Viorna quasi vias ornans*, of decking and adorning ways and hedges, where people travel, and thereupon I have named it The Traveller's Joy. (p. 97)

67–70. *Our blackbirds sang no English ... rejoiced.*) A rounded piece of idiosyncratic myth-making through which Thomas connects blackbirds, an old proverb, Lob's sweetheart and a poem by Thomas Hardy. A masculine version of the proverb is more familiar: 'Like lucky John (Jan) Toy—lost a shilling and found a tuppeny loaf.' Thomas selected for *This England* Hardy's *The Spring Call*, which begins:

> Down Wessex way, when spring's a-shine,
> The blackbird's "pret-ty de-urr!"
> In Wessex accents marked as mine
> Is heard afar and near.

The poem records diverse local pronunciations of 'pretty dear,' a traditional translation of the blackbird's call.

73. *the Hog's Back*. Travelling from 'London to Guildford' in Surrey, Thomas 'came in sight of the Hog's Back, by which I must go [from Guildford] to Farnham. That even, straight ridge pointing westward, and commanding the country far away on either side, must have had a road along it since man went upright, and must continue to have one so long as it is a pleasure to move and to use the eyes together.' (I.P.S., p. 72)

74. *Mother Dunch's Buttocks*. A local name for Sinodun Hill, near Wallingford, Berkshire. Richard Gough in his edition of Camden's *Britannia* states that Sinodun is 'vulgarly called Sandon, or Mother Dunche's buttocks, from a family of the Dunches, on whose estate it is' (vol. I, 1806, p. 225). Thomas mentions 'the clear heavings of the Sinodun Hills' in *The Icknield Way* (p. 159).

76. *Totteridge and Totterdown and Juggler's Lane.* A **70**
Literary Pilgrim in England contains a reference to
'Totteridge in Hertfordshire' in connection with Charles
Lamb (p. 24). Totterdown is in Richard Jefferies country,
situated where 'the Ermine Street . . . crosses the Ridgeway' (R.J., p. 3). It also appears several times in *The
Icknield Way*, where Thomas himself partially 'explains'
Juggler's Lane without diminishing its mystery: 'If [old
winding roads] go out of use in a new or a changed civilization, they may still be frequented by men of the most
primitive habit. All over England may be found old
roads, called Gypsy Lane, Tinker's Lane, or Smuggler's
Lane; east of Calne, in Wiltshire, is a Juggler's Lane; and
as if the ugliness of the "uggle" sound pleased the good
virtuous country folk, they have got a Huggler's Hole a
little west of Semley and south of Sedgehill in the same
county . . .' (p. 3)

77-8. *Why Tumbling Bay . . . he might say.* 'We have
need of men like that to explain "Eggpie" Lane near the
village of Sevenoaks Weald, or Tumbling Bay in a
neighbouring parish far inland' (preface to *Words and
Places* by Isaac Taylor, p. ix). Thomas has in fact, been
humorously illustrating the errors of lay etymologists,
country people ignorant of their own traditions, and
affirms: 'Better pure imagination than rash science in
handling place names.' Lob's explanation would evidently
be neither based on guesswork nor subject to the limitations of philologists who finally come up against the
'incalculable': 'Studies like Canon Taylor's can only feed
the roots of the imagination; they can colour or shape the
flowers only by means beyond anticipation or estimate'
(p. x). *Tumbling Bay* is a house in Seal parish near
Tonbridge in Kent. The English Place Name Society as

70 yet cannot say 'why [it] ... is called so' but suggests that it might be a modern name (post 1700) referring to some sort of architectural collapse in one wing of the house.

79–88. '*But little he says ... forgot and done.* A comic passage, but Thomas, like Wordsworth, believed in 'The Education of Nature.' Lob shares with his prose proto-types (see quotations above) an instinctive intelligence of the wits and senses that may atrophy under formal education or in cities. In Thomas's ideal 'Nature-study' 'knowledge aids joy by discipline, by increasing the sphere of enjoyment, by showing us in animals, in plants, for example, what life is, how our own is related to theirs, showing us, in fact, our position, responsi-bilities and debts among the other inhabitants of the earth. Pursued out of doors where those creatures, moving and still, have their life and their beauty, know-ledge is real. The senses are invited there to the subtlest and most delightful training, and have before them an immeasurable fresh field, not a field like that of books, full of old opinions, but one with which every eye and brain can have new vital intercourse' (S.C., p. 149 and P.E.T., p. 105). A Lob-like poacher in *Beautiful Wales* 'would give twelve hours a day at least to the open air, as a scholar to his books' and is 'economical' in speech (pp. 73–4).

85–6. Proverbial: 'Quietness is best, as the fox said when he bit the cock's head off.'

90–1. Proverbial: 'to skin a flint (stone) for a penny, and break a knife of twelve-pence' (hence 'skinflint'). This grudging wife contrasts sharply with Jan Toy.

96–8. *This is tall Tom ... when icicles hung by the wall.* A reference to Winter's song answering a song of Spring

('When daisies pied') at the end of *Love's Labour's Lost*. **70**
The song was a cornerstone of *This England* (see Thomas's
preface quoted above):

> When icicles hang by the wall,
>   And Dick the shepherd blows his nail,
> And Tom bears logs into the hall,
>   And milk comes frozen home in pail,
> When blood is nipp'd, and ways be foul,
> Then nightly sings the staring owl,
>   Tu-whit;
> Tu-who, a merry note,
> While greasy Joan doth keel the pot . . .

99. *Herne the Hunter*. An allusion which combines a real
person, a real place, legend and literature. In *Windsor
Castle* Thomas tells the story:

> It is supposed to have been in [Elizabeth I's] child-
> hood, in her father's reign, that the events which led
> to the story of Herne the hunter took place:

>> There is an old tale goes that Herne the hunter,
>> Sometime a keeper here in Windsor forest,
>> Doth all the winter-time, at still midnight,
>> Walk round about an oak, with great ragg'd horns;
>> And there he blasts the tree, and takes the cattle,
>> And makes milch-kine yield blood, and shakes a
>>   chain
>> In a most hideous and dreadful manner.

> So speaks Mistress Page in opening her plans for the
> discomfiture of Falstaff. It is said that a yeoman hanged
> himself on a tree for fear of the king after hunting in
> the Forest without leave. The tree was cursed, and a
> ghostly stag haunted the place and butted at the tree
> and breathed smoke and fire as it tore the roots. There
> was also a story that Herne was a keeper and went mad

70 after being gored by a stag. He tied a pair of antlers upon his head, ran naked through the Forest, and hanged himself on the tree, near Shakespeare's Oak in the Home Park, which was called Herne's Oak for centuries, and was blown down in 1863, or, according to another opinion, cut down by George III. (pp. 51-2) Thomas chose the quoted speech, from *The Merry Wives of Windsor* (IV. iv. 28 ff.), for *This England*, where he gives it in full together with two subsequent lines of comment by Page (p. 72).

71 104–12. *When there were kings in Kent . . . So they were married.* Although the name Jack is not introduced until line 123 Thomas is already drawing on the English cycle of 'Jack' tales (which includes 'Jack the Giant-Killer,' 'Jack and the Beanstalk' etc.) to illustrate Lob's shrewdness and charm. 'Jack is not the dull moral prince of the fairy tale, but rather the folk hero, sharp, gaining his ends unscrupulously or even immorally, often through luck rather than virtue, often too lazy to work at ordinary pursuits' (*Standard Dictionary of Folklore, Mythology and Legend*, Funk and Wagnall, New York 1950, vol. II, 535). In the tale of 'The Princess of Canterbury' Jack, a foolish shepherd, wins the king of Canterbury's daughter by passing various tests, one of which is to stay awake all night by her bedside. He entertains the princess by pretending to catch from his pocket fish which he has previously placed there. In the tale of 'Lazy Jack' Jack takes a series of jobs to support his widowed mother but always loses or spoils, through his folly, the various payments in kind he receives. Having dragged a piece of mutton home on a string he promises to bring home the next day's wages on his shoulders. This proves to be a donkey, and the sight of Jack with the donkey on his shoulders makes

the deaf and dumb daughter of a rich man laugh for the **71**
first time in her life. Her father has promised that any
man who achieves this feat shall marry her. See *English
Fairy Tales*, ed. Joseph Jacobs 1890–4 (repr. Bodley
Head, 1968) pp. 283–5, 95–6.

113–22. *And while he was a little cobbler's boy . . . scraped
his boots.* Thomas included in *This England* the following
extract from *Shropshire Folk-Lore* (1883) by Charlotte S.
Burne:

> Once upon a time there was a wicked old giant in
> Wales, who, for some reason or other, had a very great
> spite against the Mayor of Shrewsbury and all his
> people, and he made up his mind to dam up the Severn,
> and by that means cause such a flood that the town
> would be drowned.
>
> So off he set, carrying a spadeful of earth, and
> tramped along mile after mile trying to find the way to
> Shrewsbury. And how he missed it I cannot tell, but
> he must have gone wrong somewhere, for at last he got
> close to Wellington, and by that time he was puffing
> and blowing under his heavy load, and wishing he was
> at the end of his journey. By and by there came a
> cobbler along the road with a sack of old boots and
> shoes on his back, for he lived at Wellington, and went
> once a fortnight to Shrewsbury to collect his customers'
> old boots and shoes, and take them home with him to
> mend. And the giant called out to him. "I say," he
> said, "how far is it to Shrewsbury?" "Shrewsbury,"
> said the cobbler, "what do you want at Shrewsbury?"
> "Why," said the giant, "to fill up the Severn with this
> lump of earth I've got here. I've an old grudge against
> the Mayor and the folks at Shrewsbury, and now I
> mean to drown them out and get rid of them all at

71 once." "My word!" thought the cobbler, "this'll never do! I can't afford to lose my customers!" and he spoke up again. "Eh!" he said, "you'll never get to Shrewsbury, not today, *nor* tomorrow. Why, look at me! *I'm* just come from Shrewsbury, and I've had time to wear out all these old boots and shoes on the road since I started." And he showed him his sack. "Oh!" said the giant, with a great groan, "then its no use! I'm fairly tired out already, and I can't carry this load of mine any farther. I shall just drop it here and go back home." So he dropped the earth on the ground just where he stood, and scraped his boots on the spade, and off he went home again to Wales, and nobody ever heard anything of him in Shropshire after. But where he put down his load there stands the Wrekin to this day, and even the earth he scraped off his boots was such a pile that it made the little Ercall by the Wrekin side. (T.E., pp. 68–9)

The story is still current and is printed in *Fairy Tales of the British Isles*, ed. Amabel Williams-Ellis (Blackie, 1960), under the title 'A Spadeful of Earth.' Cooke explains the giant as specifically an image of 'the German threat' underneath his wider significance as the archetypal enemy and invader (pp. 219–20).

123. *Gotham's sages.* The proverbial expression 'as wise as a man of Gotham' derives from a group of tales based on the fabled stupidity of the inhabitants of this village in Nottinghamshire. 'The Wise Men of Gotham' perform such exploits as 'hedging the cuckoo' and drowning an eel (see Jacobs, *English Fairy Tales*, pp. 279–82). They have also inspired a nursery rhyme—'Three wise men of Gotham,/They went to sea in a bowl,/And if the bowl had been stronger/My song had been longer.'—and a

song by Thomas Love Peacock, which Thomas included
in *The Pocket Book of Poems and Songs for the Open Air*:

> Seamen three, what men be ye?
> Gotham's three wise men be we.
> Whither in your boat so free?
> To rake the moon from out the sea.
> The bowl goes trim, the moon doth shine,
> And our ballast is old wine.—
> And your ballast is old wine . . .

127–9. *Jack the giant-killer . . . bones for flour*. Most
English tales of giants and ogres, especially 'Jack the
Giant-Killer' and 'Jack and the Beanstalk,' attribute this
war-cry to the giant:

> Fee, fi, fo, fum!
> I smell the blood of an Englishman!
> Be he alive or be he dead,
> I'll grind his bones to make me bread!

The chant is, however, particularly uttered by the two-
headed giant Thunderdell who comes 'from the northern
dales to be revenged on Jack' (Jacobs, p. 68). Hence: 'The
Yorkshireman.'

133–41. *The man you saw . . . Lives yet*. Abandoning the
leisurely anecdotal pace of its middle section, the poem
quickens into a final crescendo of naming. This catalogue
epitomises and concentrates further the variety of allusion
introduced throughout. Jack, as the popular form of John,
the commonest English Christian name, has traditionally
acquired a generic and representative status ('Jack Smith').
So, to a lesser extent, has Robin or Bob.

133. *Jack Cade*: a popular demagogue and rebel who in
1450 led the men of Kent against the forces of Henry VI;
endowed by Shakespeare in *2 Henry VI* with some of the
vitality and folly of the folk-hero.

71 134. *Jack Moon.* Possibly an echo of *Four-and-Twenty Blackbirds*, where Thomas's interpretation of 'Everything comes to him who waits' (pp. 94–7) centres on 'Biddy Moon and her son John (who was always known as Half Moon).' 'Jack' Moon is presented as rather slow (see note above on lines 104–12), and the surname in tale and poem may hint at the traditional connection of the moon with lunacy or half-wittedness.

72 136. *Jack-in-the-hedge, or Robin-run-by-the-wall*: local names of several plants, which again link man and Nature, defining Lob as an elusive spirit of the countryside. In the copy of the poem he sent to Eleanor Farjeon, Thomas accidentally left out this line. Supplying the omission in a subsequent letter he remarks that it 'connects the Jacks and the Bobs too' (E.F., p. 131).

137. *Robin Hood, Ragged Robin.* 'Robin Hood' is not necessarily an intruder in this list of flower names. The legendary outlaw has given his name to various plants, among them the Ragged Robin.

138. *No Man's Land.* Originally waste land without an owner. In his chapter on Hilaire Belloc in *A Literary Pilgrim in England* Thomas mentions a No Man's Land in 'the middle part of the South Downs' (p. 160), and he uses the phrase in its general sense in *The South Country*: 'a waste place of no man's land' (p. 11). It had recently acquired a new grim significance as applied to the territory between the British and German trenches in France. The expression thus prepares for the references that follow.

139–40. *Although he was seen dying ... Sedgemoor too.* This roll-call of battles suggests different facets of English history and achievement as well as the uncrushable spirit of the common soldier still fighting to defend his country.

Cooke comments finely: 'Lob had to be both warrior and **72**
sage to protect what he held in trust' (p. 220).

141–5. *He never will admit. . . . On to the road.'* Lines
142–5 are a reinforcement of 'never'; but this parting shot
may also be an obscure, Delphic utterance, typical of folk-
tale prophecies or conditions⸢ Lob will only surrender his
occupation in the unlikely event of there being a golden
age or heaven on earth. ⸥

DIGGING   72

B.M. 4 April 1915.

Digging is anticipated by the last paragraph of a fine
essay, 'Flowers of Frost', which first appeared in *Country
Life* (13 February 1909):

> Frost seems also to play a part in sharpening the
> characteristic odours of winter, such as the smell of
> cherry-wood or the currant bushes freshly cut by the
> pruner, of tar when they are dipping hop-poles, the soil
> newly turned and the roots exposed by the gardeners.
> And there is a peculiar languid sweetness in the smell
> of grass when the rime is melting rapidly under the
> sun. Above all, the fragrance of the weed-fire is never so
> sweet as when its bluish and white smoke heaves and
> trails heavily and takes wing at dawn over the frost
> and its crimson reflections of the flames and among the
> yellow tassels of the dark hedge. (P.E.T., pp. 90–1)

At the end of *The South Country* Thomas describes an
Autumn bonfire 'of weeds and hedge-clippings' (p. 277).

1–2. *I think/Only with scents.* 'He seemed to me to be
able to use all his senses at once more acutely than most

72 people use a single one. The colour of flowers, the form of trees, the tints of dead leaves were no more and no less to him than the sound of water falling or the song of birds. Further, they were no more and no less than the scent of newly turned earth, of the wild rose, or the bitter-sweet garden herbs ... I remember that, for the whole of the last evening he spent with me, he at intervals pulled some mysterious object out of his pocket to smell. What it was I never saw, but it seemed to give him nearly as much satisfaction as his pipe' ('Edward Thomas, As I Knew Him' by J. W. Haines, in *In Memoriam: Edward Thomas*, The Morland Press, 1919, pp. 14–15). *Digging* concentrates into a single phial some of the perfumes that sweeten and spice Thomas's poetry.

3. *wild carrot's seed.* 'Mr. Torrance' in *The Happy-Go-Lucky Morgans* smells 'one of those clusters of wild carrot seeds, like tiny birds' nests, which are scented like a ripe pear sweeter and juicier than ever grew on pear-tree' (p. 133).

5–8. *Odours that rise ... celery.* The full-blooded consonantal sounds in this catalogue ('raspberry, or goutweed') seem to reproduce both the 'wounding' of the trees and the pungency of the odours.

9–12. *The smoke's smell ... all to sweetness turns.* '... the scent of the dying year is pungent as smoke and sweet as flowers' (S.C., p. 48). The bonfire becomes an image of regeneration as it purifies 'the dead, the waste, the dangerous.'

73 13–16. *It is enough ... Autumn mirth.* '... empurpled evenings before frost when the robin sings passionate and shrill and from the garden earth float the smells of a hundred roots with messages of the dark world' (S.C., p. 281).

B.M. 5 April 1915.

'The gateways show steep meadows between the woods. One shows two lovers of sixteen years old gathering nuts in the warm sun, the silence, the solitude. The boy bends down and she steps quickly and carelessly upon his back to reach a cluster of six, and then descending looks away for a little while and turns her left cheek to him, softly smiling wordless things to herself, so that her lover could not but lean forward and kiss her golden skin where it is most beautiful beneath her ear and her looped black hair' (S.C., pp. 224–7). *Lovers* and *In Memoriam* (*Easter, 1915*) seem to prepare for the 'lovers' who 'disappear into the wood' in *As the Team's Head-Brass* (p. 119).

9. '*What a thing it is*. A favourite expression of Thomas's old countryman friend David Uzzell (see general note to *Lob*, p. 234) who, despite his 'freedom' in conversation was 'not in the least unseemly or obtrusive, but grave and roused very rarely to his Shakespearian laughter and the words, 'Well, well, what a thing it is!' (C.O.E.T., p. 132). The phrase conveys genial assent, probably on the part of the more tolerant speaker (George), to the forces of Spring and love, with which 'picking may' is traditionally associated (cf. Robert Herrick, *Corinna's going a-Maying*).

IN MEMORIAM (EASTER, 1915)   73

B.M. 6 April 1915.

See general note to *As the Team's Head-Brass* (p. 351) and note on Thomas's short poems, p. 341.

73

B.M. 14 April 1915.

This oblivious drunkard contrasts with the vital subject of *The Huxter* (p. 76), written six days later. Thomas seems to juxtapose a natural progression towards death, as 'The downs will lose the sun,' against a fixed state suspended between life and death. The 'limping' couplet form is also employed in *After Rain* (p. 25) to convey a state of suspension.

1. *alyssum*: a genus of small four-petalled flowers. Thomas's 'Diary in English Fields and Woods,' 1895–1896, includes the following entry for 16 March 1896: ' "Snow on the mountains," Alyssum saxatile, a fleecy show in cottage-gardens' (T.W.L., p. 229).

74 HOME

B.M. 17 April 1915.

The second in chronological sequence of Thomas's three 'Home' poems. 'Home,' like the 'goal' or 'content,' is one of the shifting objectives he sets out to discover in his poetry. As in *I Never Saw that Land Before* (p. 114, see notes), where the basic situation is precisely contrary, a sense of belonging and peace is unusually complete. The poet shares in a 'rounded' harmony of man and Nature.

10–11. *familiar . . . and strange too.* Cf. *Words*, lines 25–7.

B.M. 18 April 1915.

Thomas's essay 'The Pride of the Morning' (H.E.,
pp. 135–7) begins (cf. a source of *The Glory*, p. 274):

The sun has been up for an hour without impediment,
but the meadows are rough silver under a mist after
last night's frost. The greens in cottage gardens are of a
bright, cold hue between blue and grey, which is fitter
for the armour of heaven, or the landscape of some strong
mystic, than for one who loathes to leave his bed. The
blackbirds are scattering the frost, and they live in
glittering little hazes while they flutter in the grass.

But the sky is of an eager, luminous pale blue that
speaks of health and impetuousness and success.
Across it, low down, lie pure white clouds, preserving,
though motionless, many torn and tumultuous forms;
they have sharp edges against the blue and invade it
with daggers of the same white; they are as vivid in
their place in that eager sky as yews on a pale, bright
lawn, or as lightning in blue night. If pure and hale
intelligence could be visibly expressed, it would be
like that. The eyes of the wayfarer at once either dilate
in an effort for a moment at least to be equal in beauty
with the white and blue, clear sky, or they grow dim with
dejection at the impossibility. The brain also dilates
and takes deep breaths of life, and casts out stale
thought and coddled emotion. It scorns afterthought as
the winds are flouting the penitent half moon.

Cooke considers that Thomas might have 'modified'
Health had he lived (p. 248). This is possible, but the
poem appears to be a unique and historically significant
experiment. It is a free verse meditation of the type being

75 developed by Ezra Pound and T. S. Eliot at the same period. Thomas proves that, given time or inclination, he could have pursued this mode himself. He combines successfully lines and sections of different lengths and rhythms, and solves the characteristic formal problem of free verse, maintaining the unity and power of the individual line, by the use of internal sound-effects and by imparting a peculiar resonance to the last word. This resonance derives from emphatic end-stopping, unobtrusive off-rhyme or assonance, and the reiteration of key terms ('land,' 'health,' 'satisfied,' 'sun'). Thomas may also be experimenting with the 'Imagist' technique practised by Pound and poets associated with him. After an initial welcome he fiercely criticised Pound and his methods (see Appendix B), but the images of 'wagtail' and 'cat' seem more impressionistically conceived and juxtaposed than is usual with Thomas. The exotic miscellany of references in lines 31–2 has a Poundian or Yeatsian sweep. Thomas seems to have chosen such a free-ranging mode for the special purpose of illustrating the liberation and power of the imagination in contrast to the weakness of the flesh.

13–14. *And what blue ... blessing the land.* 'The sky seems to belong to this land, the sky of purest blue and clouds that are moulded like the Downs themselves but of snow and sun' (S.C., p. 37). Like *The Glory, March, Ambition* and some others, *Health* is a 'Spring' poem.

15–22. *For had I health ... farther.* Internal assonance and the sequence of sounds concluding lines 19–22 give this passage a special momentum to accompany the poet's imaginative leaps. (The transition 'off'–'over' constitutes a particularly subtle effect.)

76 29–34. *With health ... sunlight upon dew.* In *The Icknield*

Way a man who represents aspects of Thomas himself **76**
'thrills' to the sound of a 'maiden' singing: 'Oh, for a
horse to ride furiously, for a ship to sail, for the wings of
an eagle, for the lance of a warrior or a standard streaming
to conquest, for a man's strength to dare and endure, for
a woman's beauty to surrender, for a singer's fountain of
precious tones, for a poet's pen!' (p. 142). Later in the
same book Thomas contrasts 'the tumultuous and violent
youth' of swifts with the 'old' appearance of the human
beings below, and thinks 'that even so must the birds
have been racing and screaming when the Danes harried
this way a thousand years ago, and thus went they over
the head of Dante in the streets of Florence. In the
warriors and in the poet there was a life clearly and
mightily akin to that in the bird's throat and wing, but
here all was grey, all was dead.' (p. 168)

Alcibiades: an Athenian general and statesman (c. 450–
404 B.C.) who was handsome, gifted and wealthy but
belied his early promise. He disappointed Socrates,
whose protégé he was, by failing to carry over the values
of philosophy into public life.

Mazeppa. Ivan Stepanovich Mazep(p)a (1644 ?–1709)
was Hetman of the Cossacks in the Russian Ukraine.
Thomas is evidently thinking, not of the rather obscure
historical figure, remembered principally for his desertion
from the Russians to the Swedes in the Northern War,
but of Byron's imaginative recreation in *Mazeppa*.
The poem commemorates a story that as a young man
Mazeppa—

> The happy page, who was the lord
> Of one soft heart, and his own sword,
> And had no other gem nor wealth
> Save nature's gift of youth and health

76 —captivated the wife of a count and in revenge the count had him tied to a wild horse. Illustrating the point that Byron 'was a man before he was a poet,' Thomas observes: 'There are finer poems than his "Mazeppa," but the poet is the equal of that wild lover and of the great king who slept while the tale was told' (S.C., p. 116). The same passage includes a reference to *Michelangelo*: 'Byron's poetry without his life is not finished; but with it, it is like a statue by Michael Angelo or Rodin that is actually seen to grow out of the material.'

35–46. *I could not be . . . four yards.* The poet implies that his aspiration (desire, dissatisfaction), and perhaps all human aspiration, is necessarily infinite, and is preferable as a state to attainment, however 'little' or 'mighty.' This may apply also to *poetic* aspiration, as Thomas seems to be exploring in *Health* that energy which is the source of both life and creativity. Thus he possibly hints here at his own status midway between the 'sun' of a great poet like Shakespeare and the minor lyric poet ('bird') such as W. H. Davies.

39. *As the hand makes sparks from the fur of a cat.* 'I passed some examination in chemistry but, as with other things, cared nothing for it, except for doing as well as most at it. For a while I played with magnets and amber, and rubbed the cat's fur in the dark.' (C.O.E.T., p. 83)

76   THE HUXTER

B.M. 20 April 1915.

Title. A *huxter* (now usually spelt *huckster*) is a retailer in a small way, sometimes at markets, sometimes from door to door.

2. *a plentiful lack.* An echo of *Hamlet*, II. ii. 198.　　　**76**

6–7. *a bottle of beer . . . a cart.* Cf. *Head and Bottle*, line 3 **77** (p. 73) and see general note.

SHE DOTES　　　**77**

B.M. 21 April 1915.

1. *dotes:* a word which appropriately combines the senses of extreme affection and craziness.

8–10. *childishness . . . carelessness . . . loverless.* These monotonous consonantal rhymes dramatise both the girl's obsession and her repeated frustration.

SONG　　　**78**

B.M. 22 April 1915.

In a letter to Eleanor Farjeon Thomas calls the poem 'a sort of a song,' tells her it was written 'under a thick cloud of [his life of] Marlborough' and asks ironically 'Does it make you larf'? (E.F., p. 132). *Song* reads like a rehearsal for *The Unknown* (p. 107, see notes).

8. *And yet she says she loves me till she dies.* The song behind *Song* may be an Elizabethan favourite of Thomas's:

> There is a Ladie sweet and kind,
> Was never face so pleased my mind,
> I did but see her passing by
> And yet I love her till I die.　　(Anon.)

(See general note to *An Old Song*, p. 176.)

B.M. 24 April 1915.

9–12. *I loathed and hated her* ... *God gave her rest.*
'... the hedges are full of strong young thrushes which
there is no one to frighten—is there any prettier dress
than the speckled feathers of their breasts and the cape of
brown over their shoulders and backs, as they stir the
dew in May ?' (S.C., p. 108) Bird-murder is calculated to
attract Thomas's deepest 'loathing,' yet he accords the
cat a certain ambiguous respect, and even some com-
passion (lines 2–4). 'God gave her rest' may bestow elsewhere a little of the odium for her place in the scheme of
things. Just after his prose celebration of a thrush's
plumage Thomas condemns 'the spirit of one who, having
been disturbed while shaving by the sight of a favourite
cat in the midst of her lovers and behaving after the
manner of her kind, gives orders during the long midday meal that she shall be drowned forthwith, or—no—
to-morrow, which is Monday' (S.C., pp. 109–10).

B.M. 25 April 1915.

'Melancholy' was only one of the terms by which
Thomas sought to define his personal unhappiness (see
From Prose to Poetry, p. 138). Coombes explains its
poetic function as follows: 'In discussing the "melancholy" in the poetry Thomas uses the word often but
never simply as a description of the mood or state we
are concerned with it as it is part of the whole sensibility

and not as having an autonomous psychological interest. **79**
The total consciousness out of which the poetry comes is
far too complex to be even faintly indicated by the word
"melancholy," and the poetry is, in fact, an affirmation
(not in the Browningesque manner) of life and living'
(p. 208). Nevertheless the poet seems to yield in this
instance to a more traditional or Keatsian melancholy.
He presses into service such Romantic properties as
'storm,' 'fever,' 'magic,' 'distant cuckoo' and 'dulcimers'
(a compendium of Keats, Wordsworth and Coleridge
perhaps). The poem shares with Keats's *Ode on Melancholy* the word 'rave,' and draws more noticeably and
consistently than usual on words like 'solitude,' 'sweetness,' 'strange,' 'vain.' Such terms, as Coombes observes,
'are almost invariably *used* as an essential element in the
whole poem, modified by and modifying other elements,
and not exploited for their stock emotional value' (p.
233). However, in *Melancholy* Thomas seems to relish
this kind of value and colour just as he does the narcotic
mood.

6–7. *What I desired I knew not, but whate'er my choice/
Vain it must be, I knew.* This sentence almost parodies
Thomas's capacity to block all hopeful exits and to convolute his syntax.

9–12. *All day long . . . or me.* The climax of the poem, like
that of *Adlestrop* (p. 38, see note), makes a wide range of
phenomena orbit around a central moment of suspended
time. The contrast in sound between 'cuckoo calling' and
the 'softness' of the next line establishes a sense of physical
and spiritual distance; while the multiple units which
compose the last two lines dramatise, in a series of
expanding ripples, the 'remoteness' of the poet's trance-
like state.

B.M. 30 April 1915.

'The true sun above a summer valley' seems to represent an open, 'natural' relationship; 'the electric light' one unacknowledged by the world. The contrast is resolved in 'ask no light' which implies that all love is one.

B.M. 2 May 1915.

Thomas wrote to Robert Frost on 3 May: 'Are the children at school now? Or are you still "neglecting" them? God bless them all. By the way, there was a beautiful return of sun yesterday after a misty moisty morning, & everything smelt wet & warm & cuckoos called, & I found myself with nothing to say but "God bless it." I laughed a little as I came over the field, think-about the "it" in "God bless it".' (D.C.L.)

Cooke considers *April* one of the poems Thomas might have 'suppressed' had he lived to collect his own work (p. 248). Scannell calls it 'almost maudlin in its senti-mentality,' but also detects 'an essential innocence of feeling that reminds one strongly of Hardy's less success-ful poems' (p. 29). Two moments of 'rapture,' when Thomas exceptionally casts aside all reservations and reserve, seem to have called forth a hyperbole as unusual as the phrase 'God bless' (see note on lines 13–14 of *February Afternoon*, p. 311). The two stanzas might be justified as equivalents of 'God bless it' and 'God bless you,' while the emotional situation defined in lines 15–21 appears sufficiently subtle.

9–10. *When earth's breath ... The richest oven's.* 'A **80**
richness, now first felt, in the atmosphere, as if the sun
drew fragrances from the earth' (entry for 21 March
1896, 'Diary in English Fields and Woods,' T.W.L.,
p. 231).

10. *loudly rings 'cuckoo.'* Perhaps an echo of Thomas's
favourite Medieval lyric (with which he concluded *The
Pocket Book of Poems and Songs for the Open Air*):
'Sumer is icumen in,/Lhude sing cuccu!'

11. *the nightingale's 'tsoo, tsoo, tsoo, tsoo.'* Earlier in his
letter to Frost Thomas announces: 'we have one piece of
luck. Two pairs of nightingales have come to us. One
sings in our back hedge nearly all day & night . . . I hope
the gods don't think I'm the sort of poet who will be
content with a nightingale, though. —You don't think
they could have made that mistake do you?'

23–4. *an isle in April lovelier/Than April's self.* Accom-
panying *a, r, i,* and *l* sounds set off the repeated 'April' –
a musical effect which illuminates Thomas's decision not
to set his poem in May.

JULY **80**

B.M. 7 May 1915.

A near-sonnet: see note on Thomas's sonnets, p. 344.
He remarks in a letter to Robert Frost: 'There is nothing
like the solitude of a solitary lake in early morning, when
one is [bathing] in deep still water' (15 August 1916,
D.C.L.).

At the river I took a dinghy and sculled for nearly two
hours, while the fresh perfumes, refined by gale and
dew—the blackbird's listless note, with a freshness as

80   if the dew were in it—the wings rising and falling in twinkling thickets—the vinous air of June, all dealt with me as they would. Hardly a thought or memory shaped itself. Nevertheless, I was conscious of that blest lucidity, that physical well-being of the brain, "like the head of a mountain in blue air and sunshine," which is so rarely achieved except in youth. Thus in a prolongation of the mood of sleep, whose powerful touch was on me still, as I knew when I could find no answer for a questioning wayfarer, I covered several miles by one impulse, and as if nothing had intervened, resumed my breakfast thoughts. For the pebbles of a shallow had been shrieking under the boat, which could go no farther. Sounds and odours suddenly invaded and startled my senses. Solitude asserted itself. The day had come: and beads of night mist were humming as they fell upon the stream from off the willows. (H.S., pp. 166–7)

July savours a Keatsian escape like that of *Melancholy* (p. 79, see notes), written a month before. Thomas seems in this later poem to 'know' and consummate his 'desire,' achieving a rare 'content.' Images of water and birds now fill his horizon and the temporary abdication froms responsibility is complete. The poem's languoroud movement rounds out a pervasive sense of suspendee- life, although there are undercurrents of potential rs,' animation (Thomas can 'break' the mood at will): 'stir 'awake.'

B.M. 8 May 1915.

Thomas devotes a whole essay to 'Chalk Pits' (L.S., pp. 27–37).

It is sometimes consoling to remember how much of the pleasantness of English country is due to men, by chance or design... among the works of men that rapidly become works of Nature, and can be admired without misanthropy, are the chalk and marl pits. (pp. 27–8)

Among the 'lesser' pits he distinguishes two types: the kind that is scooped out of a hillside and the 'hollow pit,' which often becomes a 'dell':

Some farms have one little or big dell to almost every field, and to enterprising children there must be large tracts of country which exist chiefly to provide these dells. One or two of the best of them are half-way between the hollow pit and the hill-side scoop. One in particular, a vast one, lies under a steep road which bends round it, and has to protect its passengers by posts and rails above the perpendicular. At the upper side it is precipitous, but it has a level floor, and the old entrance below is by a very gradual descent. It is very old, and some of the trees, which are now only butts, must have been two centuries old when they were felled. It is big enough for the Romany Rye to have fought there with the Flaming Tinman. But in Borrow's days it had more trees in it. Now it has about a score of tall ash trees only, ivy covered, and almost branchless, rising up out of it above the level of the road. Except at midsummer, only the tops of the ash trees catch the sunlight. The rest is dark and wild, and

81   somehow cruel. The woodmen looked tiny and dark,
as if working for a punishment, when they were felling
some of the trees below. That hundred yards or so of
road running round the edge of the ancient pit is as
fascinating as any other similar length in England.
From the rails above you could well watch the Romany
Rye and the Flaming Tinman and fair-haired Isopel.
But except the woodmen and the horses drawing out
the timber, no one visits it. It is too gloomy. This is no
vineyard, unless for growing the ruby grape of Proser-
pine, the nightshade. Though roofed with the sky, it
has the effect of a cave, an entrance to the underworld.
(pp. 32–3)

The Chalk Pit can be read as a portrait of the divided
artist which analyses the relation of art to life. The first
speaker (*A*) responds in a coarsened way to the scene,
the embryonic materials of poetry. He imposes upon it
from outside a 'fanciful' interpretation. *A* is the self-
conscious artist deploying a vocabulary of art ('amphitheatre,' 'tragical' etc.). He represents the side of himself
that Thomas progressively learned to curb in his prose
books (there are traces in the passage quoted above). It
evidently still required an occasional poetic exorcism:
cf. *Sedge-Warblers* (p. 83, see notes) in which two
equivalent 'voices' are engaged. The second speaker (*B*)
is the truer Thomas who submits his imagination to the
actualities of a situation. He 'does not understand' what *A*
is getting at, must have 'the truth/Or nothing.' *B* sticks
to the facts, to plain language, to a name ('It is called the
Dell'). He invokes and evokes, not fictional 'ghosts,' but
real people physically linked with the place. The last
word and the genuine 'mystery' is his. Nevertheless, in
lines 30–4 *A* and *B* seem to merge; and *A*'s voice is heard

in the mature blend of Thomas's poetry, a romantic **81**
colouring finely diffused. It is perhaps *A* who works up
our curiosity about the chalk pit, even though *B* satisfies
it.

3. *amphitheatre*: an appropriate term for level ground
surrounded by rising slopes.

35–46. *I used to meet a man . . . yet wild too.* Probably to **82**
some extent a self-portrait. The girl has some features
of the young Helen Thomas. Thomas once called her a
'brown earth-girl' (W.W.E., p. 125), and he mentions her
'dark brown hair' in an essay, 'July,' which recalls their
early love-making (L.A.T., p. 101).

44. *orts and crosses*: noughts (oughts) and crosses.

50–2. '*You have said enough . . . with them.*' *A*'s pre-
judiced condemnation of the 'pair' conclusively exposes
the real limitations of his sensibility, his separation of
art from life.

56–8. *imperfect friends, we men/And trees . . . breed a
mystery.*' 'I cannot walk under trees without a vague
powerful feeling of reverence. Calmly persuasive they,
ask me to bow my head to the unknown god. In the
evening, especially, when the main vocation of sight is
to suggest what eyes cannot see, the spacious and fragrant
shadow of oak or pine is a temple which seems to contain.
the very power for whose worship it is spread' (H.S., p,
183). Thomas's poetry is thoroughly, if unobtrusively,
planted with trees. The imitation of *Aspens* (p. 92) constitutes his most obvious piece of flattery; otherwise they
seem to form an essential, infinitely varied background:

> I like trees for the cool evening voices of their many
> leaves, for their cloudy forms linked to earth by stately
> stems—for the pale lifting of the sycamore leaves in
> breezes and also their drooping, hushed and massed

82   repose, for the myriad division of the light ash leaves—
for their straight pillars and for the twisted branch
work, for their still shade and their rippling or calm
shimmering or dimly glowing light, for the quicksilver
drip of dawn, for their solemnity and their dancing,
for all their sounds and motions—their slow-heaved
sighs, their nocturnal murmurs, their fitful fingerings
at thunder time, their swishing and tossing and hissing
in violent rain, the roar of their congregations before
the south-west wind when it seems that they must lift
up the land and fly away with it, for their rustlings of
welcome in harvest heat—for their kindliness and their
serene remoteness and inhumanity, and especially the
massiest of the trees that have also the glory of motion,
the sycamores, which are the chief tree of Cornwall,
as the beeches and yews are of the Downs, the oaks
of the Weald, the elms of the Wiltshire vales (S.C.,
pp. 172–3).

83   FIFTY FAGGOTS

B.M. 13 May 1915.
∠Fifty Faggots resembles a sonnet in construction,
although dependent on assonance rather than rhyme. It
is an indirect war poem anticipating the theme and
resolution of As the Team's Head-Brass (p. 119). The bare
faggots seem an image of Thomas's own possible disloca-
tion from his environment. When the 'underwood' became faggots an old natural cycle was terminated. However, 'a blackbird or a robin' will eventually establish a
new cycle, 'renaturalise' the faggots. This tenancy, too,
may be precarious, but Thomas outlines a continuity

which will at least temper the forces of change. The **83**
faggots' organic role in the life of his family also supplies
a reassuring 'warmth.' Thomas had, in fact, to confess to
Frost on 15 August 1916: 'My faggot pile is pretty nearly
used up, but it wasn't fair. We have been saving coal by
wood fires out of doors, or it would have lasted the war
out I believe.' (D.C.L.)

3. *Jenny Pinks's Copse*. In his introduction to *Words and
Places* by Isaac Taylor Thomas remarks that 'fortunately
science cannot destroy the imagination which kindles . . .
at the infinite variety of significance in names like . . .
Palfrey Green, Happersnapper Hanger, Jenny Pink's
Copse . . .' (p. x).

SEDGE-WARBLERS 83

B.M. 23–4 May 1915.
A younger Thomas romanticised the scene straight-
forwardly in his essay 'The Brook': 'Nymph-like the
brook brightens and curves its crystal flesh and waves
its emerald hair under the bridges at field corners, where
the brambles dip their blossoms, and the nightingale
sings and the sedgewarbler has its nest. For it the lonely
willows in the flat fields shed their yellow leaves most
pensively, like maidens casting their bridal garments off'
(H.E., pp. 98–9). See also prose source of *The Mill-
Water* (p. 291).

Sedge-Warblers is one of the poems quoted by James
Fisher to support his contention that 'the major English
bird poet of our century was Edward Thomas' (*The Shell
Bird Book*, Ebury Press and Michael Joseph, 1966, p.
208). Birdsong pervades both poetry and prose; and

83 Thomas's appreciative mimicry of the sedge-warbler's call confirms that his ear was as true as his eye. He could explain to Gordon Bottomley:

> The turtle dove is very much smaller than the woodpigeon & flies low as a rule & very lightly. Its voice is a soft purring, sounding as if half buried & very warm and luxurious, far softer & less articulated than the woodpigeon's "Take two cows Taffy." The stockdove is a third species, about the same size as the woodpigeon but not ringed round the neck & with a coo that is more of a grunt as a rule than the woodpigeon's, a soft grunt, but it has other very pretty notes which I can't describe. (L.G.B., p. 193)

Quoting lines 1–4 of *Under the Woods* (p. 88), Fisher observes that 'in present birds' 'Thomas saw past rural slow permanence, and history' (ibid.). As the 'voice' of Nature, birds express an instinctive and ancient wisdom from which most human beings have been cut off. Thus Thomas often gives them the last word in a poem (as here), just as they formerly set their seal on countless prose descriptions: 'Below, invisible in the dark rain but not unfelt, is the deep hollow land of the Weald. The owls whimper and mew and croon and hoot and shriek their triumphs' (S.C., p. 63).

1–12. *This beauty made me dream . . . Its poison.* Thomas establishes a dream world in an exaggeration of his Keatsian manner only to banish it ('And yet'). A Romantic vision and its vocabulary ('clime,' 'divine and feminine,' 'nymph,' 'soul unstained,' 'mortal or immortal kin') almost seduces him, but gradually retires before purer notes. Cooke connects *poison* with Thomas's remark: 'Victor Hugo has called reverie a poison of the brain' (H.S., p. 6).

26

15–17. *while it combed ... water-crowfoot*: 'the king- **84**
fishers were in pairs on the brooks, whose gentle water
was waving and combing the hair of the river moss ...'
(B.W., p. 122). 'The water of the pond was entirely
hidden by the flowers of the water crowfoot like a light
fall of snow ...' (*The Isle of Wight*, p. 26).

19–29. *And sedge-warblers ... in or out of school*. Citing
the end of this poem, Fisher observes that Thomas could
see 'birds as artists.' Conversely he saw the poet as a
bird, giving utterance to the same intuitive perceptions.
His choice of such bird-Cinderellas for a portrait of the
artist illuminates Thomas's modesty, his preference for
'truth' over 'beauty' or for discovering beauty through
fidelity to Nature ('a song to match the heat/Of the strong
sun' etc.). At the beginning of *Sedge-Warblers*, as of his
writing career, Thomas had been tempted to abstract
from Nature 'another beauty,' forcing it into the mould
of his own mythological fancies.

28. *Wisely reiterating endlessly*. 'As to the 3-word line I
thought it was right somehow, but there was nothing
intentional about it' (E.F., p. 146). The 'rightness' of the
line lies in its appropriate 'reiteration' of sounds and of
the adverbial form to create a cyclical effect.

THE GLORY **84**

No MS. or precise date for this poem can be discovered
and it has accordingly been placed between the last poem
from B.M. and the first from Bod. Thomas mentions it
in a letter to Gordon Bottomley dated 24 April 1916 in
connection with the anthology, *An Annual of New
Poetry* (L.G.B., p. 265); but as he is anxious to replace

84 it with another choice, an earlier date of composition appears likely. *The Glory* seems close, thematically and structurally, to *Ambition* (p. 48, see notes), and to explore in a more diffuse and directly speculative manner the same disharmony as *October* (p. 97, see notes).

Thomas introduces an essay, 'One Green Field,' as follows:

> Happiness is not to be pursued, though pleasure may be; but I have long thought that I should recognise happiness could I ever achieve it. It would be health, or at least unthwarted intensity of sensual and mental life, in the midst of beautiful or astonishing things which should give that life full play and banish expectation and recollection. I never achieved it, and am fated to be almost happy in many different circumstances, and on account of my forethought to be contemptuous or even disgusted at what the beneficent designs of chance have brought ... [for example] polluting, by the notice of some trivial accident, the remembrance of past things, both bitter and sweet, in the company of an old friend. Wilfully and yet helplessly I coin mere pleasures out of happiness ... Also, the flaw in my happiness which wastes it to a pleasure is in the manner of my looking back at it when it is past. It is as if I had made a great joyous leap over a hedge, and then had looked back and seen that the hedge was but four feet high and not dangerous. Is it perhaps true that those are never happy who know what happiness is? (H.E., pp. 91–2)

Besides *October*, *The Glory* also resembles *Melancholy* (p. 79, see notes) and *Liberty* (p. 98, see notes) in the Keatsian flavour of its language ('naught,' 'oft,' 'pent,' the compound adjectives) and mood. The poet's implicit

envy of the birds, as of flowers in *October*, recalls the **84**
Ode to a Nightingale; but he cannot identify with Nature's
'happiness' as can Keats, or forget even temporarily 'the
weariness, the fever, and the fret.' He refuses the glory's
'invitation' until both his own deficiencies and the inevitable setbacks of daily existence have been reviewed.

15. *And tread the pale dust pitted with small dark drops.* **85**
The minute patterning of *p*, *d*, *t* and *s* sounds in
this line, which is almost entirely composed of evenly
stressed monosyllables, seems to reflect both the 'pitted'
texture of the ground (and of life) and the poet's careful
steps.

19–20. *Or must I be content with discontent/As larks and
swallows are perhaps with wings?* Is discontent a condition
organic to man's existence, whose positive benefits we
lack the perspective to appreciate?

28. *I cannot bite the day to the core.* 'It is interesting to
note that although [Thomas] cannot "bite the day to the
core," the language and the image that he uses to tell us
this have a strength and a sharpness which show at least
that he knows fully what "biting" means and involves'
(Coombes, p. 201). Like many of Thomas's conclusions
this statement may be a scrupulous inaccuracy. The poem
has certainly pared if not bitten the day to the core.

I BUILT MYSELF A HOUSE OF GLASS   85

Bod. 25 June 1915.

1. *a house of glass.* Cf. *Gone, Gone Again* lines 29–32
(p. 128). Images of glass-houses and shattered glass
evidently haunted Thomas from childhood: 'I discovered the joy of throwing stones over into the unknown
depths of a great garden and hearing the glass-house

85 break . . .' (C.O.E.T., p. 43). The proverb: 'People who
live in glass houses shouldn't throw stones' is night-
marishly interpreted in *Four-and-Twenty Blackbirds*.
Archie Flinders, who spies on other children and tells
tales, lives 'in a big, dark house, surrounded and hidden
by a tall yew hedge.' He throws stones at the boys who
pass until in retaliation they break the glass-house in his
garden. Afterwards Archie, to whom one of the boys has
quoted the proverb, dreams

> that he was living in an enormous palace with rooms
> and halls too many for him to count. They were full of
> beautiful things, and all were his. Nevertheless Archie
> was not happy; for the walls, the floors, and the roof
> of his palace were made of glass. Nobody else was in
> the palace; yet he kept looking round, out of the glass
> walls, up out of the glass roof, and down through the
> glass floor; he was afraid to do anything lest he should
> be peeped at, and somebody should tell tales about
> him. He was afraid to eat. He did nothing but wander
> up and down the staircases and along the passages,
> from room to room, searching for a corner where there
> was no glass. His search was vain. Miserable and help-
> less, he looked out through the walls. The palace was
> surrounded by a yew hedge as high as the hills: he
> could not see over it, nor could anyone standing on the
> hill-top see into the enclosure. But though he could see
> nobody he had a feeling that he was being looked at
> through the hedge. It was more than he could endure.
> Downstairs he rushed, and out of the palace into the
> grounds. Without a pause he picked up a stone and
> hurled it at the walls. A crash, a hundred clashes, and
> a long clattering dissolved the palace to a heap like a
> pyramid. . . (pp. 67–9)

The 'house of glass' symbolises the invisible but tangible **85**
barrier which Thomas's 'self-consciousness' interposed
between him and the world (see *From Prose to Poetry*,
p. 138). However, as its last line confirms, the poem
generalises this sense of isolation and dissociation as
potential in every human being. Sylvia Plath uses a
similar image (for mental illness) in her novel *The Bell-
Jar* (Faber, 1966).

WORDS 86

Bod. 26–8 June 1915.

J. W. Haines tells us that Thomas composed the poem
'partly on a bicycle ride between Gloucester and May
Hill and partly on the Hill itself, whence, sitting down, he
could see the Hills of Wales,

> "And Herefordshire
> And the Villages there,"

as he wrote. He brought it down, written out, to breakfast
next morning, and finally polished it on the road to
Coventry in the afternoon.' ('Edward Thomas, As I Knew
Him,' *In Memoriam: Edward Thomas*, The Morland
Press, 1919, p. 14)

[John Clare] reminds us that words are alive, and not
only alive but still half-wild and imperfectly domesti-
cated. They are quiet and gentle in their ways, but are
like cats—to whom night overthrows our civilisation
and servitude—who seem to love us but will starve in
the house which we have left, and thought to have
emptied of all worth. Words never consent to cor-
respond exactly to any object unless, like scientific
terms, they are first killed. Hence the curious life of

86 words in the hands of those who love all life so well that they do not kill even the slender words but let them play on; and such are poets. The magic of words is due to their living freely among things, and no man knows how they came together in just that order when a beautiful thing is made like "Full fathom five." And so it is that children often make phrases that are poetry, though they still more often produce it in their acts and half-suggested thoughts; and that grown men with dictionaries are as murderous of words as entomologists of butterflies. (*Feminine Influence on the Poets*, pp. 85–6)

Cooke places the poem in the context of Thomas's evolving attitude to style (pp. 137–45). The studies of Maeterlinck, Swinburne and Pater may have indirectly given the kiss of life to his own prose, helped him to recognise and exorcise its 'murderous' capacities: 'the piece [*Serres Chaudes*] is hardly more than a catalogue of symbols that have no more literary value than words in a dictionary. It ignores the fact that no word, outside works of information, has any value beyond its surface value except what it receives from its neighbours and its position among them' (*Maurice Maeterlinck*, p. 27). 'Pater was, in fact, forced against his judgment to use words as bricks, as tin soldiers, instead of flesh and blood and genius. Inability to survey the whole history of every word must force the perfectly self-conscious writer into this position. Only when a word has become necessary to him can a man use it safely; if he try to impress words by force on a sudden occasion, they will either perish of his violence or betray him. No man can decree the value of one word, unless it is his own invention; the value which it will have in his hands has been decreed by his own past, by the past of his race.' (*Walter Pater*, p. 215)

Words is perhaps the most modest tribute ever paid by **86** a poet to his medium. 'Choose me' implies that poets only release the latent potential of language itself. It suggests that Thomas's own procedure was one of alert receptivity. His attitude to 'English words' connects with his attitude to English place names (see note, p. 331). Still more finely and mysteriously than place names they bear witness to the interweaving of man and his environment through time: 'Life itself is fleeting, but words remain and are put to our account. Every action, it is true, is as old as man and never perishes without an heir. But so are words as old as man, and they are conservative and stern in their treatment of transitory life. Every action seems new and unique to the doer, but how rarely does it seem so when it is recorded in words, how rarely perhaps it is possible for it to seem so. A new form of literature cannot be invented to match the most grand or most lovely life. And fortunately; for if it could, one more proof of the ancient lineage of our life would have been lost' (*George Borrow*, p. 40). But words do not only link us to the past: embryonic of the future, they comprehensively afford the continuity which every poet, and Thomas in particular, confirms through their agency. *Words* does for Thomas's medium what *Lob* (p. 68, see notes) does for his message. (It seems no accident that the poems appeared together in *Form*, a periodical edited by Austin O. Spare and Francis Marsden, I, i, April 1916.) The point is made by the happy interaction between Thomas and his materials. The poem flows richly, yet relishes each word in each short line. Thomas's very virtuosity contradicts his modesty, declares that words have indeed 'chosen him.' 35. *Worn new*. This oxymoron comprises perhaps the **87** most brilliantly succinct definition ever made of what

279

87 happens to words in speech and in poetry.

43–4. *some sweetness/From Wales*. Thomas preserved a sense of connection with this land of his fathers where he had spent memorable childhood holidays (see C.O.E.T., pp. 19–22 and pp. 53–5). The first of these 'gave me the most definite and most pleasant of my very early memories, together with some less definite ideas associated with Carleon and Wales which afterwards increased, I might almost say magically, by the aid of things heard in home talk or read in books, and of a visit several years later' (C.O.E.T., p. 22). ' "Over there," said his father, pointing beyond the ships, "is the land we have come from." It was as faint and grey and incredible in the distance as his own land was clear and true; and he sighed with happiness and security, and also with anticipation of the further deeps that were to be revealed, the battlefield, the curlew's eggs, the castles, the harps, the harpers harping all the songs of his father' ('Home,' L.A.T., p. 35). However, in *Beautiful Wales* Thomas disowns a romantic feeling for the country, attacking 'the lovers of the Celt': 'Their aim and ideal is to go about the world in a state of self-satisfied dejection, interrupted, and perhaps sustained, by days when they consume strange mixed liquors to the tune of all the fine old Celtic songs which are fashionable. If you can discover a possible Celtic great-grandmother, you are at once among the chosen. I cannot avoid the opinion that to boast of the Celtic spirit is to confess you have it not' (p. 10 and P.E.T., p. 50). Nevertheless, his admission in a letter to Ian MacAlister: 'After all Wales is good for me. In spite of my accidentally cockney nativity, the air here seems to hold in some virtue essential to my well-being, and I always feel, in the profoundest sense, at home' (Moore, p. 277) represents the real feeling which led him to repudiate a bogus response. **87**

Thomas's appreciation of the South of England was, correspondingly, sharpened by the consciousness that he was an outsider: 'Yet is this country, though I am mainly Welsh, a kind of home, as I think it is more than any other to those modern people who belong nowhere' (S.C., p. 7). His Welshness may have given him the combined gratitude and objectivity to celebrate his 'foster-mother' in a unique fashion. More positively, Wales is often on the horizon of Thomas's prose. *The Happy-Go-Lucky Morgans* are a Welsh family who spend years in a London suburb but make a symbolic return to Wales. He sought at times 'another kind of felicity than that which dwells under the Downs,' and heard ancestral voices: 'Then, or at home looking at a map of Britain, the West calls, out of Wiltshire and out of Cornwall and Devon beyond, out of Monmouth and Glamorgan and Gower and Caermarthen, with a voice of dead Townsends, Eastaways, Thomases, Phillipses, Treharnes, Marendaz, sea men and mountain men' (S.C., pp. 7–8).

45–6. *Whose nightingales/Have no wings.* Nightingales are found only on the borders of Wales: the wingless nightingales are the musical Welsh who speak and write English with a special 'sweetness.'

THE WORD **88**

Bod. 5 July 1915.

16. *the name, only the name.* cf. *Adlestrop*, line 8 (p. 38) and '*Home*,' line 28 (p. 109). In all three poems Thomas affirms the power of words or names to lodge and release a wide range of associations. *The Word* perhaps comple-

88 ments *Words* in focussing on their personal rather than their traditional suggestiveness. The 'empty thingless name,' like the 'bodiless sweet' La-la-la! of *The Unknown Bird* (p. 43), peculiarly distils all such suggestiveness because its appeal has no tangible origin. Suggesting nothing, it suggests everything.

17–19. *the elder scent . . . like memory*. Thomas fuses the physical sensations of smell and taste with the functioning of thought and memory. This is a perfectly sensitised condition in which to receive the thrush's rich, indefinable communication.

19. *the wild rose scent*. 'The air smells like the musky white wild rose; coming from the west it blows gently, laden with all the brown and golden savours of Wales and Devon and Wiltshire and Surrey which I know, and the scent lifts the upper lip so that you snuff deeply as a dog snuffs' (H.E., p. 95). '. . . the pink roses which have the pure, slender perfume connected by the middle-aged with youth' (I.W., p. 107).

88 UNDER THE WOODS

Bod. 5 July 1915.

"Now, home and the garden were so well known, so safe, and so filled with us, that they seemed parts of us, and I only crept a little deeper into the core when I went to bed at night, like a worm in a big sweet apple. But the woods on the hills were utterly different, and within them you could forget that there was anything in the world but trees and yourself, an insignificant self, so wide and solitary were they. The trees were mostly beeches and yews, massed closely together. Nothing could grow under them. Except for certain

natural sunny terraces not easily found, they covered **88**
the whole hills from top to bottom ... Nobody took
heed of the woods except the hunters. The timber was
felled if at all by the west wind. The last keeper had
long ago left his thatched cottage under the hill, where
the sun shone so hot at midday on the reed-thatched
shed and the green mummy of a stoat hanging on the
wall." ('Mr. Torrance,' H.G.L.M., pp. 149–51)

1–4. *When these old woods ... the old years.* See general
note to *Sedge-Warblers*, p. 272.

13. *Most silent beech and yew*: Most silent [were] beech **89**
and yew.

22. *And with no scent at all.* The mummy's lack of
'scent,' so important to the process of memory in Thomas's
poetry, indicates how 'barely' recollections of the keeper
have survived. The poem as a whole pushes the frontiers
of memory very far back, into 'these old woods' and 'the
old years.'

HAYMAKING   89

Bod. 6, 7, 8 July 1915.

Thomas included *Haymaking* and *The Manor Farm*
(p. 31, see notes), numbered I and II, in *This England*
under his pseudonym 'Edward Eastaway' (pp. 111–12).
The poems appear at the end of the section 'Her Sweet
Three Corners.' Both idyllic scenes embody a tradition
and 'spirit' he had often tried to capture in prose:

[The] meadows are brown with yet untouched grasses,
grey and silken with the placid ruffled waves of yesterday's new swathes, and liquid emerald where the hay
has already been carted; and now the brown, now the

89   grey, now the emerald warms and becomes visible under the feet of the light that dwells in the mist ... I turn my head and, looking again, the sun is once more in the sky, the mist has gone. The vast, hunched, hot, purring summer country is clearly enjoying the light and warmth. The swallows flying are joyous and vivid in colour and form as if I had the eyes of some light-hearted painter of the world's dawn. Where the gleam was, that haunt of the sun's, that half hour's inn to which he turns from the long white road of the sky to rest, is seen to be the white farm house that stands in the midst of woods and ricks.

Yet, though so clear, the house, half a mile off, seems to have been restored by this fair and early light and the cooing of doves to the seeming happy age in which it was built. The long, tearing crow of the cock, the clink of dairy pans, the palpitating, groaning shout of the shepherd, *Ho! ho! ho! ho! ho!* now and then, even the whirr of the mowing machines, sound as if the distance that sweetens them were the distance of time and not only of space. ('An Old Farm,' H.E., pp. 71–2)

(The following passage is a continuation of that quoted in the general note to *Adlestrop*, p. 187, q.v.)

The utmost kindliness of earth is expressed in these three houses, the trees on the flat green, the slightly curving road across it, the uneven posts and rails leaning this way and that at the edge of the pond. The trees are so arranged about the road that they weave a harmony of welcome, of blessing, a viaticum for whosoever passes by and only for a moment tastes their shade, acknowledges unconsciously their attitudes, hears their dry summer murmuring, sees the

[farm]house behind them. The wayfarer knows nothing **89**
of those who built them and those who live therein,
of those who planted the trees just so and not otherwise,
of the causes that shaped the green . . . He only knows
that centuries of peace and hard work and planning
for the undreaded future have made it possible. The
spirit of the place, all this council of time and Nature
and men, enriches the air with a bloom deeper than
summer's blue of distance. . . (S.C., p. 12)

1–6. *After night's thunder . . . divine gaiety.* Cf. lines 1–10
of *May the Twenty-third* (p. 51) and see note. Thomas's
essay 'The Artist,' which anticipates details of both
poems, includes a description of 'clouds, farther away
than [Adams] had ever before seen clouds, the most
delicate of toppling marble mountains, grey-white with
a glistening white profile towards the sun . . . Round
about the sun itself hung a mass of . . . blue-grey, edged
with fiery gold . . .' (L.A.T., pp. 133–4). These lines
stand in an interesting relation to the main body of the
poem from which the simile of lines 3–6 sets them apart.
The 'perfect blue' of the sky evokes a primal state before
the earth was contaminated by human 'misery' and
violence (the 'thunder,' perhaps, of war). Thomas delays
the introduction of Adam into Eden ('The smooth
white empty road'), although his imagery prepares for
man's presence: 'fir cones standing up stiff,' 'happier
than any crowd/Of children.'

8. *the holly's Autumn falls in June.* The evergreen holly **90**
sheds some of its leaves in June. More economically than
in *The Manor Farm* (cf. lines 18–21 and see note) Thomas
fuses the seasons.

17–18. *The swift . . . flown off with the arrow.* In 'The
Artist' the eyes of Adams the painter delight 'in the

90 silkiness and darkness of the long grass, in the towering of one tree, the forking of another, and the inexplicable ramifications of hundreds; in the flight of the swift which was as if the arrow and bow had flown away together' (L.A.T., p. 133). The combination of fancy and visual exactness in this image has often been praised. A similar clarity and intensity inform Thomas's whole portrayal of summer with its strong sunlit colours and sharply outlined detail. The reference to swallows in the passage quoted above from *The Heart of England* confirms that Thomas had long felt the need of usurping the vision and techniques of the painter in order to delineate such a scene (see note on line 35 below). At the same time he provides the aural dimension ('shrill shrieked') which words can additionally bestow.

35. *Older than Clare and Cobbett, Morland and Crome.* All interpreters of the English countryside. Thomas writes perceptively of John Clare (1793–1864) in *Feminine Influence on the Poets*: 'one of those who have in them the natural spirit of poetry in its purity' (p. 84) and in *A Literary Pilgrim in England*: 'To enumerate the flowers was a pleasure to him, and he did so in a manner which preserves them still dewy, or with summer dust ...' (p. 234). 'No man ever came so near to putting the life of the farm, as it is lived, not as it is seen over a five-barred gate, into poetry. He gives no broad impressions— he saw the kite, but not the kite's landscape—yet his details accumulate in the end, so that a loving reader, and no one reads him but loves him, can grasp them, and see the lowlands of Northamptonshire as they were when the kite still soared over them' (p. 235). Thomas evidently relished the 'long formless pieces full of place-names and of field-lore,' and all his remarks implicitly associate him

with Clare: they are probably unrivalled as naturalists **90**
among English Nature poets. *This England* contains two
extracts from Clare's poetry, one a description of birds
on Emmonsail's heath which reveals an even more
specific affinity.

'William Cobbett is one of those names which have
come to symbolise the bearer's character to perfection. It
is now impossible to say how much of the character of the
name was given to it by this one man in his seventy-two
years of life (1763–1835). It was an altogether English
name to begin with, thoroughly native and rustic; and
English it remains, pure English, old English, merry
English . . . William Cobbett is the only Cobbett in the
Dictionary of National Biography, but through him speak
a thousand Cobbetts, too horny-handed to hold a pen,
hairy, weather-stained, deep-chested yeomen and peasants,
yet not one of them, I dare say, a better man than this
Farnham farmer's boy, whose weapons included the
sword, the spade, the voice, and the pen' (Thomas's
introduction to *Rural Rides*, p. vii). Thomas in several
contexts praises Cobbett's style for qualities central to his
own and which he admired in Robert Frost's poetry: 'The
movement of his prose is a bodily thing. His sentences
do not precisely suggest the swing of an arm or a leg,
but they have something in common with it. His style
is perhaps the nearest to speech that has really survived'
(p. xi). There are four extracts from Cobbett's writings
and one reminiscence of the man in *This England*, the
reminiscence and an autobiographical passage appearing
in the 'Vital Commoners' section.

The second half of the line may owe its inspiration to a
description in Borrow's *Wild Wales* which Thomas quotes
in *George Borrow*: 'About a hundred yards distant was a

90 small watermill, built over the rivulet, the wheel going slowly, slowly round; large quantities of pigs, the generality of them brindled, were either browsing on the banks, or lying close to the sides, half immersed in the water; one immense white hog, the monarch seemingly of the herd, was standing in the middle of the current. Such was the scene which I saw from the bridge, a scene of quiet rural life well suited to the brushes of two or three of the old Dutch painters, or to those of men scarcely inferior to them in their own style—Gainsborough, Moreland, and Crome' (p. 283). George Morland (1763–1804), a painter of landscape and animals, is mentioned sympathetically by Thomas in *The Isle of Wight*: 'This most English—old English—of painters knew every corner of the island, especially those parts which are still least accessible, as he knew every fisherman and publican ... There is no cruciform or other stone to his memory: nothing left but his paintings, his pleasant name, and the stories of his merriment and after wretchedness' (p. 43). Thomas applies the simile 'as English as Morland' to 'a perfect type of the dark ancient house in a forest' in *The Happy-Go-Lucky Morgans* (p. 72). John Crome (1768–1821) was also an exponent of the English landscape tradition in art. Often called 'Old Crome' to distinguish him from his son, he founded the 'Norwich school' of painting. It seems no accident that the line is divided between writers and painters. Like Morland and Crome Thomas puts a frame around a pastoral scene, finally giving the game away at the end of the poem: 'Immortal in a *picture* of an old grange.' He arrests and stylises life in order to suggest that it distils truths which possess the permanence of art.

42. *grange*: originally a granary, then a country house **90** with farm buildings attached.

A DREAM 91

Bod. 7 and 8 July 1915.

Thomas wrote to Robert Frost on 22 July: 'A month or two [ago] I dreamt we were walking near Ledington but we lost one another in a strange place & I woke saying to myself "Somehow some day I shall be here again" which I made the last line of some verses' (D.C.L.). The poem, which presents the familiarities of landscape and friendship as overwhelmed, seems to prophesy Thomas's transition from known to 'unknown': three days after its composition he wrote informing Frost of his decision to enlist (see p. 305).

THE BROOK 91

Bod. 10 July 1915.

17. *frizzled*: literally, with short crisp curls or fried with **92** a sputter. The word's sharp visual and aural force focuses the completeness of the poet's sensuous response, 'gathers sight and sound.'

ASPENS 92

Bod. 11 July 1915 (the day Thomas wrote to Robert Frost of his decision to join up, see p. 305).

Thomas urged *Aspens* on Gordon Bottomley for *An Annual of New Poetry* in which it finally appeared: ' "Aspens," I have thought, was decidedly one of the better pieces' (L.G.B., p. 265). The following sentence concludes an essay on Christina Rossetti: 'For hers was

92 an instrument having the power to make out of little words and common things, including a discontent with this earth and life which is not too deep for tears or words and "goes not to Lethe," a music more enduring, perhaps not less monotonous or more really sorrowful, than that of a larch tree sighing in the wind' (L.S., p. 70). *Aspens* becomes plainly in its last two stanzas a portrait of the artist, but this symbolism has been implicit throughout. The trees are detached, saddened, subtle commentators on the scenes of life, 'the inn, the smithy, and the shop.' They also evoke scenes of death, call up and upon history and memory. Aspens inhabit Thomas's imaginative context of 'day and night,' seasons and weather (particularly 'wind' and 'rain'); share his method of understated suggestion ('whisper') — cf. *I Never Saw that Land Before*, lines 21–5 (p. 115) and see note. They identify him with a compulsion to expression which is an end in itself and independent of any audience: 'And it would be the same were no house near.' The last stanza further implies a view of the poetic imagination as activated rather than active: stirred to response by life and Nature. Cf. Shelley, 'Make me thy lyre, even as the forest is' (*Ode to the West Wind*) and Coleridge, *The Eolian Harp*.

5–8. *Out of the blacksmith's cavern ... have been*. The 'ringing,' emphatically stressed monosyllables and dissyllables which communicate the sounds of life indirectly enhance the superior staying-power of the aspens, whose characteristic music prevails in the poem itself.

93 20–4. *But need not listen ... like a different tree*. There is unobtrusive defiance as well as self-deprecation in the conclusion of the poem. Although editors rejected his poems, preferred 'a different tree,' Thomas instinctively

knew the worth of his work. In a letter to Gordon **93**
Bottomley he refers to 'the satisfaction of knowing that
if a man like S[turge] M[oore] misses Frost so completely I can stand being missed myself in turn' (L.G.B.,
p. 250). These lines are also prophetic of the wider
reception of Thomas's poetry. Because he 'whispers,'
never compromises with meaning or language for the
sake of a showy effect, his poems have not been easily
popular or popularised. As with aspens, their presence
and value has too often been taken for granted.

22. *We.* 'About "Aspens" you missed just the turn that
I thought essential. *I* was the aspen. "We" meant the
trees and I with my dejected shyness' (E.F., p. 152–3).

23. *That ceaselessly, unreasonably grieves.* This line
contains only one word more than the penultimate line
of *Sedge-Warblers* (p. 84) which comprises a similar
adverbial *tour de force* (see note). The *e/s* sounds, associated throughout the poem with aspens, gather strength
and persistence from the weight of the adverbs.

THE MILL-WATER   93

Bod. 12 July 1915.

One by-road went to a lifeless mill, a tall house with
upper windows of ample prospect. Above the wheel
the waters no longer slid fast with awful repose, but
cried and leapt through the broken flood-gates into a
pool in the shadow of steep banks and underwood.
The house was peopled only by the beautiful machinery
of polished wood, now still and morose. The wheel too
was still. Callosities of dry moss on the spokes, little
by little, took the place of the weed which the river

93 had combed into such excellence. And I could not but
wonder that these things had, according to Hecuba's
wish, voices "in hands and feet and hair," the eloquence
of death. The place would have been sad, had it not
been for the meadow cranesbill at the door, a mournful
flower, but here, as part of the ceremonial of decay
by which this desolation was made perfect, it left one
thought, "How beautiful is death." Each evening, just
when the first nightjar was skimming the wood, the
sedge-warblers began to sing all together round the
pool. The song might have been the abstract voice of
some old pain, feebly persistent. It went far into the
night with a power of ghostly alarms, and attuned to
such thoughts as come when night in certain places is
malign, reverses the sweet work of the day, and gives
the likeness of a dragon to the pleasant corner of a
wood. The birds were full of prelusive dark sayings
about the approaching night. (H.S., pp. 177–9)

The Mill-Water resembles *Two Houses* (p. 95, see notes)
in imagery, tension, and theme; in being a 'prelusive
dark saying about the approaching night.' Its effects,
however, are predominantly aural whereas those of the
later poem are predominantly visual.

17–20. *Solitude, company . . . haunted or concluded be.* Cf.
the third stanza of *Lights Out* (p. 132). 'Haunted' refers
particularly to 'solitude' and 'grief,' 'concluded' to
'company' and 'delight'; but both verbs also attach
themselves to all the nouns, establishing a cat's-cradle of
nuances.

94 21. *silentness.* Cf. *The Manor Farm,* line 10 (p. 31).

FOR THESE $\quad$ **94**

Bod. 13–14 July 1915.

This poem expresses a traditional wish whose classical model is Horace's second epode ('Beatus ille qui procul negotiis' etc.). Thomas may have remembered John Clare's version, *After Reading in a Letter Proposals for Building a Cottage* ('Beside a runnel build my shed' etc.), and others which he included in the 'Village and Inn' section of *The Pocket Book of Poems and Songs for the Open Air*.

1–12. *An acre of land . . . at least a pond.* Even if Thomas does not ostensibly ask 'for these' he is cataloguing most of what his poetry celebrates: 'the lovely visible earth and sky and sea,' describing a possible 'home.'

11. *the sign of the Rising Sun*: a once common inn-sign, showing a stylised sun with round disc and pointed rays.

13–16. *For these I ask not . . . Fate.* Thomas audaciously **95** delays the main verb, thus concealing his real stance in the poem until the last moment. The qualifications and syntactical upheaval introduced at this point effectively undermine the four-square solidity of the preceding stanzas, as with characteristic ambiguity he probes the nature of 'content.' He implies that he will settle for less than the idyllic harmony suggested by the details of the earlier catalogue. These, however, offer a provisional image of what 'content' might be. The poet is like a child who mentions that he 'does not want' an object of desire, simply in order to introduce the topic.

Bod. 21 July 1915.

2. *clay pipes*. *In Pursuit of Spring* reveals Thomas as a connoisseur of clay pipes (pp. 120–6).

4. *Blenheim* (1704), *Ramillies* (1706) and *Malplaquet* (1709) were victories of the Duke of Marlborough in the War of the Spanish Succession. This line constitutes the only mark left on Thomas's poetry by his last and most detested piece of commissioned writing, *The Life of the Duke of Marlborough*. John Moore comments that 'there was less of himself in it than in any of his books; it was— for him—curiously objective and impersonal' perhaps because 'now he saved himself for his poetry' (p. 224). Coombes, however, detects a negative involvement: 'his view of the Duke's times and campaigns is coolly and consistently disenchanted' (p. 42); while Cooke notices a touch of satire towards the military and political establish- ment and an embryonic identification with the ordinary soldier which, he claims, 'show how Thomas's poetry might have developed had he lived through the real thing' (p. 86). Some squibs are directed at the war poetry of the period: Thomas calls the panegyrics after Ramillies 'verses of praise and flattery that never died because they never lived' (p. 173). Shortly after finishing 'Marl- borough,' shortly before he wrote *Digging*, Thomas enlisted.

5–10. *The dead man's immortality ... light of day.* Cf. Thomas's suggestion of historical layers at the end of *The Manor Farm* (p. 32, see note). His 'digging' or imaginative archaeology uncovers the common humanity, and inhumanity, that links the ages (cf. *February After- noon*, p. 105, and see notes). 'Almighty God' is semi-

ironic; 'the mastodon,' an image at once awe-inspiring **95**
and brutal, suggests the scale and oppression of war.

TWO HOUSES   **95**

Bod. 22 July 1915.

In *The South Country* Thomas describes 'a thatched
cottage' and continues: 'The one other house is not so
high; nor has it eyes; nor do an old man and a girl and
two children go in and out of it; it is, in fact, not a house
of the living, but of the dead, a round tumulus at the
edge of the hill' (p. 202). See note on lines 17–32 of
Gone, Gone Again (p. 363). *Two Houses* confirms that
Thomas's portrayal of houses corresponds to the whole
gamut of his imagination. Sunlit ones like *The Manor
Farm* symbolise a continuing organic existence; 'dark' or
deserted dwellings suggest a darker past (or future),
death and the 'unknown.' Thomas's enlistment may be
the hinge on which the poem turns.

14. *the muslined peach*. Ripening peaches are protected **96**
by some kind of light material like muslin. This image
perfectly conveys the insulation of the scene, from the
'dust' of a 'road' that perhaps 'leads to France.' Since he
wrote *The Manor Farm* Thomas's appreciation of 'warm
tiles' has been modified by a deepening consciousness of
the war and death.

21–4. *And the black dog . . . Dark echoes reply*. Thomas
subtly evokes Cerberus, watchdog of Hades, and the
river Styx which the dead must cross to reach the Underworld. 'And presently it was dark, but for a lamp at an
open door, and silent, but for a chained dog barking,
and a pine tree moaning over the house. When the dog

96 ceased, an owl hooted, and when the owl ceased I could just hear the river Frome roaring steadily over a weir far off.' (I.P.S., pp. 178–9)

26–7. *the dead ... half hidden lie.* A fine passage in *The South Country* is inspired by the 'monuments' of the Cornish moors:

> On every hand lie cromlech, camp, circle, hut and tumulus of the unwritten years. They are confused and mingled with the natural litter of a barren land. It is a silent Bedlam of history, a senseless cemetery or museum, amidst which we walk as animals must do when they see those valleys full of skeletons where their kind are said to go punctually to die. There are enough of the dead; they outnumber the living; and there those trite truths burst with life and drum upon the tympanum with ambiguous fatal voices. (p. 164)

96   COCK-CROW

Bod. 23 July 1915.

Generated by aural memories, 'the long, tearing crow of the cock, the clink of dairy pans' (H.E., p. 72), *Cock-Crow* is one of the best of Thomas's short poems (see note, p. 341). F. R. Leavis examines its metaphor at the end of his essay, 'Imagery and Movement' (*Scrutiny*, XIII, 1945, 119–34):

> To present a "wood of thoughts" as being "cut down" by an "axe of light" looks like a bold indulgence in the pleasures of stylization. Yet we have to recognize that "wood," with its suggestions of tangled and obscure penetralia, stirring with clandestine life, is not an infelicitous metaphor for the mental life of sleep.

And when in re-reading we come to "silver blow" we **96**
have to recognize a metaphorical subtlety... "Cleaving" identifies the effect of the sound with that of the
axe, the gleam of which gives an edge to the "silver"
of the blown trumpet. The "silver-sounding" trumpet
is a familiar convention, and the element of wilful
fantasy in this translation of the cock-crow becomes
overt in the heraldically stylized twin trumpeters...
We are prepared so for the ironical shift of the last line,
where daylight reality asserts itself:

The milkers lace their boots up at the farms.

The poet, aware as he wakes of the sound and the
light together, has humoured himself in a half-waking
dream-fantasy, which, when it has indulged itself to
an unsustainable extreme of definiteness, suddenly has
to yield to the recognition of reality.

 OCTOBER **97**

Bod. 15 and 16 October 1915.

One of Thomas's richest and most celebrated poems.
He mentions tantalisingly in a letter to Eleanor Farjeon
that 'the original version was in blank verse, but quite
different' (E.F., p. 169). Cf. a fine description of the month
in *Beautiful Wales*: 'One by one I saw the things which
make the autumn hedges so glorious and strange at a
little distance: the yellow ash trees, with some green
leaves;... the green brambles with red fruit and black;
... and on the long, green, wet grass the fallen leaves
shining under red and yellow oaks... The air was full
of the sweetness of the taste of blackberries, and the scent
of mushrooms and of crumbling, wild carrot-seeds, and

97 the colour of yellow, evening grass. The birches up on the hills above the road were golden, and like flowers. Between me and them a smouldering fire once or twice sent up dancing crimson flames, and the colour and perfume of the fire added themselves to the power of the calm, vast, and windless evening, of which the things I saw were as a few shells and anemones at the edge of a great sea. The valley waited and waited.' (pp. 185–6, and P.E.T., p. 46)

The meditative aspect of the poem is more directly prefigured near the end of *The South Country*: 'This is the beginning of the pageant of autumn, of that gradual pompous dying which has no parallel in human life, yet draws us to it with sure bonds. It is a dying of the flesh, and we see it pass through a kind of beauty which we can only call spiritual, of so high and inaccessible a strangeness is it. The sight of such perfection as is many times achieved before the end awakens the never more than lightly sleeping human desire of permanence . . . The motion of the autumn is a fall, a surrender, requiring no effort, and therefore the mind cannot long be blind to the cycle of things as in the spring it can when the effort and delight of ascension veils the goal and the decline beyond' (pp. 278–9). Thomas had long been preoccupied with 'the pageant of autumn': cf. also 'In Autumn Woods' (T.W.L., pp. 85–93), discussed in relation to the poem by Cooke (pp. 109–112), and 'An Autumn House' (*Rose Acre Papers*, pp. 92–107). Cooke uses *October* to illustrate 'the number of influences which may impinge on Thomas's consciousness in the course of a single poem' (pp. 192–4).

One of these influences was Keats. In his essay 'Keats and Edward Thomas' (*Essays in Criticism*, VII, 1957, 404–15) John Burrow makes *October* his chief focus in

arguing that 'the particular strength of [Thomas's] poems **97**
testifies as much to an intelligent reading of Keats as to
the acknowledged friendship and advice of Robert
Frost.' (Cf. *Melancholy*, p. 79, *The Glory*, p. 84, and
Liberty, p. 98 and see notes.) Burrow observes that in his
short book *Keats* (written in 1913 but not published until
1916) Thomas particularly commends qualities later
evident in his own poetry; e.g. 'Keats's fidelity to the
observation or feeling of the hour' (p. 36) and his charging
of descriptive detail: '[The "Ode to a Nightingale"] and
the "Ode on a Grecian Urn" are of a texture so consummate and consistent that the simple line, "The grass, the
thicket, and the fruit-tree wild," in one of them, and an
equally simple line in the other, "With forest branches,
and the trodden weed," both gain from their environment
an astonishing beauty, profound and touching' (p. 56).

October has parallels with both *Ode to a Nightingale*
and *Ode to Autumn*; and Burrow compares the effect of
its first twelve lines with the 'arrested scenes' which
begin some of Keats's poems, e.g. *I Stood Tip-toe
upon a Little Hill* and *Hyperion*. 'The scene with which
the poem opens is "rich," "fresh again and new as
Spring," it looks warm, and has a delicate appearance of
permanence ... offering the promise of a "timeless
moment." But the promise is deceptive, for the equilibrium is easily disturbed ("At heavier steps than birds'
the squirrels scold"). The leaves are slipping from the
elm into the grass. The hesitant rhythm of a line like
"The gossamers wander at their own will" (I think it is a
phrase of Wordsworth's that leads one to expect "*sweet*
will") co-operates to produce an effect of fragility. The
scene is warm to the gaze but cool to the touch.' (p. 406)
4. *Harebell and scabious and tormentil.* Among the flowers

97 entered in Thomas's 'Diary in English Fields and Woods'
for 3 October 1895 are 'Harebells . . . sheep's scabious . . .
tormentil' (T.W.L., p. 199). '. . . the flowers of knapweed
and harebell, and golden tormentil' (S.C., p. 11). 'Hasn't
Bronwen taught you tormentil, the tiny yellow flower in
short hill grass, a flat buttercup or avens with rather
separate petals ? Tormentilla it is. The accent is on the
2nd syllable which doesn't (as I see it) affect the merit of
the line whatever it may be; I mean doesn't tell against
it.' (E.F., p. 169)

6. *the wind travels too light.* Cf. 'as the light wind lives
or dies' (Keats, *Ode to Autumn*).

8. *The gossamers wander at their own will.* The line of
Wordsworth's which haunts this occurs in his sonnet
Composed upon Westminster Bridge: 'The river glideth
at his own sweet will.' The missing unstressed syllable
between 'own' and 'will' creates a pause during which
both Thomas and the gossamers reserve to themselves a
final independence of movement. The variation in the
line between light, erratic stresses and heavy emphasis on
wander/own/will (linked by alliteration) conveys at once
the 'wandering' and the 'wilfulness' of the gossamers. For
a different reading of this subtle rhythm see C. Day
Lewis, 'The Poetry of Edward Thomas' (*Essays by Divers
Hands*, XXVIII, 82).

18–21. *But if this be not happiness . . . or obscured be.* Cf.
an ironical self-portrait in *The Icknield Way*: '. . . I fell in
with a philosopher who seemed to be equally moved [by a
beautiful evening scene] yet could not decide whether his
condition was to be described as happiness or melancholy.
He talked about himself. He was a lean, indefinite man;
half his life lay behind him like a corpse, so he said, and
half was before him like a ghost' (see p. 137 ff.). Discuss-

ing the emotion of the *Ode to a Nightingale*, Thomas **97** feels that 'melancholy (in spite of the ode) is too disparaging a name for this mood' (*Keats*, p. 55). His own 'melancholy' derives from the feeling that he is a partial discord in the harmony of Nature. Although almost able to identify with the beauty and vitality of the scene, he is excluded from the unconscious organic cycle of the year by virtue of his temperament or simply of his humanity. Yet the solution of the poem comprises more than an assurance of 'happiness' in hindsight ('Some day I shall think this a happy day'). Implicitly the seasonal metaphor does apply to man himself. 'Happiness' will evolve out of 'melancholy' as Spring out of Autumn, even if the spiritual progress is slower and more difficult. Thomas's 'happiness' in life and in poetry seems always to have been a matter of slow accumulations rather than sudden ecstasy.

THERE'S NOTHING LIKE THE SUN   **97**

Bod. 18/19 November 1915.

Written during 'beautiful cold sunny days, and the earth thick with clean snow' (E.F., p. 171).

1. *nothing like the sun*. Cf. 'My mistress' eyes are nothing like the sun' (Shakespeare, the first line of sonnet CXXX). Although 'there's nothing like' is a familiar idiomatic expression, its slight oddness in the context suggests that Thomas is consciously using Shakespeare as a launching-pad.

2. ' "This world being made so" is 5 heavy syllables unaccented' (E.F., p. 175).

20. *till we are dead*. This phrase counterpoints 'as the **98**

98 year dies' in line 1, emphasising that man is finally detached from the annual cycle. The blunt rhyme word seems distinct from the other sounds in the poem, yet not wholly alien to its tone of acceptance.

98   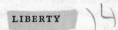 LIBERTY

Bod. 26 November 1915.

The poem derives from the first two paragraphs of a short essay, 'Cherry Blossom':

In front, a tall beechen hill closes up the gulf that runs out of the valley into the heart of the chalk down. The hill fills nearly half the sky, and just above it stands the white full moon, as one who looks over his lands. It warms the low, pale, curdled sky, but does not disturb the darkness of the beeches. All its light seems to fall and settle as if it would dwell there for ever in the cherry trees on either hand. All are blossoming, and in their branches the nightingales sing out of the blossom, dispersing what ruins remain of the world of yesterday, and building rapidly those tall watch towers that last until dawn, which men may climb and from their summits see what may make them out of love with the earth.

The past day is long past, the day of fighting, digging, buying, selling, writing; and if there are still men on the earth they are all equal in the trances of passion or sleep; the day to come is not to be thought of. The moon reigns; you rule. The centuries are gathered up in your hand. You and the moonlight and the nightingale and the cherry blossom have your own way with them all night long ... You exult because you are alive and your spirit possesses this broad, domed earth.

Poor thing as you are, you have somehow gained a **98**
power of expression like the nightingale's, a pure trans-
lucency like the petals of the flowers; and as never
before to man or woman you open your eyes widely
and frankly, even the limbs move with the carelessness
of the animals, the features lose the rigidity that comes
of compromise and suppression. (H.E., pp. 167–8 and
P.E.T., p. 77)

Like *October*, *Liberty* has much in common with Keats's
Ode to a Nightingale as the prose parallel bears out.
Keats's nightingale and Thomas's moonlight confer a
brief detachment from the everyday circumstances of life.
Thomas can imagine himself 'free,' but raises the same
kind of doubts about 'liberty' as he does in *October* about
'happiness.' The human condition seems to cheat us of
both. While Nature pursues her organic fulfilment, or the
moon preserves ultimately an Olympian aloofness, per-
plexed man is caught between the two. See John F.
Danby's discussion of the poem in 'Edward Thomas'
(*Critical Quarterly*, I, 1959, 310–11).

5. *unforgotten*. Danby calls this 'a typical surprise. It
does not mean "still remembered." It means in fact the
very opposite: these things have never been even admitted
into memory.'

17. *The wiser others*: those who accept life as it is and
remain sanely untroubled by the 'self-consciousness' and
self-questioning which, more than anything else, im-
prison the poet.

24–7. *And yet I still am half in love with pain . . . door*. **99**
Cf. *The Signpost*, lines 21–9 (p. 23) and see note. This is
perhaps Thomas's most complete statement of his
mature philosophy, which recognises that the benefits and
limitations of earthly existence are inextricable.

99 *half in love with pain.* Cf. 'half in love with easeful Death' (Keats, *Ode to a Nightingale*).

99   THE THRUSH

Bod. November 1915.

It is interesting, at several levels, to compare Hardy's *The Darkling Thrush*, which Thomas included in *The Pocket Book of Poems and Songs for the Open Air*, and from which he may have taken his inspiration ('At once a voice outburst among/The bleak twigs overhead,/In a full-hearted evensong/Of joy illimited . . .').

1–4. *When Winter's ahead . . . When Winter's dead?* A complicated series of temporal relations are here assimilated to the present tense (Winter's . . . read . . . read . . . Winter's). This, together with line constructions which reflect each other in an ABBA pattern, dramatises the cycle of the seasons which ultimately flattens out time and tense.

17. *I know the months all.* Thomas has recently proved this in *There's Nothing Like the Sun.* Months and seasons are significantly 'named' throughout his poetry: cf. also *Gone, Gone Again* (p. 127) which bears a formal resemblance to *The Thrush* and shows Thomas returning more sombrely to the same theme nearly a year later. Months are featured in the titles of eight poems and many others soon establish an extremely precise seasonal location: 'At hawthorn-time' (*Lob*), 'It was late June' (*Adlestrop*), 'It was upon a July evening' (*It Was Upon*).

100 21–32. *I must remember . . . ahead and behind.* Thomas's wordplay, connecting both April and November impartially with birth and death, implies that every situation

304

or state possesses such duality. The duality is to be **100** cherished ('I love') as part of the 'human' condition. The poet's complex awareness of 'all that's ahead and behind' is contrasted with that of the thrush (a simpler being and artist) who celebrates only the self-contained moment, however beautifully. A younger Thomas had envied the thrush in an essay called 'November Rain': 'One thrush sang heartily somewhere deep among the ash trees, and that was the only sound ... When I had walked another mile, the wood was out of sight, the thrush unheard. The wood is now purple immortally, for ever that song emerges from its heart, as free from change as one whom we remember vividly in the tip-toe of his exulting youth, and dying then has escaped huskiness, and a stoop, and foul breath, and a steady view of life. (H.E., p. 154)

THIS IS NO CASE OF PETTY RIGHT OR WRONG **100**

Bod. 26 December 1915.

(See Cooke's biographical section, pp. 74–100, and his chapter on Thomas as a war-poet, 'Roads to France,' pp. 209–42. See notes on *Lob*, pp. 230–53.)

On Sunday 11 July 1915 Thomas wrote to Robert Frost that he had decided against joining the latter in New Hampshire:

Last week I had screwed myself up to the point of believing I should come out to America & lecture if anyone wanted me to. But I have altered my mind. I am going to enlist on Wednesday if the doctor will pass me. I am aiming at the "Artists' Rifles," a territorial battalion, chiefly for training officers. So I must let them make an officer of me if they can. This

100   is easier to do than to come out to you & see what turns
up. But it will train me for the greater step.—I wish
I could explain how it came about. But I don't quite
know. (D.C.L.)

Thomas's letters to Frost during the first half of 1915
demonstrate indeed that 'it was not at all a desperate nor
yet a purposed resolution but the natural culmination
of a long series of moods & thoughts' (L.G.B., p. 253).
For some time he had been in the situation of *The Signpost*, deliberating whether to join Frost in America or
commit himself to England and the war. The possibility of adopting an alien way of life may have sharpened
a sense that he should share in the protection of his own
heritage: 'It might have been next year when we were
walking in the country that I asked him the question his
friends had asked him when he joined up, but I put it
differently. "Do you know what you are fighting for?"
He stopped, and picked up a pinch of earth. "Literally,
for this." He crumbled it between finger and thumb, and
let it fall.' (E.F., p. 154)

His writings also show that at a deep level the decision
had gradually been making itself. Commissioned by
The English Review to write some topical essays, Thomas
set out at the end of August 1914 and 'travelled through
England, from Swindon to Newcastle-on-Tyne, listening
to people, in railway carriages, trams, taverns, and
public places, talking about the war and the effects
of it' (L.S., p. 113). The fruits of this experience were
'Tipperary,' 'It's a Long, Long Way,' 'England' and
probably 'This England' (all included in *The Last Sheaf*).
The essays reveal a progressive personal involvement, as
Thomas examines the foundations of men's feeling for
their country: the relation between local, parochial love

and larger identification with England as a whole:

> I should like to know what the old soldier meant by "England," if it was anything more than some sort of a giant with Gloucestershire for its eyes, its beating heart, for everything that raised it above a personification. His was a very little England. The core and vital principle was less still, a few thousand acres of corn, meadow, orchard, and copse, a few farms and cottages; and he laughed heartily over a farmer's artfulness who had hid away some horses wanted by the War Office. If England was against Germany, the parish was against Germany, England, and all the world. ('It's a Long, Long Way,' L.S., p. 136)

> If England lies like a vast estate calm around you, and you a minor, you may find faults without end. If England seems threatened you feel that in losing her you would lose yourself . . .

> I believe the man who thought it a "quaint" idea to love England would feel very much as I do about these passages and about Walton altogether. I believe that England means something like this to most of us; that all ideas of England are developed, spun out, from such a centre into something large or infinite, solid or aëry, according to each man's nature and capacity; that England is a system of vast circumferences circling round the minute neighbouring points of home. ('England,' L.S., p. 91 and p. 111)

> At one stroke, I thought, like many other people, what things that same new moon sees eastward about the Meuse in France. Of those who could see it there, not blinded by smoke, pain, or excitement, how many saw it and heeded? I was deluged, in a second stroke, by

100   another thought, or something that overpowered
thought. All I can tell is, it seemed to me that either I
had never loved England, or I had loved it foolishly,
aesthetically, like a slave, not having realized that it
was not mine unless I were willing and prepared to die
rather than leave it as Belgian women and old men and
children had left their country. Something I had
omitted. Something, I felt, had to be done before I
could look again composedly at English landscape, at
the elms and poplars about the houses, at the purple-
headed wood-betony with two pairs of dark leaves on
a stiff stem, who stood sentinel among the grasses or
bracken by hedge-side or wood's-edge. What he stood
sentinel for I did not know, any more than what I had
got to do. ('This England,' L.S., p. 221 and P.E.T.,
p. 226; see general note to *The Sun Used to Shine*, p.
347)

Meanwhile the compilation of *This England* (see note,
p. 235) was bringing Thomas still nearer to the discovery
of 'Lob'; but a year or two earlier the cohering sense of
English landscape and tradition in his prose books had
already developed to a similar point:

Someone with a precocious sneer, asked if England was
now anything more than a geographical expression, and
Mr. Stodham preached a sermon straight away:

"A great poet said once upon a time that this earth
is 'where we have our happiness or not at all.' For most
of those who speak his language he might have said
that this England is where we have our happiness or
not at all. He meant to say that we are limited creatures,
not angels, and that our immediate surroundings are
enough to exercise all our faculties of mind and body:
there is no need to flatter ourselves with the belief

that we could do better in a bigger or another world. **100**
Only the bad workman complains of his tools."

Mr. Stodham quotes from Coleridge's *Fears in Solitude*
(later included in *This England*) and adds the conclusion
of Wordsworth's *To a Skylark* (which, with the other
reference to Wordsworth above, holds the record for
quotation in Thomas's prose):

" 'Type of the wise who soar but never roam,
　True to the kindred points of heaven and home.'
Well, England is home and heaven too. England made
you, and of you is England made. Deny England—
wise men have done so—and you may find yourself
some day denying your father and mother—and this
also wise men have done. Having denied England and
your father and mother, you may have to deny your
own self, and treat it as nothing, a mere conventional
boundary, an artifice, by which you are separated from
the universe and its creator. To unite yourself with the
universe and the creator, you may be tempted to
destroy that boundary of your own body and brain,
and die. He is a bold man who hopes to do without
earth, England, family, and self." (H.G.L.M., pp.
220–2)

It seems to be no coincidence that Thomas started to
write poetry in December 1914. Cooke valuably corrects
the notion that his work ignores the war, but goes a little
too far in calling its influence in begetting Thomas's
poetry 'decisive'; and also overstates the extent to which,
in reading Thomas, 'we are reminded . . . of Wilfred
Owen' (p. 224). The war did not transform Thomas: he
became neither patriot nor pacifist. Rather, it defined him
—or a part of him complementary to that defined by
Robert Frost—compelling the articulation of his ac-

100 cumulated sense of English tradition(Thus, with Hardy
and Yeats, Thomas is among the few poets of the period
who managed to absorb the war into a pattern at once
personal and universal. He wrote all his poetry during
the hiatus provided by his deliberations about joining
up and by nearly a year and a half of training.) This
breathing-space enabled him to write some poems
which, while they can hardly be called war poems, show
a profound assimilation of the facts and meaning of war
(see *As the Team's Head-Brass*, p. 119 and notes).(Thus
he constructed a crucially important bridge between the
world before the war and the world after it:)'And like
her mother that died yesterday.'

4. *to please newspapers*. Thomas was consistently scornful
of both popular war propaganda and the propaganda
poets: 'In print men become capable of anything. The
bards and the journalists say extraordinary things. I
suppose they do it to encourage the others. They feel
that they are addressing the world; they are intoxicated
with the social sense' (L.S., p. 92). In a long review entitled 'War Poetry,' quoted by Cooke (pp. 212–14), he
states: 'The writer of . . . patriotic verses appears to be a
man who feels himself always or at the time at one with a
class, perhaps the whole nation, or he is a smart fellow
who can simulate or exaggerate this sympathy. Experience,
reality, truth, unless suffused or submerged by popular
sentiment, are out of place . . . It is the hour of the
writer who picks up popular views or phrases, or coins
them, and has the power to turn them into downright
stanzas. Most newspapers have one or more of these
gentlemen.' Thomas seems to have suspected even his
own complex position in this poem: Eleanor Farjeon
implies that he deliberately excluded it from his first

book (E.F., p. 180)—although he did choose it for *Six* **100**
Poems by Edward Eastaway. For an oblique poet like
Thomas the writing of such a poem amounts in itself to
an act of patriotic commitment (the language betrays a
little forcing).

12. *Two witches' cauldrons roar*: the natural storm and the
storm of war.

18–19. *when perchance/The phoenix broods serene above* **101**
their ken. When the war is over and 'an England beautiful'
will have risen, like the phoenix, from its own ashes.
Thomas hints that he can more genuinely appreciate
the whole experience than future 'historians,' detached
from the conflict. 'Serene' and 'ken' recall Keats's
sonnet *On first looking into Chapman's Homer*; the
whole conception seems rather strained and literary.
20–6. *But with the best ... hate her foe.* Reminiscent of
Thomas's epigraph to the 'This England' section of *This
England*, Prince Arthur's patriotic outburst after reading
'*Briton moniments*' (*Faerie Queene*, II, x, 69):

> ... Deare countrey, O how dearely deare
> Ought thy remembraunce, and perpetuall band
> Be to thy foster Childe, that from thy hand
> Did commun breath and nouriture receaue ?
> How brutish is it not to vnderstand,
> How much to her we owe, that all vs gaue,
> That gaue vnto vs all, what euer good we haue.

RAIN **101**

Bod. 7 January 1916.

For Thomas's love of rain see general note to *After
Rain* (p. 161). A prose meditation (I.W., pp. 280–3 and

101 P.E.T., pp. 166–9) closely linked with *Rain* is perhaps the best known of the 'uncut stones which are scattered about his books' (Scannell, p. 12).

I lay awake listening to the rain, and at first it was as pleasant to my ear and my mind as it had long been desired; but before I fell asleep it had become a majestic and finally a terrible thing, instead of a sweet sound and symbol. It was accusing and trying me and passing judgment. Long I lay still under the sentence, listening to the rain, and then at last listening to words which seemed to be spoken by a ghostly double beside me. He was muttering: The all-night rain puts out summer like a torch. In the heavy, black rain falling straight from invisible, dark sky to invisible, dark earth the heat of summer is annihilated, the splendour is dead, the summer is gone. The midnight rain buries it away where it has buried all sound but its own. I am alone in the dark still night, and my ear listens to the rain piping in the gutters and roaring softly in the trees of the world. Even so will the rain fall darkly upon the grass over the grave when my ears can hear it no more ... I put my face to the window. There is nothing out there but the blackness and sound of rain. Neither when I shut my eyes can I see anything. I am alone. Once I heard through the rain a bird's questioning watery cry—once only and suddenly. It seemed content, and the solitary note brought up against me the order of nature, all its beauty, exuberance, and ever-lastingness like an accusation. I am not a part of nature. I am alone. There is nothing else in my world but my dead heart and brain within me and the rain without. ... Now there is neither life nor death, but only the rain. Sleep as all things, past, present, and future, lie

still and sleep, except the rain, the heavy, black rain **101**
falling straight through the air that was once a sea of
life. That was a dream only. The truth is that the rain
falls for ever and I am melting into it. Black and monotonously sounding is the midnight and solitude of the
rain. In a little while or in an age—for it is all one—I
shall know the full truth of the words I used to love, I
knew not why, in my days of nature, in the days before
the rain: "Blessed are the dead that the rain rains on."

Cooke quotes the passage in full and comments on the
development from prose to poem (pp. 177–82). In *Rain*
Thomas confronts the possible obliteration or meaning-
lessness of everything he cherishes. His vision is redeemed
from total 'bleakness' by the honesty with which it confronts the worst, by its 'cleanness' and clarity.

2. *bleak hut*: an army hut.

6. *this solitude.* Throughout his poetry Thomas employs
the characteristic word 'solitude' to denote happy as
well as unhappy states. Its recurrence suggests that the
individual is fundamentally alone; every man is an island
or separate point of consciousness. 'This solitude' implies
not only the poet's isolation, but that of mankind in a
universe that is ultimately alien and unfriendly.

16. *the love of death.* Thomas was always attracted to the
solution and dissolution of death (see *From Prose to
Poetry*, p. 138). He analyses this attraction in a description of 'Morgan Rhys' (partly a self-portrait, partly a self-
parody) which anticipates the reservations of lines 17–18:

As will happen with men who love life too passionately,
he was often in love with death. He found enjoyment in
silence, in darkness, in refraining from deeds, and he
longed even to embrace the absolute blank of death, if
only he could be just conscious of it; and he envied the

101   solitary tree on a bare plain high up among the hills, under a night sky in winter where the only touch of life and pleasure was the rain. And now, with his fantastic belief that the corpse is life's handiwork and its utmost end, he is humanised only by a dread of the blank to which he is going:

> When we shall hear
> The rain and wind beat dark December, how,
> In that our pinching cave, shall we discourse
> The freezing hours away?

He has made a heaven and he fears it. (B.W., pp. 94–5; the quotation is from *Cymbeline*, III, iii)

Suicide remained an imaginative possibility for Thomas even when it had ceased to be a personal temptation. As an agnostic he could envisage no transcendence of 'life and earth' (*Liberty*) when these became intolerable. However, the death-wish in his poetry is generally answered by a life wish (*The Signpost, Home* p. 54). *Rain* represents the 'dark December' or deepest winter of his spirit, and death is not elsewhere envisaged as an 'absolute blank' or 'perfect' full-stop. At other seasons Thomas integrates his love of death with his love of life: conceives death as a natural sleep or evolution, a continuing journey into the 'unknown' (*The Green Roads, Lights Out*). John F. Danby implicitly answers both those critics who condemn Thomas's 'death-wish' and those who too vigorously defend him from the charge of possessing one, when he comments on the 'strength' present in *Lights Out*: 'Life is not being denied. It is only that life does not cover everything. There is sleep, and death, and forgetting, and leaving behind.' ('Edward Thomas,' *Critical Quarterly*, I, 1959, 317)

Bod. 15 January 1916.

Thomas's starting point is an evening scene as described in *The Icknield Way*: 'The air was now still and the earth growing dark and already very quiet. But the sky was light and its clouds of utmost whiteness were very wildly and even fiercely shaped, so that it seemed the playground of powerful and wanton spirits knowing nothing of earth. And this dark earth appeared a small though also a kingly and brave place in comparison with the infinite heavens now so joyous and so bright and out of reach.' (p. 137)

9–16. *But clouds . . . it were not.* A similar idea is more indirectly framed in *After You Speak* (p. 120), which also exhibits traces of Shelley's influence. Thomas tends to idealise his 'not impossible shees' or imagined Muses (see general note to *The Unknown*, p. 325), but a firm grasp of the earthly and earthy curbs the transcendental element in his aspiration. He suggests here, as in other poems, that the finite world gives human desire its shape, context and meaning. *As the Clouds that are so Light* affirms the complementary roles of earth and sky, lover and beloved, body and spirit.

Bod. 22 January 1916.

The epigraph to *The South Country* is a speech of Paul Ruttledge's in *Where There is Nothing* by W. B. Yeats:

As I can't leap from cloud to cloud, I want to wander from road to road. That little path there by the clipped

102   hedge goes up to the high road. I want to go up that
path and to walk along the high road, and so on and on
and on, and to know all kinds of people. Did you ever
think that the roads are the only things that are endless;
that one can walk on and on, and never be stopped by
a gate or a wall? They are the serpent of eternity. I
wonder they have never been worshipped. What are the
stars beside them? They never meet one another. The
roads are the only things that are infinite. They are all
endless.

Several passages in *The South Country* (e.g. pp. 64–5 and
153–4), which follows and celebrates a number of roads,
anticipate Thomas's more extended meditation in the
dedication and first chapter of *The Icknield Way*:

To-day I know there is nothing beyond the farthest of
far ridges except a signpost to unknown places. The end
is in the means—in the sight of that beautiful long
straight line of the Downs in which a curve is latent—in
the houses we shall never enter, with their dark secret
windows and quiet hearth smoke, or their ruins friendly
only to elders and nettles—in the people passing whom
we shall never know though we may love them ... I
could not find a beginning or an end of the Icknield
Way. It is thus a symbol of mortal things with their
beginnings and ends always in immortal darkness. I
wish the book had a little more of the mystery of the
road about it. (pp. vi–vii, and P.E.T., pp. 163–4)

Much has been written of travel, far less of the road.
Writers have treated the road as a passive means to an
end, and honoured it most when it has been an ob-
stacle; they leave the impression that a road is a connection between two points which only exists when the

traveller is upon it ... [Yet] we still say that a road **102**
"goes" to London, as we "go" ourselves ... We may
go or stay, but the road will go up over the mountains
to Llandovery, and then up again over to Tregaron.
It is a silent companion always ready for us, whether
it is night or day, wet or fine, whether we are calm or
desperate, well or sick. It is always going: it has never
gone right away, and no man is too late ...

Why go straight? There is nothing at the end of any
road better than may be found beside it, though there
would be no travel did men believe it. The straight
road, except over level and open country, can only be
made by those in whom extreme haste and forethought
have destroyed the power of joy, either at the end or at
any part of its course. Why, then, go straight? (pp. 1–5)
The Icknield Way and *In Pursuit of Spring* are to some
extent constructed as symbolic journeys which look
forward to those of the poetry. *Roads* gives explicit and
mythological form to the assumptions that underlie a
whole complex of poems. Roads, paths, lanes comprehensively reflect man's progress through life, his spiritual
development and quest. Thomas's very syntax is an
imaginative equivalent of the network of highways and
by-ways criss-crossing the 'South Country.' The 'incon-
clusiveness' of his poetry is sometimes attacked: but
its road symbolism insists that man's life, a poet's vision,
does not really begin or end: 'the end is in the means.'
1–4. *I love roads ... gods.* Thomas's ABBA rhyme
scheme, the last line picking up the first, suggests through
the poem the continuity of roads, as does the sinuous
brevity of his quatrains.
25–8. *The next turn ... Hell conceal.* Line division and **103**
syntax dramatise the different surprises of a journey.

103 This is the most directly allegorical stanza in the poem, perhaps flavoured by Thomas's admiration for Bunyan: '*Pilgrim's Progress* is full of the sense of roads ... How full of plain English country wayfaring is the passage where Hopeful and Christian take a road by a river-side, and then when it turns away from the water they see a stile leading into a path which keeps on, as a path would do, along the bank through By-path Meadow: only, as it happens, the river is in flood and they must turn back again towards the stile. This man knew roads ...' (I.W., pp. 5–6)

29–32. *Often footsore, never ... As it winds on for ever.* Not only the last line but the general rhythm of this stanza echoes Tennyson's *The Brook*:

> ... And out again I curve and flow
>> To join the brimming river,
>> For men may come and men may go,
>>> But I go on forever.

Thomas may have been influenced by Tennyson's conception (cf. lines 5–8) and quatrains, but his own approach is thematically, structurally and metrically more sophisticated.

33. *Helen of the roads*: 'Helen is the lady in the Mabinogion, the Welsh lady who married Maxen the Emperor and gave her name to the great old mountain roads—Sarn Helen they are all marked on the maps. Do you remember the "Dream of Maxen"? She is known to mythologists as one of the travelling goddesses of the dusk' (E.F., p. 182). Thomas recounts 'The Dream of Maxen' in *Celtic Stories* (pp. 121–5) and more briefly in the first chapter of *The Icknield Way*. Maxen dreams of a beautiful girl in a castle and finally tracks her down after years of searching: 'She became his bride, and he gave her three castles—

318

one at Arvon in North Wales, one at Carleon, and one at **103**
Caermarthen in the South. Then, says the tale, "Helen
bethought her to make high-roads from one castle to
another throughout the Island of Britain. And the roads
were made. And for this cause are they called the roads
of Helen Luyddawc, that she was sprung from a native
of this island, and the men of the Island of Britain would
not have made these great roads for any save her" '
(pp. 7–8). Thomas probably enjoyed the coincidence with
his wife's name.

35. *the Mabinogion tales.* Thomas provides a note on his
sources at the end of *Celtic Stories*: 'The Welsh tales
come from a book now known as the *Mabinogion*. They
were written down at the end of the Middle Ages, and
translated from Welsh into English by Lady Guest in the
nineteenth century. The original Welsh manuscript
(called "The Red Book of Hergest," because it was once
at Hergest in Radnor) belongs to the fourteenth and
fifteenth centuries, but the stories had been told over and
over again, and probably written down many times, before
they were copied into "The Red Book".' (p. 126)

38. *The threes and fours so wise.* Clumps consisting of a **104**
few trees which seem to be communing together.

50–6. *Troops that make loneliness . . . the dead/Returning
lightly dance.* 'I wish you had liked "Roads" more. I
thought the particular ghosts came in comfortably
enough after the ghosts in general' (L.G.B., p. 260).
'Troops' links the two, and the repetition of 'light.' The
poem acquires a new dimension or definition with
Thomas's evocation of the war, which is 'lightened' by
the sense that 'the dead' have been relieved of a burden
and join a timeless procession.

53. *Now all roads lead to France.* Robert Frost wrote to

104 Edward Garnett after Thomas's death: 'His poetry is so very brave—so unconsciously brave. He didn't think of it for a moment as war poetry, though that is what it is. It ought to be called Roads to France.' (*Selected Letters*, p. 217)

59. ' "They" in [stanza] 15 refers to "the dead" ' (E.F., p. 184).

105   THE ASH GROVE

Bod. 4, 5, 6, 7, 8 and 9 February 1916.

5. *the interval*: the clearing. The moments of profoundest peace and poise in Thomas's poetry occur during 'intervals' of time or space when the tensions before and after are suspended if not forgotten. Cf. *Interval* (p. 24), *The Bridge* (p. 56), *Good-Night* (p. 57) and *I Never Saw that Land Before* (p. 114) and see notes. *The Ash Grove* resembles *Good-Night* in length of line and stanza, but its highly individual rhyme-scheme (AABA, BBCB etc.), an adaptation of terza rima, gives additional emphasis to the effect of suspension.

10–16. *And now an ash grove . . . or cost.* Cf. the last two stanzas of *I Never Saw that Land Before* and Wordsworth, *Tintern Abbey*, 23–31:

> Though absent long,
> These forms of beauty have not been to me
> As is a landscape to a blind man's eye;
> But oft, in lonely rooms, and 'mid the din
> Of towns and cities, I have owed to them,
> In hours of weariness, sensations sweet,
> Felt in the blood, and felt along the heart,
> And passing even into my purer mind

With tranquil restoration ...   **105**
The conditions which enable Thomas, like Wordsworth, to 'see into the life of things,' are linked with 'singing' or poetic expression.

13. *The song of the Ash Grove.* 'The Ash Grove' is a traditional Welsh air to which many sets of words have been put. See note on Thomas's interest in folk songs, p. 176.

FEBRUARY AFTERNOON   **105**

Bod. 7 and 8 February 1916.

See note on Thomas's sonnets, p. 344. He teased Eleanor Farjeon: 'you didn't realise it was a sonnet I suspect' (E.F., p. 187). The poem looks forward to *As the Team's Head-Brass* (p. 119, see notes) in its use of the plough as a slightly ambiguous symbol of continuity in the context of war.

4–5. *So that the first are last ... last are first again.* In view of lines 13–14 (see note below) probably an intentional biblical echo: 'If any man desire to be first, the same shall be last of all, and servant of all' (*Mark*, IX, 35). The birds who first reach what the plough casts up are then left behind as they enjoy their pickings. The image dramatises the inexorable 'law' of destiny.

8. *shaw*: a strip of wood or underwood forming the border **106** of a field.

13–14. *And God still sits aloft ... stone-deaf and stone-blind.* The only respectful references to God in Thomas's poetry are the exceptional 'God bless you' in *April* and an incidental or accidental 'God save England' in *This is No Case of Petty Right or Wrong*. Both phrases are conven-

106 tional, with 'you' and 'England,' rather than 'God,' in the foreground. More calculated allusions tend towards the tone of these lines: Thomas's attitude in *Digging* (p. 95), *A Cat* or *No one Cares Less than I* is equally, though more obliquely, sceptical. Here, indignation at the human cost of war compels him to be uniquely outspoken. The evocation of an oblivious tyrant interestingly resembles Wilfred Owen's portrayal of 'Field-Marshal God' in several poems.

Thomas's anger, like Owen's, may be fundamentally directed at the men who have made a god of war in their own image. He had been, however, a natural agnostic from childhood, detesting organised religion as a dark force or spiritual suffocation: '[My grandmother] first took me to church. Clad in those uncomfortable clothes, I walked beside her, who looked more uncomfortable in her layers of black. I felt that everyone enjoyed being stiff, solemn, black, except myself. On entering the church she bent forward to pray, dragging me down with her to blur my sight for a similar period. I rose with an added awkwardness in gazing at the grim emotionless multitudes of hats, bonnets, and bare heads. It was an inexplicable conspiracy for an hour's self-torture. The service was a dreary discomfort in which the hymns were green isles. When all was over, we crept with a shuffle, a pause, a shuffle, a pause, out to the tombstones and the astonishing fresh light' (C.O.E.T., p. 48). 'Perhaps my weariness in chapel was mingled with something which specialists would label as religious. I only know that where people were sad and solemn I was overcome, half-suffocated by the sadness and solemnity. What was read and preached was to me airy nothing' (p. 75). See *The Mountain Chapel*, lines 34–42 (p. 30) and note.

Bod. 9 February 1916. Preceded in the MS. by *P.H.T.*
(8 February) and followed by *No One So Much As You*
(11 February).

See note on Thomas's love poetry, p. 324. *These Things
that Poets Said* occupies an interesting position in an
interesting sequence of poems. *P.H.T.* (C.P., p. 189) is
virtually a hate-poem to Thomas's father ('But not so
long as you live/Can I love you at all') and in *No One So
Much As You* (C.P., p. 186) he explains to his mother
the inadequacies of his love. Then Thomas wrote *The
Unknown*, a poem to an ideal woman, and *Celandine*, an
evocation of young love. *These Things that Poets Said* is
a theoretical statement about love poetry which covers
the range of attitudes exhibited in this group of poems.
Feminine Influence on the Poets contains much thoughtful
analysis of the mode, but now Thomas evidently feels
obliged to distinguish his own aesthetic from that of other
poets. Its special quality is honesty, fidelity to the facts, as
he admits he cannot identify his experience with theirs.
No One So Much As You is the practical embodiment of
this aesthetic. Yet, Thomas retains some traditional attributes of both lover and love poet. He recognises that he
has loved and that love transformed him: 'I, loving not,
am different'; and has sufficient confidence in his own
vision to appeal, conventionally, to a personified 'Love'
for adjudication. Line 8, in music as well as diction,
manifests Thomas's underlying wistfulness to relate his
own poem to 'These things that poets said /Of love.'

3–4. *When I loved . . . love and poetry equally.* 'How many
times has Shelley—Shelley and the daffodils of Devon or
the wild thyme of Wiltshire—been the half of a first love?

323

106 To how many does his poetry not seem, during a great lovely tract of life, to have been the half of spring and summer and autumn, of night and dawn and noon, and of youth enjoying these things ? At the time when youth is most exultant, this poetry is thumbed night and day; a page is opened at random, as Virgil used to be, for a word big with fate ...' (*Feminine Influence on the Poets*, p. 78 and P.E.T., p. 127). See the first three chapters of *As It Was*.

107   THE UNKNOWN

Bod. 14 February 1916.

Thomas is reworking Richard Crashaw's famous conceit in *Wishes to his (supposed) Mistresse*:

Who ere shee bee,

That not impossible shee

That shall command my heart and mee ...

In *Feminine Influence on the Poets* Thomas calls Crashaw's poem 'remarkable for its grave original beauty and its being apparently inspired by the thought of a woman who may some day appear before him, and also because the woman is to be not merely beautiful and virtuous, but intelligent ...' (p. 264). Thomas wrote little love poetry in the ordinary sense of the term. *And You, Helen*, virtually apologises for not being a love poem. Yet despite his conviction of emotional incapacity or inadequacy, and despite the ultimate truth and stability of his marriage, Thomas consistently sought further fulfilment in friendship with both men and women. The letters to Gordon Bottomley indicate his need for a male confidant and intellectual whetstone (see general note to *The Sheiling*,

p. 376); there was his platonic and literary relationship **107**
with Eleanor Farjeon; and there was, of course, Robert
Frost. In *The Sun Used to Shine* (p. 117, see notes)
Thomas shows himself able to celebrate friendship if not
love.

In addition, he retained the notion of a 'not impossible shee' throughout his writing career: 'something
floated under the trees, turning an unknown face towards
me; then passed away as softly as the day was fading.
I just saw the pale glorious face' (H.S., p. 184). This
vision, whom Thomas finally hails as 'Isoud with the
White Hands' (p. 186), is only one of many idealised
'maidens' featured in his prose. In poetry *After You
Speak* (p. 120) and *As the Clouds that are so Light* (p. 102)
invoke a transcendental creature, almost out of reach
of the 'dust' or 'earth' that typify the poet. Such goddesses
seem to be composite or 'unknown' figures with origins
deep in Thomas's past and imagination. His remarks
about Shelley's love poetry apply to this branch of his
own: 'Even in [the poems sent to a particular lady]
the character of the woman, in body or mind, is barely
hinted at. In the poems of passion the woman is invisible;
the emotion is everything; and what is brought before
us is the desire of a man, and the idea of a woman
rising in hesitating reply' (*Feminine Influence on the Poets*,
p. 223). Thomas's curious emphasising of the word 'poet'
in this poem and in *Song* (p. 78) suggests that 'the
Unknown' may also be the Muse, inspiration as well as
aspiration. In *Feminine Influence on the Poets*, after saying
that 'individual women ... give the impulse and the
subject,' he affirms: 'When the subject changes, the
impulse will remain, and the influence, though not easily
definable, is not the less great' (p. 5). This is expanded in

107 *The Tenth Muse*: 'Their chief direct influence has been exerted by the stimulation of desire—desire to possess not only them but other known and unknown things deemed necessary to that perfection of beauty and happiness which love proposes. It is a desire of impossible things which the poet alternately assuages and rouses again by poetry, in himself and in us' (p. 8 and P.E.T., p. 128). He also observes that just as 'the sight of a fine landscape, recovery from sickness, rain in spring, music of bird or instrument or human voice' may bring love poems to mind, so they must have inspired poets to write poems in which 'the figure of a woman is introduced unwittingly as a symbol of they know not what, perhaps only of desire...' (*Feminine Influence on the Poets*, p. 77 and P.E.T., p. 126)

29–30. *she/May not exist*. The drama of this deceptively low-keyed statement is accentuated by a line-division which delays Thomas's final revelation.

108   CELANDINE

Bod. 4 March 1916.

See note above on Thomas's love poetry. The poem has connections with an essay, 'July' (L.A.T., pp. 96–116), which Thomas called 'one of those crude mixtures of experience & invention which prove me no artist' (L.G.B., p. 206). The essay, and perhaps the poem, draws on his courtship of Helen; both may also revive some adolescent experience. Although the girl in the poem is perhaps dead only in the sense that the past is, *Celandine* seems to be related to *Eluned*, a poem written in Thomas's teens—'Her nature and name/Were like those flowers'—

and quoted anonymously in *Beautiful Wales* (pp. 82–3). **108**
Eluned (Helen) ends:

> She is dead, Eluned,
> Who was part of Spring,
> And of blue Summer and red Autumn,
> And made the Winter beloved:
> She is dead, and these things come not again.

19–23. *But this was a dream . . . Gone like a never perfectly recalled air.* This conclusion does not invalidate the middle section of the poem: although memory loses its grip of the experience (leaving behind its usual lieutenant in Thomas's poetry, smell), the maiden has in fact been 'perfectly recalled' in the 'short swift eternity' of imaginative embodiment.

'HOME' **108**

Bod. 7 and 10 March 1916.
This is the only poem in which Thomas directly explores his reaction to life in the limbo of an army camp. 'Somebody said something about homesickness the other day. It is a disease one can suppress but not do without under these conditions' (letter to Eleanor Farjeon postmarked 27 February 1916, E.F., p. 188). *'Home'* focuses too on the strange artificial comradeship born of the 'conditions.' Previously, in camp at High Beech, Thomas 'found I could get on with people I had nothing in common with & almost get fond of them. As soon as we were in London the bond was dissolved & we had blank looks for one other' (L.G.B., pp. 255–6). Thomas had at

108 least something in common with the other two figures in
'*Home.*' On 5 March he wrote to Robert Frost: 'We got a
walk, three of us, one a schoolmaster, the other a game-
breeder who knows about horses & dogs & ferrets. We
heard the first blackbird, walked 9 or 10 miles straight
across country (the advantage of our uniform—we go
just where we like): ate & drank (stout) by a fire at a big
quiet inn . . .' (D.C.L.). Later there was to be more
genuine contact with some new arrivals at Hare Hall, including Gordon Bottomley's friend, the painter Paul
Nash: 'I am really lucky to have such a crowd of people
always round & these 2 or 3 nearer: You might guess
from "Home" how much nearer' (letter to Frost on
21 May, D.C.L.).

    3–5. *the untrodden snow . . . rustic and old.* 'It is fine and
wintry here, very dirty though underfoot. The hills look
impassable and make me think they must have looked
like that 2000 years ago' (letter to Eleanor Farjeon,
'*probably* March 11th,' E.F., p. 191). 'The untrodden
snow' suggests the erasure of life's usual landmarks, as in
'The Barge': 'We were in a primitive world. In those short
days the world seemed to have grown larger; distance
was more terrible. A friend living thirty miles off seemed
inaccessible in the snow. The earth had to be explored,
discovered, and mapped again; it was as it had been
centuries ago, and progress was not very real to our minds.'
(H.E., p. 157)

109 12. *the cold roofs*: evidently those of Hare Hall Camp.

    20–1. *Between three counties . . . We were divided.* Never-
theless Thomas sometimes felt that 'England' provided
a link between himself and his army companions: 'I
furbish up my knowledge of England by finding some
place that each man knows & I know & getting him to

talk. There isn't a man I don't share some part with.' **109**
(L.G.B., p. 259)

28. *only the word.* Cf. *Adlestrop* (p. 38) and *The Word* (p.
88): 'only the name.'

30–5. *If I should ever . . . an evil dream.* 'It is curious how
the mind steadily refuses to hanker after what it knows is
absolutely forbidden for (it believes) a comparatively
short time. So far I don't think I have resented or regretted
anything or longed for the impossible' (letter to Gordon
Bottomley, 6 November 1915, L.G.B., p. 256). A week
later, describing a sudden fit of depression to Frost,
Thomas asked: 'Does one really get rid of things at all by
steadily inhibiting them for a long time on end? Is peace
going to awaken me as it will so many from a drugged
sleep? Am I indulging in the pleasure of being someone
else?' (D.C.L.). In his second-last letter to his wife he
wrote: 'I, you see, must not feel anything. I am just, as it
were, tunnelling underground and something sensible in
my subconsciousness directs me not to think of the sun,
at the end of the tunnel there is the sun. Honestly this is
not the result of thinking; it is just an explanation of my
state of mind which is really so entirely preoccupied with
getting through the tunnel that you might say I had
forgotten there was a sun at either end, before or after
this business . . .' (Moore, p. 264). '*Home,*' like Thomas's
army letters, implies the buried resentment ('captivity')
and perplexities beneath his surface composure. Moore
oversimplifies in stating: 'he had changed his whole
attitude to life, shaken hands with the past and shut his
eyes to the future, so that he was troubled neither with
regrets nor apprehensions' (p. 228). Thomas was indeed
deeply sure of the rightness of his decision—or of the
rightness of decision. He repressed literary and personal

109 hopes for after the war. But his letters to Frost after enlistment also display a familiar oscillation of mood. The letter which contains the origin of '*Home*' announces a total relapse: 'Well, the long & short of it seems to be that I am what I was, in spite of my hopes of last July. The only thing is perhaps I didn't quite know what I was. This less active life you see gives me more time & inclination to ruminate.'

110   THAW

Bod. 10 March 1916.

See note on lines 1–2 of *The Manor Farm* (p. 173) and on Thomas's short poems (p. 341).

3. *delicate as flower of grass*. Thomas employs this simile in 'Flowers of Frost' (1909): 'The beeches that were yesterday a brood of giantesses are now insubstantial and as delicate as flowers of grass' (P.E.T., p. 88).

110   IF I SHOULD EVER BY CHANCE

Bod. 6 April 1916.

This poem and the three that follow were written on consecutive days and obviously form an interconnected group, although each preserves its independent life. Thomas wrote to Gordon Bottomley with reference to a projected anthology (*An Annual of New Poetry*): 'The household poems ought perhaps to appear as a bunch' (L.G.B., p. 266). The place names (names of village, parish, field, farm, house and brook) in the poems were all taken from the country around Hare Hall Camp—near

Romford in south-east Essex. Thomas liked this area 'more and more' (E.F., p. 170) and the names indicate that camp life had not dulled his interest in his surroundings.

The 'household poems' are unified by a number of factors: the motif of 'giving'; the place names; the couplet form; the expression of desirable human attributes in terms of the countryside. They constitute the apotheosis of all Thomas's 'catalogues,' his exhaustive detailing of the natural scene (see note, p. 332). But although these poems form a peak of celebration and tenderness in his work, each exhibits a characteristic reservation or undertow. The conditions attached to the 'gifts' recall the tests or drawbacks which accompany fairy gifts in folk lore. Various techniques reinforce this traditional element: sing-song rhythms, exaggerated feminine rhymes, incantatory refrains. Certain phrases are hallowed by time and use: 'shall all forever be hers,' 'once on a time,' 'As far as a man in a day could ride.' The poems' format and phrasing also suggest that the poet is making his imaginative will and testament.

2–3. *I'll buy Codham . . . Lapwater.* 'If only those poems which are place-names could be translated at last, the pretty, the odd, the romantic, the racy names of copse and field and lane and house. What a flavour there is about the Bassetts, the Boughtons, the Worthys, the Tarrants, Winterbournes, Deverills, Manningfords, the Suttons: what goodly names of the South Country—Woodmansterne, Hollingbourne, Horsmonden, Wolstanbury, Brockenhurst, Caburn, Lydiard Tregoze, Lydiard Millicent, Clevancy, Amesbury, Amberley (I once tried to make a beautiful name and in the end it was Amberley, in which Time had forestalled me) . . .' (S.C., p. 153).

110 Thomas's relishing of this 'roll-call'—he refers in *The Icknield Way* to 'the fascination of a roll-call of country names' (p. 22)—anticipates the effects he secures in the 'household poems' and in *Lob*. Place names seem to mark a nodal point in his imagination. They testify to the interaction between man and Nature, between landscape and language, and thus embody cultural continuity in a peculiarly rounded sense. This particular 'roll-call,' like the others in the 'household poems,' is not arbitrary. Thomas's delight in naming is communicated by his orchestration of sound. A rich cluster of hard 'c's and 'd's gives way to lighter consonants ('r' emerging in its own right) and broad, open vowels. The names further suggest physical properties of the countryside, as they do in all this group of poems.

4. *my elder daughter*: Bronwen Thomas, born in October 1902.

5–10. *The rent ... all for ever be hers.* 'Bronwen was Edward's most eager sharer of wild-flower lore; she knew as many as he did, had an eye almost as quick ... In his happiest poem ... Edward offers to bestow on his elder daughter half a dozen sweet-named places ... provided she finds the first white violet of the year before he does. Every spring it was a race between them.' (E.F., p. 22)

110   IF I WERE TO OWN

Bod. 7 April 1916.

See general note to *If I Should Ever by Chance*, p. 330.

If I were to Own includes a rather more varied catalogue of the countryside than the other poems of the group (lines 8–14). Thomas's lists of place names exaggerate, in fact, a pervasive tendency of these poems and **110** of his poetry in general. He 'knows the months all,/And their sweet names.' He names birds, flowers, trees, seasons, and neglected or unobtrusive phenomena like 'copses, ponds, roads, and ruts,' 'Twig, leaf, flint, thorn,/Straw, feather' (*November*, p. 19). This loving exactitude passes into the detail of all Thomas's scenes, and the outer ripples of such naming cover all his poetry. Thomas's catalogues seem to derive from the twin instincts to celebrate and to commemorate every aspect of the English landscape. The habit of cataloguing is already entrenched in his first book, *The Woodland Life*, a naturalist's inventory of a year's observations in the countryside. Its concluding 'Diary in the English Fields and Woods,' in which the lusher elements of Thomas's youthful prose are pruned away, curiously anticipates the foundation of many poems:

> Feb. 21 Long tangle of bedstraws in the ditches.
> (1896) Yellow-ammers sing.
> Bees on the sunny walls.
> Companies of wood-pigeons digging for new-sown vetches.
> Young rabbits already strong and abroad.
> Coltsfoot blossoming.
> Peewits swerve in their flight like one bird— as sandpipers wheel on the sea-shore. (p. 221)

3. *the Tyes*. In Essex 'tye' seems originally to have meant an outlying common, later an enclosed field.

5–7. *Skreens, Gooshays . . . and Lillyputs*. The names ending in 's' either have their origin in a local manorial family name, or have been assimilated to this form.

15. *my son*. Thomas's eldest child, Mervyn (Merfyn) **111** Thomas was born in January 1900.

III **15–25.** *I would give them ... not I.* The poet will bestow the villages, and all that goes with them, on his son provided that his own interest in them be maintained by appropriate payment. This will be an apparently nominal ('peppercorn') rent: 'a blackbird's song' (whose 'value' is equivalent to that of 'each year's first violets' etc. in *If I Should Ever by Chance*). But if Thomas should himself abuse his condition, repudiate the values located in the blackbirds by some brutality, he loses all his rights in the heritage. He will become an outcast ('old and alone') unless he can make suitable amends. This violent imagery may reflect a potentially destructive element in Thomas's relationship with Mervyn (see notes on *Parting*, p. 205). There are undertones of the kind of taboo associated with the killing of a bird in 'Who Killed Cock Robin?' or at a higher level in Coleridge's *Ancient Mariner*. Thomas's ability to fuse different kinds of reference (see p. 237) appears in the progression from the cliché 'for a song,' to an actual 'blackbird's song,' to the nursery rhyme:

> Sing a song of sixpence
> A pocket full of rye:
> Four and twenty blackbirds
> Baked in a pie.

He wrote a book of fanciful tales woven around proverbs, called *Four-and-Twenty Blackbirds* (see note, p. 237).

30. *till the cart tracks had no ruts*: i.e. forever, a traditional form of hyperbole; cf. 'Till a' the seas gang dry' (Burns, *My Love is like a Red Red Rose*). A cart track without ruts would not be a cart track—but see note (p. 253) on lines 141–5 of *Lob*.

WHAT SHALL I GIVE ?

Bod. 8 April 1916.

See general note to *If I Should Ever by Chance*, p. 330.

1. *my daughter the younger*: Myfanwy (Baba) Thomas, born in August 1910.

3. *I shall not give her anything.* Thomas implicitly contradicts this declaration in the course of the poem. His imaginative progression from 'South Weald and Havering' to the stars serves to enhance as well as define the homely values of 'Steep and her own world' until they become themselves a 'gift.' The poem recalls both the simpler sentiment of W. H. Davies's *Sweet Stay-at-Home*:

> Sweet Stay-at-Home, sweet Well-content,
> Thou knowest of no strange continent . . .

and the grander conception of W. B. Yeats's *A Prayer for my Daughter*, but more exactly parallels Philip Larkin's *Born Yesterday (for Sally Amis)*, which ends:

> May you be ordinary;
> Have, like other women,
> An average of talents:
> Not ugly, not good-looking,
> Nothing uncustomary
> To pull you off your balance,
> That, unworkable itself,
> Stops all the rest from working.
> In fact, may you be dull—
> If that is what a skilled,
> Vigilant, flexible,
> Unemphasised, enthralled
> Catching of happiness is called.

(*The Less Deceived*, The Marvell Press, 1955, p. 24)

111 4–9. *Havering, Havering Bower*. Reviewing a book called *Romantic Essex* in 1901 Thomas remarks: 'We are grateful . . . for the mere repetition of such names as Ashingden, Cressing, Havering-atte-Bower . . .' The manor of Havering was held by the kings of England for several centuries. The word 'Bower' indicates that it became particularly associated with their queens, beginning with Queen Eleanor of Provence in 1267. Among the queens who actually resided there were Isabella, child-bride of the deposed Richard II, and Joanna, widow of Henry IV, who was imprisoned on a charge of treason and witchcraft and returned to Havering to die. Thomas's reference, however, may be less specific.

112 11. *Samarcand*. More usually, Samarkand: one of the oldest cities of Central Asia, now part of the U.S.S.R. It had great commercial importance because of its position at the junction of trade routes from India and China. The exotic associations of Samarkand may have been sharpened for Thomas by the publication in 1913 of James Elroy Flecker's lyric sequence, *The Golden Journey to Samarkand*, in the volume of that name.

17. *Steep*. See general note to *When First*, p. 370.

112   AND YOU, HELEN

Bod. 9 April 1916.

See general note to *If I Should Ever by Chance*, p. 330. Through the sequence Thomas's joyous giving has been gradually tempered by subtler qualifications. This poem to his wife, the most direct and comprehensive of the group, confirms that the poems are not just pieces of

escapist fantasy but deal with the real gifts of life ('that **112**
great treasure-house'), the human possibilities which so
often become stunted. He is also putting in order the
most outstanding of his emotional affairs. Thomas's
failures to love clearly reflect his failures to live (see *From
Prose to Poetry*, p. 137 and Biographical Extracts, p. 383).
Helen Thomas has recorded his terrible withdrawals
from her when afflicted by the depression that blighted
all around it. In *As It Was* she anticipates and sum-
marises:

> ... there were to come dark days when his brooding
> melancholy shut me out in a lonely exile, and my heart
> waited too eagerly to be let into the light again ...
> But this was to come, and it was only now and then
> that I had hints of this darkness in his soul, this fierce
> unrest which beyond all found peace in nature, but
> not in me. Alone he had to be in his agony, but when
> he emerged from it, exhausted by God knows what
> bitter contest, he looked for me and needed me, and
> our love was always the firm ground on which we
> stood secure and that no storm ever swept away. (p. 47)

Or, as Thomas more wryly stated it: 'Helen usually gets
a share of my depression, & in fact has done so for so
many years now that she is always too near the edge, has
lost her buoyancy & is thin & often poor-spirited: but
she still has a lot of courage & whenever I let her, gets
hopeful again' (L.G.B., p. 162). Introversion often
drove underground the main current of Thomas's
emotional life: yet the compensating fineness of his self-
scrutiny enabled him to build up, as in this 'love poem,'
rich alternative modes of feeling (see note on Thomas's
love poetry, p. 324): he gives Helen 'an infinite great
store.'

112 7. *A clear eye as good as mine.* Helen Thomas was short-sighted. 'The amazing keenness of Edward's sight was brought home to me on these walks; he would remark on some bird in a distant tree when to me the tree was only a blur on the landscape. (Once when we were riding on an open bus-top in town, he pointed out to me the curious difference in the two eyes of a dog sitting in a window. I took his word for it)' (E.F., p. 24). Coombes (p. 53) quotes a passage from *Richard Jefferies* to show how Thomas 'valued the eye as more than a recorder':

> The clearness of the physical is allied to the penetration of the spiritual vision. For both are nourished to their perfect flowering by the habit of concentration. To see a thing as clearly as [Jefferies] saw the sun-painted yellow-hammer in Stewart's Mash is part of the office of the imagination. Imagination is no more than the making of graven images, whether of things on the earth or in the mind. To make them, clear concentrated sight and patient mind are the most necessary things after love; and these two are the children of love. (R.J., p. 44)

113 21–2. *And myself, too ... proved kind.* This couplet condenses one of Thomas's deepest and darkest themes, assimilating it to the terminology of a fairy tale quest.

113   LIKE THE TOUCH OF RAIN

Bod. 30 April 1916.

See notes on Thomas's love poetry (p. 324) and 'rain' poetry (p. 161).

9–12. *Those two words shut a door ... And will not open again.* Robert Graves, who emerged like Thomas from

a Georgian context and may have been influenced by **113**
the latter's poems of statement, expresses love's arrival
and withdrawal in a similar image (*The Door*):

> When she came suddenly in
> It seemed the door could never close again,
> Nor even did she close it—she, she—
> The room lay open to a visiting sea
> Which no door could restrain.

> Yet when at last she smiled, tilting her head
> To take her leave of me,
> Where she had smiled, instead
> There was a dark door closing endlessly,
> The waves receded.

Thomas's last stanza perfectly concludes a perfectly
orchestrated lyric. The apparent simplicity of form and
diction (every word is a monosyllable or dissyllable)
conceals his profound development of the central image.
Thomas refers to the poem as "Go now" (E.F., p. 194),
and this stark phrase effectively 'shuts a door' between
the exuberant feeling of the middle stanza and the stoic
understatement of his conclusion.

WHEN WE TWO WALKED   **113**

Bod. 1 May 1916.
7–8. *Who acted in their pride/Juno and Jupiter*. Thomas **114**
may refer to a version of the classical fable of King
Ceyx and his queen Alcyone in which they aped Zeus
and Hera, king and queen of the gods (Jupiter and Juno
in Roman mythology): 'These perished by reason of
their pride; for he said that his wife was Hera, and she

114 said that her husband was Zeus. But Zeus turned them into birds; her he made a kingfisher (*alycon*) and him a gannet (*ceyx*)' (Apollodorus, *The Library*, I. vii. 4; Sir James Frazer's translation). Men traditionally attract the wrath of the gods if they presume to equal them in any respect. It is 'wiser' to propitiate Fate with some kind of tribute (perhaps a 'Lenten' penance) or dissimulation. Humbler ambitions and passions escape the thunderbolt. 'The Gods,' however, supply an image for the destructive properties of arrogance itself. A 'cottage woman' in *The Happy-Go-Lucky Morgans* recalls the family, several of whom die: ' "You never saw the like of them for happiness. When I used to stop at the gate and see them in the grass, perhaps soaking wet, tumbling about and laughing as if they weren't Christians at all, I said to myself: 'Oh, dear, dear me, what trouble there must be in store for those beautiful children, that they should be so happy now. God preserve them, if it be his will.' I whispered: 'Hush, children, be a bit more secret-like about it.' It don't do to boast about anything, let alone happiness".' (p. 270)

114 TALL NETTLES

Bod. 1 May 1916.

There are several prose descriptions of this deserted farmyard: 'The walnut tree among the ricks is dead. Against its craggy bole rest the shafts of a noble, blue waggon that seems coeval with it; long ladders are thrust up among its branches; deep in the brittle herbage underneath it lean or lie broken wheels, a rude wooden roller, the lovely timber of an antique plough,

a knotted and rusted chain harrow ...' (H.E., p. 108 **114**
and P.E.T., p. 75). 'Mr. Torrance' in *The Happy-Go-
Lucky Morgans* recalls what is clearly the same spot:
'the barn and sheds, apparently tumbling but never
tumbledown, were ... surrounded by a disorderly
region of nettles' (p. 130). In 'In a Farmyard' Thomas
refers to a pond 'lying deep among tansy flowers, grey
nettles ...'; the farmyard is 'always dusty'; and the
pond lies 'unused' 'in a corner' (H.E., p. 57). His feeling
for such a disregarded 'corner' is typical.

The perfection of *Tall Nettles* suggests a 'corner' of
Thomas's poetry which should not be disregarded: his
mastery of the short lyric. In such poems as *A Tale*
(p. 64), *In Memoriam (Easter, 1915)* (p. 73), *Cock-Crow*
(p. 96), *Thaw* (p. 110) and *The Cherry Trees* (p. 115)
he turns a single natural phenomenon with similar skill
into an image precise and resonant. His ability to
'miniaturise' the components of a poem appears in the
economical selection of detail ('Only the elm butt'), the
concentration shaping a phrase ('I like most') or single
word ('prove'), the hoarding of dramatic and rhythmic
climax until exactly the right moment. Philip Larkin
may be Thomas's truest heir in this mode.

I NEVER SAW THAT LAND BEFORE **114**

Bod. 5 May 1916.
    I rode ... into the valley of the Sheppey. To within
a mile of Wells I was to have this little river always
with me and several times under me ... It was a
delightful exit ... On both hands grassy banks rose
up steeply. The left one, when the rookery was

114   passed, was topped with single thorn trees, and pigs
       and chickens did their duty and their pleasure among
       the pollard ashes below ... The left bank being
       steeper, is either clothed in a wood of ivied oaks, or
       its ridgy turf and scattering of elms and ash trees
       are seldom interrupted by houses ... Then on both
       hands the valley does without houses. The left side
       is a low, steep thicket rising from the stream, which
       spreads out here into a sedgy pool before a weir, and
       was at this moment bordered by sheaves of silver-
       catkined sallow, fresh-cut. (I.P.S., pp. 235–6)

115   17–18. *some goal/I touched then.* Cf. *Some Eyes Con-
       demn*, line 12 (p. 117) and *The Other*, line 32 (p. 27).
       Coombes finds 'something *relatively* immature in the
       way Thomas often refers to happiness and beauty as
       "goals" that can conceivably be reached and retained,
       as if he hoped a golden land existed at the end of a
       journey. He was never, of course, a romantic yearner;
       he was never complacent, he was always questioning
       himself. But his frequent longing for a perfect "home"
       seems to be an inevitable outcome of his failure to
       achieve the kind of integration that we associate with a
       great tragic poet, the adjustment that comes with
       passing through personal suffering to a more inclusive
       vision and view of life' (p. 209). But to imply that
       Thomas falls short only of a Shakespearean synthesis is
       a high tribute. In fact his 'goal' functions as a working
       hypothesis rather than as a fixed objective. It is not a
       destination but a direction in which he steers. Thomas's
       'agnosticism' did not supply the final certainties of a
       more confident or Christian poet. His conception of
       'the unseen moving goal' keeps all questions open up to
       and beyond the last moment. The 'maturity' and 'inte-

gration' of his poetry lies in this very open-endedness. **115**
The resolution of poems like *Old Man* and *The Other*
depends on a courageous recognition that there are
always fresh possibilities to be faced. But if the 'goal' as
a fixed point of contentment or self-knowledge is a
mirage, it may occasionally, as here, take Thomas by
surprise. His 'golden land' turns out to be the most
homely and ordinary of landscapes, his 'goal' a temporary
but solving moment of rest.

21–5. *I should use . . . such whispers bid.* Cf. *Aspens*
(p. 92) and see notes. Thomas's fidelity to 'whispers,'
his use of 'a language not to be betrayed' may explain
the comparative neglect of his poetry.

THE CHERRY TREES   **115**

Bod. 7 and 8 May 1916.

IT RAINS   **116**

Bod. 11, 12, 13 May 1916.

See note on 'rain' in Thomas's poetry, p. 161. An
essay called 'Rain' includes the following: 'One shower I
remember that wrought magic in a London garden . . .
At the bottom of the garden, beyond the lawn, was an
enclosed space of warm rank grasses, and, rising over
them a vapour of cow-parsley flowers. A white steam
from the soil faintly misted the grass to the level of the
tallest buttercups. Rain was falling, and the grasses and
overhanging elm trees seemed to be suffering for their
quietness and loneliness . . . For the time, that garden

116 was the loneliest place on earth, and I loved and feared
its loneliness.' (R.A.P., pp. 112–13)

12–15. *When I turn away ... revisits the light.* 'Far
away a gate is loudly shut, and the rich blue evening
comes on and severs me irrevocably from all but the
light in the old wood and the ghostly white cow-
parsley flowers suspended on unseen stalks. And there,
among the trees and their shadows, not understood,
speaking a forgotten tongue, old dreads and formless
awes and fascinations discover themselves and address
the comfortable soul, troubling it, recalling to it un-
remembered years not so long past but that in the end
it settles down into a gloomy tranquillity and satisfied
discontent, as when we see the place where we were
unhappy as children once' (H.E., p. 55). 'The white
cow-parsley flowers hovered around me on invisible
stems . . .' (H.E., p. 217).

12–13. *on its fine stalk/Twilight has fined to naught.* 'Its'
refers to 'the parsley flower' and 'that' should be understood after 'stalk.'

116   SOME EYES CONDEMN

Bod. 13 and 14 May 1916.

'I am glad you liked the sonnet, I suppose it was one.
My fear was that it ended with a click. "One" is, I
suppose, a weakness' (E.F., p. 198). Perhaps wary of the
'click' Thomas wrote only six sonnets in all, although he
seems to coquette with the form by producing so many
rhymed and unrhymed pentameter structures of between
ten and eighteen lines. He wrote to Jesse Berridge in
1902: 'Personally, I have a dread of the sonnet. It must

contain 14 lines, and a man must be a tremendous poet **116** or a cold mathematician if he can accommodate his thoughts to such a condition. The result is—in my opinion—that many of the best sonnets are rhetoric only' (Moore, p. 284). He later wrote in the same vein of the Elizabethan sonneteers: 'The sonnet had become, in fact, so powerful a thing of itself that the chances were against a man who set out to use it as a medium of "emotion remembered in tranquillity." He might as well hope to be the saviour of mankind in a well-ironed silk hat' (*Feminine Influence on the Poets*, p. 98). He did, however, qualify this extreme position: 'As the sonata can be true-hearted as the folksong, so the elaborate sonnet or epithalamium can be no less so than "Whistle and I'll come to ye, my lad"' (p. 104).

Some of Thomas's own performances bear this out. Of his sonnets two are Shakespearean in form, *It Was Upon* (p. 122), and *That Girl's Clear Eyes* (*Handel Street*) (p. 128); two are composed of couplets, *A Dream* (p. 91) and *The Wind's Song* (C.P., p. 188); and two are semi-Petrarchan, *Some Eyes Condemn* and *February Afternoon* (p. 105). This structural variety, together with subtle rhyming (internal rhyme is exploited in *Some Eyes Condemn*) and a marked counterpointing of form and syntax, manifests in practice Thomas's stated fear of 'mathematics,' his recognition that a steady submission to the sonnet's imperious patterns might inhibit the rhythmic flexibility he valued. Throughout his poetry he implicitly denies this form as he denies a smoothly regular iambic pentameter; avoids it as he avoids the obvious. When he cannot escape the sonnet the result occasionally, in fact, suggests a set piece: the 'eye' conceit of *Some Eyes Condemn* is given a slightly

345

116 pompous or even absurd Elizabethan elaboration.
9–10. *Others, too . . . Dance, shoot.* Here Thomas pushes
the sonnet form to the point of disintegration.

117 13–14. *But thinking of your eyes . . . it was me they
burned.* The notion of his mistress's eyes burning,
wounding, or slaying the lover is a traditional motif of
the sonnet sequence Thomas's abrupt shift or revelation of focus at this late stage of the poem follows another
convention: cf. 'alas the race/Of all my thoughts hath
neither stop nor start,/But only Stella's eyes and Stella's
heart' (Sidney, *Astrophil and Stella*, sonnet XXIII). The
sonnet as a whole, and line 14 in particular, has a
Sidneyan movement, cf. 'True, and yet true that I must
Stella love' at the end of Sidney's sonnet V. Thomas's
extensive reading of English literature is very deeply
absorbed in his poetry.

117   THE SUN USED TO SHINE

Bod. 22 May 1916.
This fine poem commemorates Thomas's friendship
with the American poet Robert Frost (see Appendix A
for its literary aspect), whom he met at the end of 1913,
and in particular the month of August 1914, when the
Thomases were staying near the Frosts in Ledington,
on the Gloucestershire–Herefordshire border. It was
the golden, threatened summer of the outbreak of the
First World War (on 4 August). Thomas's essay 'This
England' (L.S., pp. 215–21 and P.E.T., pp. 222–6),
which explains some of the feelings that led him to enlist
(see general note to *This is No Case of Petty Right or
Wrong*, p. 307), covers the same ground as the poem.

346

The sun shone, always warm, from skies sometimes **117**
cloudless, sometimes inscribed with a fine white scatter
miles high, sometimes displaying the full pomp of
white moving mountains, sometimes almost entirely
shrouded in dull sulphurous threats, but vain ones.

Three meadows away lived a friend, and once or
twice or three times a day I used to cross the meadows,
the gate, and the two stiles ... How easy it was to
spend a morning or afternoon ... strolling with my
friend, nearly regardless of footpaths, in a long loop,
so as to end either at his house or my lodging. It was
mostly orchard and grass, gently up and down, seldom
steep for more than a few yards. Some of the meadows
had a group or a line of elms; one an ash rising out of
an islet of dense brambles; many had several great
old apple or pear trees. The pears were small brown
perry pears, as thick as haws, the apples chiefly cider
apples, innumerable, rosy and uneatable, though once
or twice we did pick up a wasp's remnant, with slightly
greasy skin of palest yellow, that tasted delicious.
There was one brook to cross, shallow and leaden,
with high hollow bare banks ...

If talk dwindled in the traversing of a big field, the
pause at gate or stile braced it again. Often we pro-
longed the pause, whether we actually sat or not, and
we talked—of flowers, childhood, Shakespeare,
women, England, the war—or we looked at a far
horizon, which some dip or gap occasionally disclosed.
Thomas's meditation on England and the war begins:
'Then one evening the new moon made a difference';
and includes a reference to 'the purple-headed wood-
betony with two pairs of dark leaves on a stiff stem, who
stood sentinel among the grasses or bracken by hedge-

117 side or wood's-edge.'

Frost sailed for America in February 1915, so their Ledington holiday represented a high watermark of leisurely intercourse between the poets. On 9 August 1915 Thomas wrote to Frost: 'Ledington & Whiteleaved Oak seems purely paradisal, with Beauty of Bath apples Hesperidean lying with thunder dew on the warm ground. I am almost old enough not to make any moan of it' (D.C.L.). Writing of Edward Thomas to Amy Lowell in October 1917, Frost recalled the year of which Ledington was the epitome: 'He more than anyone else was accessory to what I had done and was doing. We were together to the exclusion of every other person and interest all through 1914—1914 was our year. I never had, I never shall have another such year of friendship' (*Selected Letters*, p. 220). Helen Thomas generously affirms Frost's importance to her husband: 'He believed in [Edward] and loved him, understanding, as no other man had ever understood, his strange complex temperament' (W.W.E., p. 159). Understanding, the keynote of *The Sun Used to Shine*, was the core of their relationship. In his letter to Helen Thomas after Thomas's death (see Biographical Extracts, p. 385) and in his poem *To E. T.* Frost finds most intolerable the fact that they could no longer communicate: 'I meant, you meant, that nothing should remain/Unsaid between us, brother.' There was a scheme for the Thomases to join the Frosts farming in America. But first Thomas's decision and then his death prevented this fruition of the poets' relationship. *The Sun Used to Shine* remains the ultimate testimony to the spiritual and imaginative mating that took place, together with Frost's plain statement of the facts: 'Edward Thomas was the only brother I ever had.

I fail to see how we can have been so much to each **117**
other, he an Englishman and I an American and our first
meeting put off till we were both in middle life. I hadn't
a plan for the future that didn't include him.' (Letter to
Edward Garnett, *Selected Letters*, p. 217)

15–17. *or crocuses . . . In sunless Hades fields.* An ominous
image which Thomas had previously worked on in
prose: 'the tenderest green and palest purple of a thick
cluster of autumn crocuses that have broken out of the
dark earth and stand surprised, amidst their own weak
light as of the underworld from which they have come'
(S.C., p. 278); 'the purple crocuses of Autumn seemed
but then to have broken out of the underworld, a little
band of fugitives, and trembled affrighted in their
pallor amid all the gorgeousness of the flowers of red
and gold' (L.S., p. 82).

28. *like memory's sand.* Although apparently of equal **118**
status with 'like those rumours' etc., this illustration
really defines the effect of the others. Time erodes the
vividness of every idyll. As so often, Thomas's poem is
a means of conserving 'memory's sand,' of handing on
the experience intact to 'other men.'

NO ONE CARES LESS THAN I   118

Bod. 25 and 26 May 1916.

This poem predates by over four months Thomas's
twin response to the trumpet calls at Trowbridge—*The
Trumpet* (p. 129) and *Lights Out* (p. 132), see notes.
Moore mistakenly links all three poems as contemporary
when, after referring to *The Trumpet*, he speaks of
Thomas setting 'some more words to the brave bugle-

118 call' and quotes the first stanza of *No One Cares Less than I* (p. 236). Cooke attacks Moore's terminology:

> The impression which is conveyed (and which is certainly intended from that transferred epithet "brave") is that Thomas was careless of personal risk and eager to join the fray. In fact he is saying no such thing. The romantic response of the first stanza is deliberately undercut by the heavy "God"—"clod" rhyme. Significantly, it is "a foreign clod," which may have been Thomas's personal reaction to Brooke's "corner of a foreign field/That is for ever England." The second stanza points to the possible discrepancy (in the conjunction "But") between the words he makes to that call and what the bugles may really be saying. (p. 237)

119   AS THE TEAM'S HEAD-BRASS

Bod. 27 May 1916.

Thomas mentions the poem in a letter to Eleanor Farjeon postmarked 4 June which she mistakenly attributes to June 1915: 'I don't know about a title for the blank verse ... What about "The Last Team"?' (p. 144). He seems never to have made up his mind on this point.

> How nobly the ploughman and the plough and three horses, two chestnuts and a white leader, glide over the broad swelling field in the early morning! Under the dewy, dark-green woodside they wheel, pause, and go out into the strong light again, and they seem one and glorious, as if the all-breeding earth had just sent them up out of her womb—mighty, splendid, and

something grim, with darkness and primitive forces **119**
clinging about them, and the night in the horses'
manes. (H.E., p. 21 and P.E.T., p. 67)

As the Team's Head-Brass seems to be Thomas's
mature assessment of the impact of the First World
War on his own life and on the lives of others (see
general note to *This is No Case of Petty Right or Wrong*,
p. 305). It is the culmination and distillation of a pervasive imaginative reaction. None of Thomas's poems
was written in the trenches, although the darker side
of his art may anticipate them. His real experience of the
war derived from his period of training as a soldier.
Accordingly his poetry complements that of Wilfred
Owen in focusing on the profound disturbance of life
at home. The war's disruption of pattern and habit is
the subject of such poems as *A Private*, *The Owl*, *In
Memoriam (Easter, 1915)* and *'Home.'*

Thomas's perspective in *As the Team's Head-Brass*
recalls in some respects Hardy's *In Time of 'the Breaking
of Nations*,' written at the same period:

I

Only a man harrowing clods
    In a slow silent walk
With an old horse that stumbles and nods
    Half asleep as they stalk.

II

Only thin smoke without flame
    From the heaps of couch-grass;
Yet this will go onward the same
    Though Dynasties pass.

III

> Yonder a maid and her wight
> Come whispering by:
> War's annals will cloud into night
> Ere their story die.

Yet Thomas's relation of distant catastrophe to the ordinary human and seasonal cycles is more complex. His poem in fact consists of inter-related cycles. Structurally it returns full circle, and its rhythm is determined by the regular rotation of the plough which shapes the ruminative ebb and flow of conversation. Thematically the team suggests the cycle of the year while further cycles are hinted at through the 'lovers' and the elm with its 'woodpecker's round hole.' However, most of these cycles have been interrupted or disrupted: the elm has 'fallen,' the ploughman's 'mate' is dead; and the poem's movement is broken up by an extended conversation about the war. Yet this conversation is not wholly alien to its context or to the overall rhythm. Thomas implicitly assimilates the war to natural hazards like the blizzard (the elm has 'fallen' like a soldier) or even the cruelty involved in man's attack on the earth itself. The plough just suggests a menacing or military engine (cf. the prose passage quoted above) in words like 'flashed' 'scraping' 'screwed' or the phrase 'Instead of treading me down.' Thus, although 'Everything/Would have been different' without the war, the fact of it has been absorbed, and alternative cycles and possibilities set in motion.

Even when he reached the front, Thomas did not regard life as radically changed. He wrote to his brother Julian on 30 March 1917: 'I wonder will you find out for yourself some equilibrium in this mix-up, the War,

and of course everything else. War, of course, is not **119**
altogether different from peace, except that one may be
blown to bits and have to blow others to bits. Physical
discomfort is sometimes so great that it seems a new
thing, but of course it is not. You remember cycling in
the rain towards Salisbury. It really is seldom quite a
different thing from that. Of course, one seems very
little one's own master, but then, one seldom does seem
so. Death looms, but however it comes it is unexpected,
whether from appendicitis or bullet. An alternation of
comfort and discomfort is always a man's lot. So is an
alternation of pleasure or happiness or intense interest
with tedium or dissatisfaction or misery. I have suffered
more from January to March in other years than in this'
(Moore, p. 261). In the poem, the lovers reappear, their
private world apparently still valid; the clods again
'crumble and topple over.' The poet (ominously) may be
watching them 'for the last time,' and at another level
this phrase and the poem may prophesy the social
changes brought about by the war. However the main
stress is on an essential continuity: human progress is
like that of 'the stumbling team.'

1. *head-brass*: the brasswork on the harness about the
horses' heads.

22. *I should want nothing more.* Ironical: on the surface
this suggests that the poet will have reached the summit
of his wishes, but it literally asserts that death will have
put an end to his 'wanting.'

120   AFTER YOU SPEAK

Bod. 3 June 1916.

See note on Thomas's love poems, p. 324.

10–24. *Even so the lark . . . no light*: a simile which may owe something both to Shelley's aspiring *Skylark* and to the later of Wordsworth's *To a Skylark* poems ('Type of the wise who soar, but never roam;/True to the kindred points of Heaven and Home!').

121   BRIGHT CLOUDS

Bod. 4, 5 June 1916.

The 'Diary in English Fields and Woods' which concludes Thomas's first book, *The Woodland Life*, contains the following entry for 8 August 1895: 'Wind breaks up the sheets of scum upon the ponds, so that it appears to sink, but collects again in calm' (p. 191).

The poem is founded upon the visual precision and verbal economy of this kind of field observation. Cooke suggests that its extra dimension partly derives from Thomas's awareness of the war while becalmed in training camp, and stresses the image 'Like criss-cross bayonets': 'Momentarily, as the tall reeds flash upon the inward eye, the surface calm is broken. Like the scene in the poem, the poet's mind embraces both sunlight and shade' (see pp. 107–8). Even this image, however, originated in a 'Diary' entry for 21 April 1895: 'Reeds piercing the ripples of the brook, with twin blades curved and meeting like calipers' (T.W.L., p. 165), or perhaps in an earlier description of bluebell leaves: 'These dark green sword-like blades, as of some strong grass, curve gracefully with their own weight' (p. 36).

Bod. 8, 9, 10, 11 June 1916.

Thomas wrote to Eleanor Farjeon: 'I am sending you a sober set of verses to the tune of Rio Grande, but I doubt if they can be sung' (E.F., p. 199). He had included the song in his *Pocket Book of Poems and Songs for the Open Air* (p. 159):

> O where are you going to, my pretty maid?
> O, away to Rio;
> O where are you going to, my pretty maid?
> We're bound for Rio Grande.
> Away to Rio, away to Rio,
> So fare thee well, my bonny young girl,
> We're bound for Rio Grande . . .

'It has a glorious tune which I prefer to Westminster Abbey just now' (L.G.B., p. 94). See note on Thomas's interest in folk songs, p. 176. 'Early One Morning' is the title and opening phrase of another folk song, also included in the *Pocket Book*.

Edward Garnett's view of the poem (and of Thomas) is somewhat sentimental: 'The fascination of his shy, evasive nature and other-worldliness is caught in the charming lilt of "Early one Morning" ' (introduction to *Selected Poems*, 1927, p. xvi). Scannell more acutely detects the poem's 'sober' side, analysing the 'sombre undertone' that progressively invades it until 'the last four lines make it plain that the poem is not the jolly away-from-it-all piece of Georgian nonsense that the first six lines appeared to promise' (see pp. 23–4).

Bod. 21 June 1916.

See note on Thomas's sonnets, p. 344. His 'Diary in English Fields and Woods' which concludes *The Woodland Life* contains the following entry for 30 June 1895: 'Grass of the rising aftermath or "lattermath" beautifully green after a quickening rain, while the thistled pastures are grey' (p. 185). The literal meaning of 'lattermath' and 'aftermath' is second or later mowing, the crop of grass which springs up after the first cutting in early summer. The poem turns on a characteristic penetration of one season by another, and of the present by past and future.

1. *a July evening*. Thomas seems to have selected 'July' rather than 'June' for rhythmical reasons.

9–14. *And as an unaccomplished prophecy ... this hoar Spring*? The object of 'recall' and 'question' is 'The stranger's words.' The 'hoar' or elderly Spring seems to represent the late flowering of Thomas's poetry (and life), 'this unexpected ebullition' (L.G.B., p. 251), about whose issue he is still uncertain.

Bod. 22 June 1916.

Women He Liked draws on 'Mr. Torrance's' portrait of an old-fashioned squire in *The Happy-Go-Lucky Morgans*: 'he was pure rustic English, and his white hair and beard had an honourable look as if it had been granted to him for some rare service ... I think he knew men as well as horses; at least he knew everyone

in that country, had known them all when he and they **123**
were boys. He was a man as English, as true to the soil,
as a Ribston pippin' (pp. 148–9).

'Shovel-bearded Bob' demonstrates that Lob 'lives
yet' in Thomas's poetry, although the poem is tinged
by his darker preoccupations at this period. Bob, like
Lob, cherishes continuity and invests in it by planting
trees. His dividend is the naming of the lane which
consummates and renders indissoluble his organic
relationship with landscape. This consummation is,
however, achieved in a paradoxical manner. Bob's act
of love has proved literally destructive, reducing the
lane to 'slough/And gloom'; yet also obliquely creative,
rescuing it from the alternative oblivion of nameless-
ness.

2. *Old Farmer Hayward of the Heath.* The poem may
have started off as a dual 'explanation' of Hayward's
Heath (a small town in east Sussex) and some actual
Bob's Lane. Working back from the place names, and
using 'pure imagination' rather than 'rash science' (see
note, p. 245) Thomas reconstructs history and turns it
into myth.

7. *the stormcock*: the missel-thrush, whose song presages
bad weather.

THERE WAS A TIME   **123**

Bod. 23 June 1916.

This poem confirms Robert Frost's feeling that the
war 'has made some sort of new man and a poet out of
Edward Thomas' (*Selected Letters*, p. 193), even if other
factors must also be given credit. Thomas offers a frank

123 account of his previous personal history, and may be interpreting a curious passivity or perversity of temperament, which needed the external challenges of war and of Frost himself as a stimulus to full self-realisation. 1. *There was a time when this poor frame was whole.* Probably a conscious reference to the first line of Wordsworth's *Ode* on *Intimations of Immortality from Recollections of Early Childhood*:

There was a time when meadow, grove, and stream,
The earth, and every common sight,
   To me did seem
  Apparelled in celestial light,
The glory and the freshness of a dream.
It is not now as it hath been of yore;—
   Turn wheresoe'er I may,
    By night or day,
The things which I have seen I now can see no more . . .

Thomas's experience has, in fact, been the *reverse* of Wordsworth's. For him it is 'now' much better than 'it hath been of yore.'

124   THE GREEN ROADS

Bod. 28 June 1916.

One of Thomas's 'forest' poems, antedating *The Dark Forest* (see notes) and *Lights Out* (p. 136, see notes). 'The green roads' lead into the forest as life leads into death. The cottages etc. represent different stages or perspectives on this path to the 'unknown.' The dead oak at the heart of the forest concentrates a sense of the fathomless oblivion that can engulf man and his history.

Thomas's reiteration of 'the forest' becomes increasingly **124**
ominous, while the wandering internal rhyme in the
second line of each couplet unfailingly trips us up with a
sense of mystery or unease ('But he has never come back').
Edward Garnett comments: ' "The Green Roads"
appears somewhat indecisive and empty till one finds
that it is this very feeling of vacancy that conveys the
forest's vanished memories' (introduction to *Selected
Poems*, 1927, p. v).

10. *a thrush twiddles his song.* The thrush is like the
poet who also sings at the brink of the 'unknown' and
alone registers its existence. *Twiddles*: idly improvises.
The propriety of this word (which basically means to
twirl with the fingers) has been questioned, but its
onomatopoeic quality emphasises that the bird's song is
the sole sound in the 'vacancy.' It also implies the blithe
inconsequence of the thrush, undauntedly practising his
art. Bird and poet are reassuring presences in the poem.
Together with a sense that transition into the forest is
natural and inevitable, they mitigate the more menacing
overtones.

THE DARK FOREST   **125**

Bod. 1 and 10 July 1916.

Thomas had doubts about this poem, felt that 'the
forest is perhaps a too obvious metaphor' (E.F., p. 202).
But this reservation is mentioned in a letter postmarked
10 July and may apply only to an earlier draft sent previously to Eleanor Farjeon: 'This is the latest . . . The
forest is a fragment left 6 miles from here [Hare Hall
Camp], the best of all this county. I go there every time
I can.' (ibid.)

125 "Forest" is one of the most frequent symbols in the poetry, but when we attempt to fix its significance we find not only that it varies subtly according to the context, but also that our terms of explanation tend to sound heavy and clumsy in comparison with the poet's touch. In rather general terms we might say that "forest" in Thomas's poetry is the dark region of human experience which cannot be illuminated by thought or reason, a pathless region; it is the gulf of nothingness or eternity that waits behind the temporal and the tangible; or it is simply sleep, or death. (Coombes, p. 220)

5–8. *And evermore mighty multitudes ride/About . . . seen.* The shadowy 'multitudes' to which it is impossible to assign any precise physical or psychological shape, concentrate the 'imagist' suggestiveness of the poem.

9–12. *The forest foxglove . . . day or night.* There may be undertones of Thomas's favourite myth of Persephone, compelled to spend six months of the year in the Underworld because she had eaten pomegranate seeds there. 'Purple' is a colour traditionally associated with death and mourning: cf. *The Sun Used to Shine,* lines 15–17

125 THE GALLOWS

Bod. 3 and 4 July 1916.

Thomas and his wife were staying with Vivian Locke Ellis at Selsfield House, East Grinstead. 'At Ellises I could not help writing these 4 verses on the theme of some stories I used to tell Baba there' (E.F., p. 202). Elements of the poem, and possibly of the stories, appear in a strange essay called 'Sunday' (H.E., pp. 191–5), where Thomas dreams in a country church

'that I saw these men and women in a kind of heaven **125**
where all day long for ever they did those things which
had most pleased or most taken hold of them in life':

The gamekeeper stood, with smoking gun barrels, and
a cloud of jay's feathers still in the air and among the
May foliage about him. Pride, stupidity, servility
clouded his face as in his days of nature, and above
him in the oaks innumerable jays laughed because
beauty, like folly, was immortal there.

The squire, more faint, and whether to his joy or
not I could not discern, was standing under a bough
on which hung white owls, wood owls, falcons, crows,
magpies, cats, hedgehogs, stoats, weasels, some bloody,
some with gaping stomachs, some dismembered or
crushed, some fleshless, some heaving like boiling fat,
and on them and him the sun shone hot.

Thomas's impassive recording of the creatures' fate
(which, like their frailty, resembles man's) is more
powerful than his evident anger in the prose version. He
borrows folk-song techniques (see note, p. 176), so that
the poem chills by its lack of comment and by the
cumulatively cruel neutrality of its refrain lines. It is
interesting to compare the last two stanzas of Ted
Hughes's poem *November* (*Lupercal*, Faber, 1960, p.
50):

  . . . The keeper's gibbet had owls and hawks
  By the neck, weasels, a gang of cats, crows:
  Some, stiff, weightless, twirled like dry bark bits

  In the drilling rain. Some still had their shape,
  Had their pride with it; hung, chins on chests,
  Patient to outwait these worst days that beat
  Their crowns bare and dripped from their feet.

Bod. 15 July 1916.

The 'wiser' man is not only intelligent but kind, because he protects the feelings of 'all such as are foolish and slow of thought and slower of speech, and laugh at what they love because others do and then weep in solitude' (H.E., p. 151). It is a 'Lob' character whom Thomas credits with this wisdom in the prose passage.

127   HOW AT ONCE

Bod. 10 August 1916.

Written when Thomas was 'upset by vaccination' (L.G.B., p. 270) and bored in hospital. 'I . . . shall be lucky to do more [verses] till the swifts are back again' (E.F., p. 209). By 'next May' Thomas had been killed. He told Eleanor Farjeon that she had 'misread' the poem 'missing the point that year after year I see them, *realising it is the last time*, i.e. just before they go away for the winter (early in August). Perhaps it is too much natural history.' (p. 213)

127   GONE, GONE AGAIN

Bod. 3 September 1916.

Thomas again betrays an autumnal preoccup aaits with the passage of time. Cooke discusses the poem on a culmination of Thomas's 'insistence on facing an unvarnished reality' (pp. 140–1).

11. *Blenheim or anges*: a variety of eating apple.

12. *grubby*. Cooke points out that this word 'combines **127** the sense of "dirty" and "eaten by grubs" ' (p. 141).

17–32. *Look at the old house . . . broken every one*. The **128** image of a 'dark house' (*The Long Small Room*, p. 133, see notes), like that of *The Dark Forest*, haunts Thomas's later poetry. It conveys, if not death, an almost extinguished vitality. Thomas employed the image when writing to Gordon Bottomley in 1908 about the characteristic depression brought on by his parting from a young girl with whom he had a platonic friendship: 'I dimly foresee a guttering candle, a flicker, another flicker, a smell & an awakening to find the fire as well as the light gone out, the house cold & dark & still . . .' (L.G.B., p. 159). Houses bear much significance throughout Thomas's prose and poetry (see general note to *Two Houses*, p. 295). They function as complex symbols of man's tenancy of his body and the earth:

A house is a perdurable garment, giving and taking of life. If it only fit, straightway it begins to chronicle our days. It beholds our sorrows and our joys; its untale-bearing walls know all our thoughts, and if it be such a house as grows after the builders are gone, our thoughts presently owe much to it; we have but to glance at a certain shadow or a curve in the wallpaper pattern to recall them, softened as by an echo, and that corner or that gable starts many a fancy that reaches beyond the stars, many a fancy gay or enriched with regrets. It is aware of birth, marriage and death; and who dares say that there is not kneaded into the stones a record more pleasing than brass?
(S.C., pp. 243–4)

Thomas has earlier described a derelict house which resembles the house in the poem:

128   Hanging from the wall in rags, too wet even to flap, are the remains of an auctioneer's announcement of a sale at the house behind. Mahogany—oak chests—certain ounces of silver—two thousand books—portraits and landscapes and pictures of horses and game—of all these and how much else has the red house been disembowelled? It is all shadowy within, behind the windows, like the eyes of a corpse, and without sound, or form, or light... The martins are still there, and their play up and down before the twenty windows is a senseless thing, like the play of children outside a chamber of agony or grief. They seem to be machines going on and on when their master and purpose are dead... The moss is beginning to encrust the gravel for the soft feet of the ghosts, of the old men and the mothers and the maids and the schoolboys and tottering babes that have trodden it or ce. (pp. 240–1)

28. *dark*: the only unrhymed last word of a stanza in this unobtrusively but disturbingly irregular poem. I calls attention both to itself and to the bleak closing statement.

30–2. *Not one pane ... broken every one.* Cf. *I Built Myself a House of Glass* (p. 85) and see note.

128   THAT GIRL'S CLEAR EYES
               (*Handel Street*)

Bod. 10 September 1916.

See note on Thomas's sonnets, p. 344. Coombes supplies the following information: 'At the end of Handel Street, in the parish of St. Pancras, is the

Foundlings' Hospital, founded by Thomas Coram in **128**
1739. A statue of Coram, with that date on it, was
standing in Thomas's day; it has since been removed.
"The stony square sunlit" is Brunswick Square. Many
tombstones remain in the gardens thereabouts, and the
plane trees are still there. The hospital band still plays
the ranks of children through the gates next to which the
statue stood' (p. 223). In September 1916 Thomas was
training as an officer cadet at the Royal Artillery School
in Handel Street and *Handel Street* was originally a
registering in his usual manner of the poem's place of
composition. It is unclear whether Thomas himself or
his editors later incorporated this heading as an indica-
tion of setting and subject-matter. The subtitle was
first attached to the printed poem in 1936.

Coombes remarks: 'The structure looks simple
enough: the first eight lines belong to the main title,
That Girl's Clear Eyes, the last six to *Handel Street*' (p.
224). But the poem seems rather to divide in the middle
of line 6. His experience with the girl causes the poet to
recall an earlier and parallel experience at the School in
Handel Street, and clarify his response to it ('Nor until
now could I admit'). Coombes observes:

> The poem works round the idea of "reality": the
> poet is asking himself what is most real, real for him.
> He states that the girl's eyes (the eyes, the very feature
> that should most vividly convey and express), say, or
> said, nothing except that they are concealing some-
> thing. His own eyes are like the girl's: a significant
> reality is being concealed, and there can be no
> "meeting" between the two human beings, saying so
> much and at the same time so little to each other.
> Even if death should reveal what this reality is (he

365

128   does not say it will, for the document, envelope, that
is sealed may have nothing inside), the knowledge
will be useless because there will then be no possibility of any "meeting." (p. 223)

129   13–14. *While music blazed* . . . '*Seventeen Thirty-
Nine.*' . . . in the very last phrase of the poem the poet
comes back, seems just to manage to come back, to the
theme of the first part, to the idea of concealment: these
things that now attract him, the blazing music, the
marching children, are themselves hiding a reality; in
their attractiveness they (almost) blot out the memory
of the pity and profound devotion of the founder of
the hospital, a *Foundlings'* hospital. By that last phrase,
"hiding the Seventeen Thirty-Nine," we are taken
a little distance from the present, which we are
now likely to see as rather showy; we may wonder,
too, whether that "marched" is not, despite its splendour, half deprecatory, suggesting as it does the regi-
mentation of children. (Coombes, p. 224)

A further integrating factor must surely be the war.
The companions unable to communicate at their morning
tasks seem to be Thomas's fellow-cadets ('tombs' has
a grim prophetic resonance). The poem examines the
same self-imposed numbness as '*Home*' (p. 108, see
notes). For practical reasons the poet has chosen to live
in the present and its sensations. However, the sensations
themselves 'reveal' what he has buried, break the 'seal.'
They combine 'pleasure and pain,' sunlight and darkness, while the children marching to music mimic the
deceptive panoply of war.

Bod. 15 September 1916.

Thomas still seems to be meditating on possible departure for France. He often suffered from the feeling that he was less visible or necessary to others than they to him. At a performance of Gordon Bottomley's *King Lear's Wife* he was almost perversely pleased when the change effected in his appearance by an army haircut confirmed this: 'Nobody recognises me now. Sturge Moore, E. Marsh, & R. C. Trevelyan stood a yard off & I didn't trouble to awake them to stupid recognition' (letter to Robert Frost, 21 May 1916, D.C.L.). The poem's attitude is slightly self-pitying.

10–12. *Almost I thought ... and lightly laughed.* The poet tentatively admits the notion that he ('the blossom') means as much to other people ('rain') as they do to him: that all relationship is based on *mutual* need. But this brief vision is apparently negated by line 12, although the power of the image persists. Coombes suggests in his discussion of the poem (pp. 225–6) that Thomas 'half-surrenders the dream, realizing that it involved a certain self-importance, and progresses to a further knowledge.'

THE TRUMPET   129

Bod. 26–7–8 ? September 1916.

The Trumpet was composed when Thomas, training as an officer cadet in the Royal Artillery, spent nearly two months at firing camp in Trowbridge. He wrote to Eleanor Farjeon: 'I have written some verses suggested by the trumpet calls which go all day. They are not well done and the trumpet is cracked, but the Reveillé

129 pleases me (more than it does most sleepers)' (E.F., p. 219). *Lights Out*, Thomas's next poem but one, was also suggested by the trumpeting at Trowbridge and complements this inferior and less well known reveillé.

Cooke comments on the fact that *The Trumpet* stands first in both P. and C.P.: 'It is not a good introduction to Thomas's poetry, yet it has retained its position as first poem in almost every collection of his work. Possibly it is for this reason that it is sometimes read as a poem of the "visions of glory" category. It is, however, wholly different from such poems and testifies more to the ambiguity of Thomas's commitment. It was as if he had to pervert his own nature to adapt himself to the war, and the impotent climax of the first stanza

> Rise up and scatter
> The dew that covers
> The print of last night's lovers

amounts almost to an act of desecration against the lovers, who represent a norm of sanity in his other poems' (p. 235). The poem's inspiration, and its traditional position, may owe something to A. E. Housman's *Reveille*, with which Thomas began *The Pocket Book of Poems and Songs for the Open Air*:

> Wake: the silver dusk returning
>   Up the beach of darkness brims,
> And the ship of sunrise burning
>   Strands upon the eastern rims.
> Wake: the vaulted shadow shatters,
>   Trampled to the floor it spanned,
> And the tent of night in tatters
>   Straws the sky-pavilioned land.
> Up, lad, up, 'tis late for lying:
>   Hear the drums of morning play;

Hark, the empty highways crying   **129**
   "Who'll beyond the hills away ?" ...

Thomas's poem is more complex than Housman's, but he seems principally concerned to imitate the urgent clarity of a trumpet call. Twisting repetition/variation in vocabulary, line-length, rhyme-scheme, stress and refrain makes *The Trumpet* a technical *tour de force* of the same order as *Two Pewits* (p. 61, see note). Thomas's identification with the call may license any temporary amnesia about the war: through the music of this 'instrument' he can briefly recover innocence.

4–6. *As the dawn glowing/The stars that left unlit/The* **130** *land and water*. 'Chases' is understood after 'glowing.' The ellipsis, together with a general syntactical and rhythmical fluidity, enhances this impressionistic evocation of the rout of darkness.

21. *To the old wars*. Thomas's own voice seems to enter the poem at this point, producing a slurred note which drags down with the weight of its last two monosyllables the final 'Arise, arise!' Apart from its immediate reference to the First World War, the phrase suggests man's continuing struggles on earth in the largest sense.

WHEN FIRST   **130**

No MS. of this poem can be traced, but Thomas wrote to Gordon Bottomley on 2 October 1916 'I have just seen Steep for the last time' (L.G.B., p. 271). It seems possible that *When First* was written some time in October (Thomas's letters to Eleanor Farjeon for the month have been lost). At any rate it must have been among his last few poems.

130   In November 1906 the Thomases moved into Berryfield Cottage, Ashford, in the parish of Steep, Petersfield,
Hampshire. 'This house & the country about it make the
most beautiful place we ever lived in' (L.G.B., p. 126).
'It stood on a little rise of a winding lane which ran at
the foot of the steep sides of a vast raised plateau. The
irregular sloping edge was in some parts bare like the
downs; in other parts covered in a thick growth of
trees—beech and yew for the most part—called hangers'
(W.W.E., p. 113). Three years later they moved to a
house built specially for them by Geoffrey Lupton at
the edge of the plateau itself. A separate study was
erected for Thomas at the end of the garden. He retained the study, when, dissatisfied with their new house
at Wick Green (see general note to *Wind and Mist*,
p. 225), the Thomases again moved a short distance—to
Yewtree Cottage in the village of Steep (July 1913).
Thomas walked up the hanger to this hilltop study to
write his first poems: 'I can hardly wait to light my fire'
he told Eleanor Farjeon (E.F., p. 108); and he wrote
there when on leave. In June 1916 Helen Thomas was
told by Mrs. Lupton to remove all Edward's books and
belongings from the study, which was needed for a
companion (W.W.E., p. 166–8). This unhappy incident
precipitated the Thomases' decision to leave Steep
altogether. Helen Thomas's farewell (W.W.E,. pp.
168–9) complements *When First*: 'this hill which had
become almost human for us with its austerity, friendliness and tenderness, is more than any other place in
England linked with [Edward] in my memory and my
dreams.'

131   17. *Just hope has gone for ever*. Not a statement of un-
relieved pessimism, since 'health,' 'cheerfulness,' and

fresh discoveries remain possible. 'Hope' seems to **131**
signify a kind of youthful expectancy that has irrevocably yielded to maturer awareness of life's complexity
and pattern. The poem, in fact, ends 'hopefully' and
explores acceptance, middle-age, coming-to-terms rather
than 'melancholy.' The last stanza suggests that retrospective appreciation has taken the place of anticipation
in the poet's life. Rhythmically, too, it recaptures the
pounding 'heart-beat' of the first stanza in contrast to
the low pulse-rate of the poem's middle section. This
dramatic function of the rhythm may answer Scannell's
criticism that *When First* is an instance of Thomas's
attempting 'to impose an arbitrarily chosen form on
matter which simply refuses to submit' (p. 29). 'The
heart's dance' pulls against the stanzaic control which
Thomas's mature, rational self attempts to enforce.

THE CHILD IN THE ORCHARD   **131**

Bod. October 1916.

See general note to *The Child on the Cliffs* (p. 59).
This is Thomas's last, a belated, 'English' poem.
Possibly as an unconscious precaution against the
chance of being killed, he seems to be designating an
ideal heir to the culture and tradition he cherishes. The
child's 'education' will keep him in touch with 'Lob':
he can already associate a familiar 'earthy' animal with
literature/geography/history/mythology, and conceive
an archetypal English folk hero and heroine. Like
Thomas the child asks questions and knows the names
of birds.

5. *hern*: an archaic and dialect form of 'heron.'
7–10. '*Who was the lady . . . take for a ride?*' Two answers

131 offered by *The Oxford Dictionary of Nursery Rhymes* to the child's first question are Queen Elizabeth I and Lady Godiva (p. 66).

132 14. *the Westbury White Horse.* 'High above me, on my left hand, eastward, was the grandest, cliffiest part of the Plain wall, the bastioned angle where it bends round southward by Westbury and Warminster, bare for the most part, carved with the White Horse and with double tiers of chalk pits ...' (I.P.S., p. 176).

20. 'I see that "At the age of six" is a rather rough way of explaining who speaks. But he did tell me he was six too and seemed to realise he had a long way to go.' (E.F., p. 218)

16. *or had he a fall?* Perhaps an echo of another nursery rhyme: 'Humpty Dumpty sat on a wall,/Humpty Dumpty had a great fall.'

132 LIGHTS OUT

Bod. November 1916.

Thomas wrote to Eleanor Farjeon on 6 November: 'Now I have actually done still another piece which I call "Lights Out." It sums up what I have often thought at that call. I wish it were as brief—2 pairs of long notes. I wonder is it nearly as good as it might be' (E.F., p. 218). The reveillé at Trowbridge had inspired *The Trumpet* (p. 129, see notes) at the end of September. Coombes warns against the kind of reaction which may have helped to make *Lights Out* a much anthologised poem: 'we should disregard as far as we are able what it may seem to possess of prophecy; the poignancy doesn't need any adventitious stimulus' (p. 212). Like *The Green Roads* (p. 124, see notes), though more ominously, *Lights*

Out marks the point at which the 'roads' of life converge **132**
on the 'forest' or 'unknown.' In all Thomas's later poems
his poise between 'known' and 'unknown,' 'familiar' and
'strange,' 'home' and a lonely journey, appears to tilt
towards the darker alternatives. He sets out to encounter
not only sleep and death but those aspects of man which
lie outside his conscious awareness. The poet is crossing
the 'borders' of the mind. A passage of meditation in
The South Country (pp. 24–8) which has verbal affinities
with *Lights Out* illuminates the agnostic Thomas's view
of 'eternity' and 'immortality' as a development of
natural existence. At the end of his essay, 'An Autumn
House,' he meditates on sleep: 'It seems indeed to me
that to sleep is owed a portion of the deliberation given
to death. If life is an apprenticeship to death, waking
may be an education for sleep. We are not thoughtful
enough about sleep; yet it is more than half of that great
portion of life spent really in solitude . . . we truly ought
to enter upon sleep as into a strange, fair chapel. Fragrant
and melodious antechamber of the unseen, sleep is a
novitiate for the beyond.' (R.A.P., pp. 105–6)

1–6. *I have come . . . They cannot choose.* Between the
self-contained statements of the first and last lines, enjambement and syntactical detours enact the twists and
turns of the labyrinth.

10–12. *Deceived the travellers . . . And in they sink.* These
lines are consecutively composed of six, five and four
syllables. The short lines at the end of each stanza particularly suggest the inevitability of what is happening,
as does Thomas's emphatic rhyming throughout. The
'travellers'/'blurs' rhyme, however, appropriately 'blurs'
this stanza's pattern of monosyllabic rhyming on crisp
'k' sounds.

132 13–14. *Here love ends . . . ends*: an interesting variation on the usual rhyme-scheme.

133 21–2. *That I would not turn from now/To go into the unknown.* 'Turn from' and 'go' suggest that the poet is not yielding himself with entire passivity to sleep or death, but in part taking a positive decision. 'The unknown' anticipates (despite the repeated 'ends' of the third stanza) some extension as well as extinction of consciousness.

25–30. *The tall forest . . . And myself.* In an essay called 'The Passing of Pan' Thomas falls asleep and dreams: 'A great forest hung round about. The might of its infinite silence and repose, indeed, never ceased to weigh upon me in my dream. I could hear sounds: they were leagues away. The trees which I could see were few: I felt that they must be thousands deep on every hand' (H.S., p. 72). *The Childhood of Edward Thomas* ends with an account of a recurring phenomenon which first appeared in Thomas's early teens: 'It happens mostly when I am lying down in bed waiting for sleep, and only on nights when I sleep well. I close my eyes and I find myself very dimly seeing expand before me a vague immense space enclosed with invisible boundaries. Yet it can hardly be called seeing. All is grey, dull, formless, and I am aware chiefly by some other means than sight of vast unshapely towering masses of a colourless subject which I feel to be soft. Through these things and the space I grope slowly. They tend to fade away, but I can recover them by an effort perhaps half a dozen times, and do so because it is somehow pleasant or alluring. Then I usually sleep. During the experience I am well awake and am remembering that it is a repetition, wondering what it means and if anything new will occur,

374

and taking care not to disturb the process.' (p. 152)

Bod. November 1916.

The house in the poem resembles 'Aunt Rachel's' house at Lydiard Constantine in *The Happy-Go-Lucky Morgans*, which 'was hidden by ivy, which thrust itself through the walls and up between the flagstones of the floor, flapped in at the windows, and spread itself so densely over the panes that the mice ran up and down it, and you could see their pale, silky bellies through the glass—often they looked in and entered. The ivy was full of sparrows' nests . . .' The house has 'a large fireplace' and 'Everything had been as it was in Aunt Rachel's house for untold time; it was natural like the trees; also it was never stale; you never came down in the morning feeling that you had done the same yesterday and would do the same to-morrow, as if each day was a new, badly written line in a copy-book, with the same senseless words at the head of every page.' (pp. 85–7)

2. *Narrowed up to the end the fireplace filled.* The stanza itself 'narrows up' from the spaced monosyllables and open vowels of its first line to the cluttered consonants of 'fireplace filled.'

11. *the dark house.* See note on lines 17–32 of *Gone, Gone Again* (p. 363).

13. *Crawling crab-like over the clean white page.* Thomas's years of literary drudgery made the movement of pen over paper an inevitable image of human bondage.

16. *The hundred last leaves stream upon the willow.* 'I am worried about the impression the willow made on you. As a matter of fact I started with that last line as

133 what I was working to. I am only fearing it has a sort of
Japanesy suddenness of ending' (E.F., p. 221). Even
though Thomas decided to introduce the willows in
the first line, thus integrating the poem more tightly,
this conclusion still appears 'Japanesy' and 'sudden.'
The poem shares an oddness with the room it describes
and its tangential images have a disturbing resonance.
It seems, like other poems of this period, to take a provisional farewell of life.

134   THE SHEILING

Bod. 23 November 1916.

'The Sheiling' (from the Scottish term, also spelt
'shieling,' for a piece of pasture or a building on such
land) was the name of Bottomley's house at Silverdale,
three miles north-west of Carnforth in Lancashire, on
the edge of the Lake District. Thomas wrote the poem
while returning from his last visit there (20 to 23
November). He had just been commissioned as a second
Lieutenant in the Royal Garrison Artillery and was to
volunteer (7 December) for service in France.

The friendship and correspondence between Edward
Thomas and Gordon Bottomley (1874–1948) began in
September 1902, when Thomas was twenty-four and
Bottomley twenty-eight. The latter, a poet and verse-
dramatist, was a chronic invalid constantly endangered
by lung haemorrhages. Thus physically immobilised he
tried to live 'a life of passionate, intense meditation and
contemplation—a life of the spirit concentrated upon the
nature and processes of spiritual creation, as that is mani-
fested in the arts which are man's most permanent
achievement' (see Claude Colleer Abbott's introduction

to a selection of Bottomley's *Poems and Plays*, The **134**
Bodley Head, 1953, p. 10). He was a prolific letter-
writer (a later correspondent was the painter Paul Nash),
and maintained a respected position in literary circles.
His poems or plays appeared in all but the last of the
'Georgian' anthologies (see Appendix B) and he was able
to persuade Lascelles Abercrombie and R. C. Trevelyan
to include eighteen poems by 'Edward Eastaway' in *An
Annual of New Poetry* (1917).

The friendship was also a working partnership. For
six years Bottomley corrected the proofs of Thomas's
prose books, occasionally suggesting structural or
stylistic alterations. In return Thomas read and frankly
criticised his friend's poems and plays. His scrupulous
standards would not permit him to compromise even in
a review: 'Mr. Bottomley's newest verses are difficult,
we think, because they are not always wrought up to the
condition of poetry, but seem to have been left in a raw
state that can appeal to the intelligence only, except in a
few places ... They seem to us to be in their present
stage short of poetry, to demand the amplification of
prose, and not the sensuous and elliptical forms of
verse' (review of *Chambers of Imagery* in August 1907,
quoted by R. George Thomas, L.G.B., p. 145 n.). But
although Thomas perceived the local failings of Bottomley's poetry, he always appreciated its motivation:
'Honestly, I do think we aim at very similar things ...'
(L.G.B., p. 74); 'we do resemble one another, in spite
of my opinion of your pastoralism' (p. 122). Thomas
may have recognised in Bottomley's work some kindred
qualities of observation and, more important, an embryonic understanding of the new kind of blank verse
later brought to fruition by Frost and himself:

134   For more than three days now the snow had
                 thatched
            The cow-house roof where it had ever melted
            With yellow stains from the beasts' breath inside . . .
                 (*The End of the World, Poems and Plays*, p. 29)

His letters to Bottomley contain literary discussion and
gossip which nourished Thomas for a number of years.
The impressive powers of insight and judgement which
his letters, like his critical works, reveal were evidently
stropped by the interchange.

But Thomas's letters also turned inward, and he
derived a more personal kind of nourishment from this
unusual relationship. Professor Thomas observes that
'their natures and experiences interlocked with complementary exactitude' (L.G.B., introduction, p. 3).
Bottomley, physically handicapped, lived a peaceful
life for art's sake; Thomas, spiritually handicapped,
'ever your hurried & harried prose man' (L.G.B., p.
203), was to prove the truer poet in the end—as Bottomley
generously acknowledged. Bottomley's difference and
distance enabled Thomas to use him for ten years as
confessor or analyst, to speak more intimately of his
suffering than to anyone else: 'Oh Comforter, goodbye.
It is in my mind today that you are alive & quite real &
that—well, very few others are with whom I exchange
talk & letters' (L.G.B., p. 123). The house in the poem
may partly represent Bottomley's benign therapy; the
'land of stone,' with its 'cold heart,' Thomas's isolation
and desolation. Perhaps, too, Thomas subconsciously
implies awareness of his own more fundamental strengths.
2. *a land of stone.* As in *The Mountain Chapel* (p. 29)
Thomas is coming to terms with a nearly but not quite
alien landscape. Barren or mountainous regions are on

the frontier of his poetic territory (perhaps because **134** spiritually too close), remote from the softer centre and sanctuary of his 'South Country.' A passage in which he probes the 'hold upon the spirit' of Cornish barrows develops a similar contrast to that of the poem: 'In Cornwall as in Wales, these monuments are the more impressive, because the earth, wasting with them and showing her bones, takes their part. There are days when the age of the Downs, strewn with tumuli and the remnants of camp and village, is incredible; or rather they seem in the course of long time to have grown smooth and soft and kind, and to be, like a rounded languid cloud, an expression of Earth's summer bliss of afternoon. But granite and slate and sandstone jut out, and in whatsoever weather speak rather of the cold, drear, hard, windy dawn.' (S.C., p. 163)

13. *But music, pictures see.* Men only hear the storm as music, see it as pictures.

OUT IN THE DARK   **134**

Bod. 24 December 1916.

The last poem in Bod., and Thomas's last published poem, *Out in the Dark* was written during the Christmas leave which preceded his departure for France. It inevitably reflects the tensions of a time movingly commemorated by Helen Thomas in *World Without End* (pp. 176–183). There is an interesting resemblance between *Out in the Dark* and Thomas Hardy's *The Fallow Deer at the Lonely House*:

> One without looks in tonight
> Through the curtain-chink
> From the sheet of glistening white;

134
> One without looks in tonight
> As we sit and think
> By the fender-brink.
>
> We do not discern those eyes
> Watching in the snow;
> Lit by lamps of rosy dyes
> We do not discern those eyes
> Wondering, aglow,
> Fourfooted, tiptoe.

Hardy's poem was almost certainly written at a later date than Thomas's, so he may have been influenced by the younger poet. It is curious that James Granville Southworth should call it 'uncharacteristic' and observe: 'A first possible reaction to this poem is that it has somewhat the quality of a poem by Robert Frost . . .' (*The Poetry of Thomas Hardy*, second edition, Russell & Russell, New York, 1966, p. 189).

If Hardy *was* influenced by Thomas, he may have unconsciously recognised and reclaimed a debt. Thomas's diction is unusually Hardyesque—'haunts,' 'sage,' 'drear' —and helps to make *Out in the Dark* his most obvious tribute to one who must in some respects have been his master. He greatly admired Hardy (see I.P.S., pp. 192–8 and L.P.E., pp. 144–54) and, exceptionally at that period, preferred the poetry to the novels. Thomas appreciated Hardy's 'rusticity,' use of place names, sense of the past and of landscape. 'Country life . . . he handles with a combination of power and exactness beyond that of any poet who could be compared to him . . .' (I.P.S., p. 198). He deplored as 'superstitious' the gloomier aspects of Hardy's vision, 'that most tyrannous obsession of the blindness of Fate, the carelessness of Nature, and the insignificance of Man' (p. 194), but seems finally to have required some of its vocabulary.

Sending *Out in the Dark* to Eleanor Farjeon Thomas **134** remarked: 'It is really Baba who speaks, not I. Something she felt put me on to it' (E.F., p. 237). Nevertheless Thomas's own 'universe of sight' and 'light' is presented as almost overwhelmed by the 'night' which has encroached through several later poems. The monotonously rhymed stanzas emphasise the inexorability of this process. A childhood memory of Thomas himself may have contributed to the poem, as to *The Happy-Go-Lucky Morgans*:

> In the library I found Aurelius reading, with his back to the uncurtained window, by a light that only illuminated his face and page. Running at first to the window, I pressed my face on the pane to see the profound of deepening night, and the lake shining dimly like a window through which the things under the earth might be seen if you were out. The abyss of solitude below and around was swallowing the little white moon and might swallow me also; with terror at this feeling I turned away ... Aurelius lighted another lamp. I went over again to the window and looked out. In a flash I saw the outer vast world of solitude, darkness, and silence, waiting eternally for its prey, and felt behind me the little world within that darkness like a lighthouse. (pp. 54–6)

2–3. *The fallow fawns ... the fallow doe.* Fallow deer are a species of deer, smaller than red deer, originally so called because of their pale brown or reddish yellow colour. Thomas described the cottage at High Beech to Robert Frost in a letter of 19 October 1916: 'It is right alone in the forest among beech trees & fern & deer ...' (D.C.L.).

Biographical Extracts

Talking, and looking at the earth and the sky, we [John and I] just walked about until it was dark. Students we were not: nothing was pursued to the uttermost. We merely became accustomed to the general life of the common birds and animals, and to the appearances of trees and clouds and everything upon the surface that showed itself to the naked eye. Some rare thrush or robin we might stop to listen to; or we might watch a wren threading a bush or a tit on a birch-spray, or look at a mossy greenfinch's nest or climb up with some sort of unfounded hope to a big nest which had escaped us in spring; but for the most part we were moving and usually fast ... If the weather was bad and we were not together and no school work had to be done, I read books of travel, sport and natural history. I remember those of Waterton, Thomas Edward, Buckland, Wallace, Charles Kingsley, but above all Richard Jefferies. If I say little of Jefferies it is because not a year passed thereafter without many copious draughts of him and I cannot pretend to distinguish amongst them. But very soon afterwards I was writing out in each one of his books and elsewhere—as in a cousin's album—when I had the opportunity, those last words of *The Amateur Poacher*: "Let us get out of these indoor narrow modern days, whose twelve hours somehow have become shortened, into the sunlight and the pure wind. A something that the ancients thought divine can be found and felt there still." They were a gospel, an incantation. What I liked in the books was the free open-air life, the spice of illegality and daring, roguish characters—the opportunities so far exceeding my own, the gun, the great pond, the country home, the apparently endless leisure—the glorious moments that one could always recapture by opening the

Poacher—and the tinge of sadness here and there as in the picture of the old moucher perishing in his sleep by the lime kiln, and the heron flying over in the morning indifferent. Obviously Jefferies had lived a very different boyhood from ours, yet one which we longed for and supposed ourselves fit for. He had never had to wear his best clothes for twelve or fourteen hours on Sunday.

> From: *The Childhood of Edward Thomas*
> (Faber, 1938), pp. 133–5.

How anxiously I waited for [Edward's] homecoming on these days, and how with the first glance at his face I knew what the day had been. If it had been a bad one there was no need of words, and none were uttered. I could do nothing, for if I said one word which would betray that I knew what he had endured and was enduring, his anger and despair and weariness would break out in angry bitter words which would freeze my heart and afterwards freeze his for having uttered them. So as he ate the evening meal in silence, I talked quietly about the doings of the day, of the baby, of the walk we had been; and soon in our pretty room he would lie back in his big Oxford chair by the fire, smoking his pipe, while I sat on a stool near and sewed; and gradually the weariness would go out of his face, and the hard thin line of his mouth would relax to its lovely curve, and he would speak of an essay that had been suggested to him by something he had seen in London, or of a notable volume of poems that Nevinson had promised he should review for the *Daily Chronicle*. Then I would slip from my stool to the floor between his knees, and he would put out his hand and rest it on my neck, and I would know that the cloud had passed.

But sometimes when his spirit had been more than usually affected by the too great strain that his circumstances put upon it, the cloud did not pass, and my chatter ran dry in the arid silence. After a ghastly hour or two with the supper still uneaten on the kitchen table he would say: "Go to bed, I'm not coming," and I would know that he would sit up all night, and in the morning would be deeper in despair than ever—or he would go out and walk till morning, and perhaps from the silence of night and from the natural sounds of early dawn, and from the peace of solitude and the beauty of intangible things he would find healing and calm.

From: World Without End (Faber, 1956 ed.)
by Helen Thomas, pp. 82–3.

I don't want postcards from you, except that they would put me at my ease, especially in these days when to write more than a page means attempting the impossible and wearying myself and uselessly afflicting others with some part of my little yet endless tale. It has got to its dullest and its worst page now. The point is I have got to help myself and have been steadily spoiling myself for the job for I don't know how long. I am very incontinent to say these things. If I had never said them to anyone I should have been someone else and somewhere else. You see the central evil is self-consciousness carried as far beyond selfishness as selfishness is beyond self denial, (not very scientific comparison) and now amounting to a disease and all I have got to fight it with is the knowledge that in truth I am not the isolated selfconsidering brain which I have come to seem—the *knowledge* that I am something more, but not the belief that I can reopen the connection between the brain and the rest.

From: letter of Thomas to Eleanor Farjeon in 1913,
in *Edward Thomas: The Last Four Years* by
Eleanor Farjeon (O.U.P., 1958), p. 13.

God bless us all, what a thing it is to be nearing 40 & to know what one likes & know one makes mistakes & yet is right for oneself. How many things I have thought I ought to like & found reasons for liking. But now it is almost like eating apples. I don't pretend to know about pineapples & persimmons, but I know an apple when I smell it, when it makes me swallow my saliva before biting it. Then there are pears, too, & people who prefer pears. It is a fine world & I wish I knew how to make £200 a year in it ...

> *From:* letter to Gordon Bottomley in 1915, in
> *Letters from Edward Thomas to Gordon*
> *Bottomley* (O.U.P., 1968), p. 249.

People have been praised for self-possession in danger. I have heard Edward doubt if he was as brave as the bravest. But who was ever so completely himself right up to the verge of destruction, so sure of his thought, so sure of his word ? He was the bravest and best and dearest man you and I have ever known. I knew from the moment when I first met him at his unhappiest that he would some day clear his mind and save his life. I have had four wonderful years with him. I know he has done this all for you: he is all yours. But you must let me cry my cry for him as if he were *almost* all mine too.

Of the three ways out of here, by death where there is no choice, by death where there is a noble choice, and by death where there is a choice not so noble, he found the greatest way. There is no regret—nothing that I will call regret. Only I can't help wishing he could have saved his life without so wholly losing it and come back from France not too much hurt to enjoy our pride in him. I want to see him to tell him something. I want to tell him, what I think he liked to hear from me, that he was a poet.

> *From:* letter of Robert Frost to Helen Thomas
> after Thomas's death, in *Selected Letters*
> *of Robert Frost* (Cape, 1965), p. 216.

Critical Extracts

J. MIDDLETON MURRY

Year by year the universe grows vaster, and man, by virtue of the growing brightness of his little lamp, sees himself more and more as a child born in the midst of a dark forest, and finds himself less able to claim the obeisance of the all. Yet if he would be a poet, and not a harper of threadbare tunes, he must at each step in the downward passing from his sovereignty, recognise what is and celebrate it as what must be. Thus he regains, by another path, the supremacy which he has forsaken.

Edward Thomas's poetry has the virtue of this recognition. It may be said that his universe was not vaster but smaller than the universe of the past, for its bounds were largely those of his own self. It is, even in material fact, but half true. None more closely than he regarded the living things of earth in all their quarters. "After Rain" is, for instance, a very catalogue of the texture of nature's visible garment, freshly put on, down to the little ash-leaves

> ". . . thinly spread
> In the road, like little black fish, inlaid
> As if they played."

But it is true that these objects of vision were but the occasion of the more profound discoveries within the region of his own soul. There he discovered vastness and illimitable vistas; found himself to be an eddy in the universal flux, driven whence and whither he knew not, conscious of perpetual instability, the meeting place of mighty impacts of which only the farthest ripple agitates the steady moonbeam of the waking mind. In a sense he did no more than to state what he found, sometimes in the more familiar language of beauties lost, mourned for lost, and irrecoverable . . .

Sometimes he looked within himself for the monition which men have felt as the voice of the eternal memory; sometimes, like Keats, but with none of the intoxication of Keats's sense of a sharing in victory, he grasped at the recurrence of natural things, "the pure thrush word," repeated every spring, the law of wheeling rooks, or to the wind "that was old when the gods were young," as in this profoundly typical sensing of "A New House."

> "All was foretold me; naught
> Could I foresee;
> But I learned how the wind would sound
> After these things should be."

But he could not rest even there. There was, indeed, no anchorage in the enduring to be found by one so keenly aware of the flux within the soul itself. The most powerful, the most austerely imagined poem in this book is that entitled "The Other," which, apart from its intrinsic appeal, shows that Edward Thomas had something at least of the power to create the myth which is the poet's essential means of triangulating the unknown of his emotion. Had he lived to perfect himself in the use of this instrument, he might have been a great poet indeed . . .

No; not a great poet, will be the final sentence, when the palimpsest is read with the calm and undivided attention that is its due, but one who had many (and among them the chief) of the qualities of a great poet. Edward Thomas was like a musician who noted down themes that summon up forgotten expectations. Whether the genius to work them out to the limits of their scope and implication was in him we do not know. The life of literature was a hard master to him; and perhaps the opportunity he would eagerly have grasped was denied him by circumstance. But, if his compositions do not, his themes will never fail—of so much we are sure—to awaken unsuspected echoes even in unsuspecting minds.

> *From:* 'The Poetry of Edward Thomas' in *Aspects of Literature* (Collins, 1920), pp. 33–4, 36–8. The essay originally appeared in the *Nation* as a review of *Last Poems*.

F. R. LEAVIS

Only a very superficial classification could associate Edward Thomas with Mr. Blunden, or with the Georgians at all. He was a very original poet who devoted great technical subtlety to the expression of a distinctively modern sensibility. His art offers an extreme contrast with Mr. Blunden's. Mr. Blunden's poems are frankly "composed," but Edward Thomas's seem to happen. It is only when the complete effect has been registered in the reader's mind that the inevitability and the exquisite economy become apparent. A characteristic poem of his has the air of being a random jotting down of chance impressions and sensations, the record of a moment of relaxed and undirected consciousness. The diction and movement are those of quiet, ruminative speech. But the unobtrusive signs accumulate, and finally one is aware that the outward scene is accessory to an inner theatre. Edward Thomas is concerned with the finer texture of living, the here and now, the ordinary moments, in which for him the "meaning" (if any) resides. It is as if he were trying to catch some shy intuition on the edge of consciousness that would disappear if looked at directly. Hence, too, the quietness of the movement, the absence of any strong accent or gesture . . .

A phrase in [*Old Man*]—"listening, lying in wait for what I should, yet never can, remember"—describes admirably Thomas's characteristic manner. The intimations that come, as here, are not of immortality. And it would be difficult to set off Hardy's Victorian solidity better than by contrast with this poem. A far larger proportion of Thomas's work is good than of Hardy's (indeed, the greater part of the collected poems is good), but, on the other hand, one cannot say "great" confidently of anything of Thomas's, as one can of Hardy's best. The very fidelity with which Thomas records the modern disintegration, the sense of directionlessness

> —How dreary-swift, with naught to travel to,
> Is Time—

implies limitations. But Thomas's negativeness has nothing in common with the vacuity of the Georgians. He was exquisitely sincere and sensitive, and he succeeded in expressing in poetry a representative modern sensibility. It was an achievement of a very rare order, and he has not yet had the recognition he deserves.

From: New Bearings in English Poetry (Chatto, 1932 and Peregrine, 1963), p. 61, pp. 63–4 (Peregrine ed.).

H. COOMBES

There are, of course, among Thomas's poems some which do not fully show his unique qualities, slight poems in which he is not fully engaged; and there are poems which are not wholly successful. Occasionally his use of words like "dearest" and "fairest" may be felt to have no great depth or very strong pressure behind it; and he sometimes allows himself to be satisfied (because of his dislike of rhetoric) with a rhythm that has little impulse in it, a movement and tone that are too conversational. But there are extraordinarily few places where we can point to perfunctory rhythms or to actual faults in tone, and even in the very short and the less ambitious poems, and in those parts where we may feel a lack of "bite," a careful reading will almost always reveal some characteristic attitude and touch. Thomas's poetry is notable for the consistency with which it displays his particular excellences.

If we say it is minor poetry, it is chiefly because his range is limited; the preoccupation is personal, he is concerned with his own condition and moods. But though the poetry does not take in much of the outward circumstance of the age he lived in, the mind and spirit in and behind it is modern in its delicately exploring tendency, its refusal to accept any of the old sanctions and forms simply because they are sanctions and forms, its chastening but not overwhelming apprehension of time and eternity, its sense of isolation. Possibly we might postulate a more positive attitude to experience as essential to a writer if he is to be reckoned "major," though I should say that those by whom Thomas might be considered unduly negative would turn out to be, in the main, those who believe they find or hope to find strength and salvation in a creed or programme of one sort or another, religious, social, economic, political. In any case, our final emphasis must fall not on stature but on the sensitive life. He made poems out of what would be called slight events and unimposing situations, poems that are fresh and beautiful on the surface and rich underneath. He had the eye to see and the voice to tell that bare elm-tops are "delicate as flower of grass"; and the whole body of his poetry is there to show that when he writes

> As well as any bloom upon a flower
> I like the dust on nettles, never lost
> Except to prove the sweetness of a shower,

the affirmation that he is making, with its suggestion of a depth which both modifies and enhances the surface meaning, is simply true.

From: Edward Thomas (Chatto, 1956), pp. 245–6.

WILLIAM COOKE

As a war poet Thomas is virtually ignored. His poems are seldom included in anthologies of war poetry, and if his name is mentioned in critical studies it is largely for the sake of comprehensive appearances. The general feeling was summarized in 1947 by Athalie Bushnell:

> Although the background to his writing was often an army hut or trench, yet very little of his poetry actually takes war or war incidents as its subject. His poetry is nature poetry, taking simplicity, wonder and longing as its keynotes.

In *Edward Thomas* (1956), H. Coombes categorized "between eighty and ninety" of his poems as "nature poems" (this description is qualified) but found only "six or seven war poems." John H. Johnston in *English Poetry of the First World War* (1964) dismissed him in a single reference:

> Unlike Francis Ledwidge and Edward Thomas, who refused to let the conflict interfere with their nostalgic rural visions, Blunden successfully adapted his talent for unpretentious landscape description to the scenes of war.

Only a year later in *Heroes' Twilight* (1965), Bernard Bergonzi compared Thomas with Blunden:

> ... like Blunden he found a therapeutic and sanative value in contemplating nature, or remembering rural England, in the midst of violence and destruction. But very few of Thomas's poems are actually about the war, even obliquely: in his loving concentration on the unchanging order of nature and rural society, the war exists only as a brooding but deliberately excluded presence.

The inadequacy of these comments may be seen if they are considered alongside extracts from poems already discussed:

> His poetry is nature poetry, taking simplicity, wonder and longing as its keynotes. (Athalie Bushnell)

> wondering,
> What of the lattermath to this hoar Spring?

("It Was Upon")

> Before the might,
> If you love it not, of night.

("Out in the Dark")

> Edward Thomas ... refused to let the conflict interfere with [his] nostalgic rural visions. (Johnston)

> Tall reeds
> Like criss-cross bayonets ...

("Bright Clouds")

> Now all roads lead to France
> And heavy is the tread
> Of the living; but the dead
> Returning lightly dance ...

("Roads")

... very few of Thomas's poems are actually about the war, even obliquely: in his loving concentration on the unchanging order of nature and rural society, the war

exists only as a brooding but deliberately excluded presence·
(Bergonzi)

And when the war began
To turn young men to dung.
("Gone, Gone Again")

Helpless among the living and the dead,
Like a cold water among broken reeds,
Myriads of broken reeds all still and stiff . . .
("Rain")

The "unchanging order of . . . rural society" is not as unchanging as Bergonzi maintains; nor are these "nostalgic
rural visions" as remote from the conflict as Johnston would
have us believe. Thomas was that rare poet for whom the
division between the "two Englands" did not exist, and he
faced the tragedy of war, the waste and the pity, with an
awareness beyond most of his contemporaries. In reading
his poetry we are reminded not of Francis Ledwidge nor
Edmund Blunden, but of Wilfred Owen. A friend of Owen's
wrote that the keynote of his character was "an intense pity
for suffering humanity—a need to alleviate it, wherever
possible, and an inability to shirk the sharing of it, even when
this seemed useless." It is the keynote of such poems as "The
Owl," "In Memoriam (Easter, 1915)" and "The Cherry
Trees." "The pity of war" entered Thomas's poetry before
Owen had even enlisted.

From: ch. IX ('Roads to France') of *Edward Thomas:
A Critical Biography* (Faber, 1970), pp. 209–10, p. 224.

Appendix A

EDWARD THOMAS AND ROBERT FROST

Robert Frost came to England in September 1912 at the age of thirty-eight seeking, and finding, recognition for his poetry which it had not received in America. Within two months his first book, *A Boy's Will*, had been accepted for publication by David Nutt and Company. Frost's gratitude to 'the country that has made me a poet' (*Selected Letters*, p. 131) may have appeared in his helping to make a poet for England. Edward Thomas received from Frost a stimulus which liberated him both personally and imaginatively (see general note to *The Sun Used to Shine*, p. 346). In May 1914, a few months after Thomas's first meeting with Frost, the latter's second book, *North of Boston*, was published. Thomas's reviews of this volume in *The New Weekly*, *The English Review* (see Cooke, pp. 71–3) and *The Daily News* form the first public testaments to Frost's effect on him:

> This is one of the most revolutionary books of modern times, but one of the quietest and least aggressive. It speaks, and it is poetry . . .

> These poems are revolutionary because they lack the exaggeration of rhetoric, and even at first sight appear to lack the poetic intensity of which rhetoric is an imitation. Their language is free from the poetical words and forms that are the chief material of secondary poets. The metre avoids not only the old-fashioned pomp and sweetness, but the later fashion also of discord and fuss. In fact, the

medium is common speech and common decasyllables ...
Yet almost all these poems are beautiful. They depend not
at all on objects commonly admitted to be beautiful;
neither have they merely a homely beauty, but are often
grand, sometimes magical. Many, if not most, of the
separate lines and separate sentences are plain and, in
themselves, nothing. But they are bound together and
made elements of beauty by a calm eagerness of emotion.

Having commented on the lyrical aspect of Frost's achievement, Thomas continues:

The more dramatic pieces have the same beauty in solution,
the beauty of life seen by one in whom mystery and tenderness together just outstrip humour and curiosity. This
beauty grows like grass over the whole, and blossoms with
simple flowers which the reader gradually sets greater and
greater value on ... The book is not without failures.
Mystery falls into obscurity. In some lines I cannot hit
upon the required accents. But his successes, like "The
Death of the Hired Man," put Mr. Frost above all other
writers of verse in America. He will be accused of keeping
monotonously at a low level, because his characters are
quiet people, and he has chosen the unresisting medium of
blank verse. I will only remark that he would lose far less
than most modern writers by being printed as prose. If
his work were so printed, it would have little in common
with the kind of prose that runs to blank verse: in fact, it
would turn out to be closer knit and more intimate than
the finest prose is except in its finest passages. It is poetry
because it is better than prose. (*Daily News*, 22 July 1914)

Thomas vigorously championed Frost's poetry to his literary
friends:

[T. Sturge] Moore was excellent in principle. But in con-
demning Frost I think still that he had been misled into

supposing that Frost wanted poetry to be colloquial. All he insists on is what he believes he finds in all poets—absolute fidelity to the postures which the voice assumes in the most expressive intimate speech. So long as these tones & postures are there he has not the least objection to any vocabulary whatever or any inversion or variation from the customary grammatical forms of talk. In fact I think he would agree that if these tones & postures survive in a complicated & learned or subtle vocabulary & structure the result is likely to be better than if they survive in the easiest form, that is in the very words & structures of common speech, though that is not easy or prose would be better than it is & survive more often . . .

Frost's vocabulary & structure deceive the eye sometimes into thinking it is just statement more or less easily put into easy verse forms. But it is not.

His theory is only an attempt to explain & justify observed facts in Shakespeare for example & in his own earliest efforts. (L.G.B., pp. 250–1)

But Thomas was soon to become more than Frost's apostle. His always dormant notion, that one day he might write poetry, gradually quickened between them. On 19 May 1914 Thomas wrote to his friend: 'I wonder whether you can imagine me taking to verse. If you can I might get over the feeling that it is impossible—which at once obliges your good nature to say "I can"' (D.C.L.). In November Frost made a positive and specific suggestion:

Edward Thomas had about lost patience with the minor poetry it was his business to review. He was suffering from a life of subordination to his inferiors. Right at that moment he was writing as good poetry as anybody alive, but in prose form where it did not declare itself and gain him recognition. I referred him to paragraphs in his book

In Pursuit of Spring and told him to write it in verse form in exactly the same cadence. That's all there was to it. His poetry declared itself in verse form, and in the year before he died he took his place where he belonged among the English poets. (Letter from Frost to Harold Roy Brennan in 1926, quoted by Eckert, p. 150)

Some critics have questioned the weight traditionally given to Frost's impact and advice. Cooke asserts: 'Thomas's friendship with Frost was important. It was not *that* important'; arguing that the war rather than Frost constituted 'the decisive influence' (see Cooke, pp. 182–90). Professor R. George Thomas points out that Thomas's 'changing attitude to prose rhythms' as evinced in *Walter Pater* was 'a clear anticipation of his own poetry long before he had met Robert Frost' (L.G.B., p. 220 n.). Thomas himself makes the same claim in the letter to Frost quoted above: 'you really should start doing a book on speech & literature, or you will find me mistaking your ideas for mine & doing it myself. You can't prevent me from making use of them: I do so daily & want to begin over again with them & wring all the necks of my rhetoric—the geese. However, my "Pater" would show you I had got on to the scent already.' Dislike of Pater's 'hard and stationary refinement' (p. 118), the sculptural and pictorial qualities of his prose, led Thomas to affirm 'the necessity for the aid of speech in literature. Nothing so much as the writer's rhythm can give that intimate effect "as if he had been talking." Rhythm is of the essence of a sincere expressive style' (p. 218). Like Frost, Thomas emphasises that literature cannot be a mere transcription of the spoken word; it must discover its own means of evoking the rhythms of speech, the animation of life:

The more we know of any man the more singular he will appear, and nothing so well represents his singularity as style. Literature is further divided in outward seeming from speech by what helps to make it in fact more than ever an equivalent of speech. It has to make words of such a spirit, and arrange them in such a manner, that they will do all that a speaker can do by innumerable gestures and their innumerable shades, by tone and pitch of voice, by speed, by pauses, by all that he is and all that he will become. (p. 210)

Reviewing a book on English prosody as early as 1902 Thomas had praised its author for emphasising stress rather than quantity or accent:

Quite naturally, without education, we distribute stress "with unerring accuracy of position, and deftly shaded precision of intensity" ... It is not a new system of prosody, though it makes the old one ridiculous. It affords no basis for a clarification of metres; it leaves blank verse, as before, an infinitely varied line usually of ten syllables. Its strongest quality is that it states the grounds for the appreciation of verse which have been used by the best writers of every age ... (*Daily Chronicle*, 18 September 1902)

The ground had indeed been fertilised for Frost's seed by a number of factors (see *From Prose to Poetry*, p. 136): Thomas was in an ideally receptive condition. Nevertheless, it seems inadequate to say with Cooke that 'Frost's advice was no more than what he claimed it was—the appreciation and encouragement of a friend' (p. 186), or that it 'amounted to no more than what Thomas's friends had been telling him and each other for years' (p. 185). Thomas's reading and understanding of Frost's poetry governed his response to the direct suggestion. Here was the breakthrough so long anticipated (see Appendix B). Thomas had always been a learner rather than a pioneer, as the slow development of his prose

indicates. Frost's poetry accelerated all his imaginative processes by its practical demonstration of what was possible.
Similarly, a certain passivity of temperament may have
required Frost's greater thrustfulness as an energising principle. His friend's example and encouragement thus worked
together to impel Thomas further and faster along his own
path. On 15 December 1914 Thomas sent some of his early
poems to Frost in a letter which acknowledged the debt:
'I won't begin thanking you just yet, tho if you like I will put
it down now that you are the only begetter right enough'
(D.C.L.). He never forgot his obligation—*Poems* is dedicated to Frost—though sensitive that it might be too obvious
to others: 'I wish I could see Frost's poems. Were you re-
minding me of my inspiration when you said *he* showed the
influence of *my* things? I couldn't help thinking it possible'
(L.G.B., p. 270). Thomas asked Frost of *Fifty Faggots*: 'Are
they *north* of Boston only?' (15 May 1915, D.C.L.), and
was hurt when W. H. Davies mistook some of his poems for
Frost's work.

The affinity between the subject matter of Frost's poems
and that of his own prose must have been immediately
obvious to Thomas. As Coombes points out, he recognised
rather than took over some imaginative furniture: 'lonely
houses, dark trees, tramps and miscellaneous workers, paths,
the edge of the forest, the wind in the dark, sounds of flowing
water' (p. 243). But Frost's form affected him more powerfully than his content, and his rhythms more powerfully than
his style. All Thomas's statements of Frost's 'revolutionary'
method turn on the aural innovations he introduced into
poetry. The Frost 'sentence-sound' or 'sound of sense' showed
him how English poetry could be reconnected with its origins
in English speech. In his letters Frost often explains the
theory lying behind, or deduced from, lines such as these:

399

Something there is that doesn't love a wall,
That sends the frozen-ground-swell under it,
And spills the upper boulders in the sun;
And makes gaps even two can pass abreast . . .

(Mending Wall)

The living part of a poem is the intonation entangled somehow in the syntax idiom and meaning of a sentence. It is only there for those who have heard it previously in conversation . . . It is the most volatile and at the same time important part of poetry. It goes and the language becomes a dead language, the poetry dead poetry. With it go the accents the stresses the delays that are not the property of vowels and syllables but that are shifted at will with the sense. Vowels have length there is no denying. But the accent of sense supercedes all other accent overrides and sweeps it away. (*Selected Letters*, p. 107)

I give you a new definition of a sentence:

A sentence is a sound in itself on which other sounds called words may be strung.

You may string words together without a sentence-sound to string them on just as you may tie clothes together by the sleeves and stretch them without a clothes line between two trees, but—it is bad for the clothes . . .

[The sentence-sounds] are apprehended by the ear. They are gathered by the ear from the vernacular and brought into books. Many of them are already familiar to us in books. I think no writer invents them. The most original writer only catches them fresh from talk, where they grow spontaneously. (pp. 110–11)

We must write with the ear on the speaking voice. We must imagine the speaking voice (p. 159).

Frost's new sound did not entail a rejection of traditional metre:

I have nothing in common with the free-verse people. There is no more distressing mistake than to assume that I have ... summoning [the sentence tones] is not all. They are only lovely when thrown and drawn and displayed across spaces of the footed line. Everyone knows that except a free-verser. (pp. 191–2)

Thomas's poetry exhibits, like Frost's, 'sentence tones' 'thrown and drawn and displayed across spaces of the footed line':

The rock-like mud unfroze a little and rills
Ran and sparkled down each side of the road
Under the catkins wagging in the hedge.
But earth would have her sleep out, spite of the sun ...
(*The Manor Farm*)

Iambic beat is interrupted, though not abandoned, while stress follows dramatic and conversational emphasis (Rán, spárkled, spíte), or clusters of unstressed syllables accommodate the natural phrasing of spoken English ('each side of the road,' 'spite of the sun'). Thomas may indeed have carried the whole revolution further than Frost. Regular iambic movement is not so conspicuous in his poetry; there is less end-stopping; and blank verse lines run much more frequently to an extra half or full foot. A far greater proportion of Frost's poetry than of Thomas's is overtly dramatic, incorporating different speakers. (Significantly, he liked 'the first half of Lob best' because 'it offers something more like action with the different people coming in and giving the tones of speech.') Thomas perhaps achieves more variously Frost's ideal of 'making the sentences talk to each other as two or more speakers do in drama' (*Selected Letters*, p. 427). He absorbs 'sentence-sounds' deeply into the whole structure of a rhymed lyric:

> Whatever wind blows, while they and I have leaves
> We cannot other than an aspen be
> That ceaselessly, unreasonably grieves,
> Or so men think who like a different tree.   (*Aspens*)

Here again stress follows emphasis (other, aspen, céaselessly, unréasonably), while syntax intimately plots the movement of the poet's imagination through every unexpected twist and qualification. By playing clause against line, as well as sentence against stanza, Thomas dramatises the tones and half-tones of his own voice.

Thomas's debt to Frost can be detected locally in various similarities and echoes (see Coombes, p. 244; Cooke, pp. 194–7); but only in *Up in the Wind* (C.P., p. 96), his first poem, does he truly imitate the long blank verse structures he chiefly admired in *North of Boston* and which constitute perhaps Frost's most characteristic achievement. *Up in the Wind* employs Frost's unmistakable blend of dialogue/monologue, narrative and description, and particularly resembles *A Servant to Servants* in plot and setting. Thomas returns only once to this extended mode (*Lob* is a special case): to rework more symbolically in *Wind and Mist* much the same theme. After *Up in the Wind* he seems to have instinctively occupied new territory of his own: 'I have been shy of blank verse tho (or because) I like it best. But the rhymes have dictated themselves decidedly except in one case' (letter to Frost, 15 December 1914, D.C.L.). '... since the first take off they haven't been Frosty very much or so I imagine and I have tried as often as possible to avoid the facilities offered by blank verse and I try not to be too long— I even have an ambition to keep under 12 lines (but rarely succeed)' (letter to John Freeman, 8 March 1915, Moore, p. 326). Scannell, who interestingly contrasts the poets (pp. 13–16), believes that had he lived Thomas 'would have developed [his] narrative gifts' (p. 31). But in 1916 the proportion of poems with a narrative element, and of blank verse, was already declining, while Thomas became still more occupied with taut stanzaic structures. From the outset, in fact, Thomas's poetry was both more introverted and more concentrated than Frost's. If he lacks Frost's architectonic energy, he is also without his occasional prosaic diffuseness. The more scrupulous if less bold orchestration of Thomas's rhythms reflects the minuter grain of his countryside and character, the greater complexity of his 'outer' and 'inner' weather.' For all their descriptive basis, his poems exhibit an extraordinarily rich and fine local texture. They inscribe almost invariably a perfect lyric curve.

Appendix B

EDWARD THOMAS AND THE GEORGIANS

The historical–critical label 'Georgian' primarily denotes the hard core of poets whose work appeared in the five anthologies of *Georgian Poetry*, edited by Edward Marsh (E.M.) during the decade 1912–1922. Such poets are: Walter de la Mare, W. H. Davies, Rupert Brooke, John Masefield, James Stephens, Ralph Hodgson, W. W. Gibson, T. Sturge Moore, James Elroy Flecker, Gordon Bottomley, Lascelles Abercrombie. Certain contributors to *Georgian Poetry*—for instance, D. H. Lawrence, Robert Graves, Siegfried Sassoon and Isaac Rosenberg—only figure intermittently in accounts of the archetypal Georgian poet; while non-contributors, like A. E. Housman, occasionally lend him features. Two younger poets, Edmund Blunden (represented in the last *Georgian Poetry*) and Andrew Young, are felt to have observed a Georgian aesthetic up to the present day.

Marsh's preface to the first *Georgian Poetry* affirmed the 'belief that English poetry is now once again putting on a new strength and beauty,' that 'we are at the beginning of another "Georgian period" which may take rank in due time with the several great poetic ages of the past.' However, the 'age' was to last only a few years, while the name lived on principally as a term of abuse. To Robert Graves and Laura Riding, for example,

Georgianism was a dead movement contemporary with Imagism. Although not so highly organised as Imagism, it

404

had a great vogue between the years 1912 and 1918 and was articulate chiefly upon questions of style. Its general recommendations seem to have been the discarding of archaistic diction such as "thee" and "thou" and "floweret" and "whene'er" and of poetical constructions such as "winter drear" and "host on armèd host" and of pomposities generally. Another thing understood between the Georgians was that their verse should avoid all formally religious, philosophic or improving themes, in reaction to Victorianism; and all sad, wicked café-table themes in reaction to the 'nineties. It was to be English yet not aggressively imperialistic; pantheistic rather than atheistic; and as simple as a child's reading book. This was all to the good, perhaps, but such counsels resulted in a poetry that could rather be praised for what it was not than for what it was. Eventually Georgianism became principally concerned with Nature and love and leisure and old age and childhood and animals and sleep and other uncontroversial subjects. (*A Survey of Modernist Poetry*, Heinemann, 1927, pp. 118–19; reprinted with slight variations in *The Common Asphodel* by Robert Graves, 1949, pp. 112–13).

John Press, in a currently more favourable climate, offers a neutral 'description' of the Georgians: 'They were poets who began to publish verse during the first two decades of the present century; they were content to employ the conventions of diction and the forms of verse favoured by almost all English poets from Wordsworth to Hardy; they looked for guidance to Milton, the major Romantics, and the Victorians rather than to Donne, the Metaphysicals, Dryden and Pope; they felt an intuitive sympathy with the specifically English elements of English poetry rather than with its European aspects; they remained ignorant, indifferent or hostile to the revolution in sensibility and technique inaugurated by

Pound and Eliot' (*A Map of Modern English Verse*, O.U.P., 1969, pp. 105–6). Recent revaluations of the Georgians have emphasised the real if limited achievement of the group: 'The Georgians can offer virtues which seem to have deserted modern poetry and which might be regained if we want to see poetry once more in its wholeness. These qualities are: natural simplicity, emotional warmth, and moral innocence' (James Reeves, introduction to *Georgian Poetry*, Penguin, 1962, p. xx). Some critics have also demonstrated the way in which the Georgians' reputation has been distorted by the success of the 'revolution' Press mentions.

In his significantly titled *The Georgian Revolt* (Faber, 1967) Robert H. Ross shows that Marsh's first anthology, seen in historical context, indeed heralded or endorsed a new poetic age. It is true that in 1911, as Ross remarks, 'British poetry had almost no place to go but upwards' (p. 29). As C. K. Stead has also indicated (in ch. III of *The New Poetic*, Hutchinson, 1964; Pelican, 1967), the Georgians were in conscious reaction against a poetic establishment that included Rudyard Kipling, Henry Newbolt, Alfred Noyes and William Watson. Bolder revolutionaries, like the Imagists, were soon to emerge, and Ross adopts political categories to define the resulting ferment in English poetry. On the Right were the poets of Empire and fossilised tradition; on the Left the Modernists, experimenting to find a completely new aesthetic basis; and in the Centre the Georgians, attempting a liberal compromise. Since the Right was moribund, the real action took place on the wavering frontier between Centre and Left. Modern English poetry was arguably born out of this controversy and cross-fertilisation. It was only after the First World War (in which some natural champions of the Centre had died) that the Left held almost undisputed sway, Georgianism became the Aunt

Sally of Modernism, and the literary history of the period prior to 1918 was correspondingly rewritten. One monument to 'de-Georgianisation' is Michael Roberts's *Faber Book of Modern Verse* (1936). Roberts excluded the Georgians: he also excluded Edward Thomas.

Since critics like F. R. Leavis and H. Coombes have worked valiantly to disentangle Edward Thomas from the Georgians it may seem reactionary to imply a connection. However, Thomas is still firmly claimed by anthologists of the movement like Reeves and Alan Pryce-Jones (*Georgian Poets*, Hulton, the Pocket Poets, 1959), while the term itself has ceased to be automatically pejorative. It is true that none of Thomas's poems ever appeared in *Georgian Poetry*. He met Marsh in 1913, before he began to write poetry, but the meeting does not seem to have been a success on either side (see Christopher Hassall, *Edward Marsh*, Longmans, 1959, p. 211). Later Thomas was cool in a letter to Gordon Bottomley: 'I am sending you a few more verses. If Marsh likes any of them well & good. But I should not be vastly interested in his adverse opinion' (L.G.B., p. 254). His poetry did not get into *Georgian Poetry 1913–1915*; nor into the next of the series, because Marsh had made a somewhat arbitrary rule against posthumous representation and resisted the pleas of Thomas's friends. But if Marsh continued blind or conservative, all Thomas's advocates were Georgians— de la Mare, John Freeman, W. J. Turner—who evidently regarded *Georgian Poetry* as an appropriate context for his work. It had indeed already appeared in a 'Georgian' anthology, *An Annual of New Poetry* (Constable, 1917) edited by Lascelles Abercrombie and R. C. Trevelyan. This volume included poems by Davies, Sturge Moore, Gibson and John Drinkwater, as well as by Robert Frost.

One result of wholly repudiating a link between Thomas and the Georgians has been to leave him without any literary context whatsoever, apart from his alliance with Robert Frost. This is a paradoxical position, not only for a poet whose roots sink so deeply into the English tradition, but for one so well acquainted with the poetry of his own day. Professor R. George Thomas calls him as a reviewer 'the premier interpreter of modern poetry' up to 1915 (L.G.B., introduction, p. 10). In reviews Thomas steered a characteristically independent course, saluting only what 'fed' him, and sometimes offending poet-friends with uncompromising criticism. Nevertheless, until his discovery of Frost (and of himself) Thomas's taste tilted decisively towards poets who may be labelled 'Georgian': 'I should be inclined to call [Bridges] "the chief of living poets" tho I would usually rather read De la Mare or Davies, or the best of Yeats, Sturge Moore or Abercrombie' (Moore, p. 317). Except for W. B. Yeats, all Thomas's favourites appear in *Georgian Poetry*. His friendships with Bottomley, de la Mare, Davies, Abercrombie and Gibson provide complementary evidence of the direction of his sympathies.

Thomas's position in the aesthetic arguments of the day was somewhat left of Centre—a position afterwards confirmed by his practice as a poet. He was certainly not of the Right, remarking of Newbolt in 1902 that 'all his verse might be described as an elaborate corollary to "Rule Britannia".' He did not align himself absolutely with the Georgians; having greeted the first anthology ironically in one review: 'Not a few of these [poets] had developed their qualities under Victoria and Edward,' he went on to define the general flavour with some of the astringency of later critics: 'It shows much beauty, strength, and mystery, and some magic— much aspiration, less defiance, no revolt—and it brings out with great cleverness many sides of the modern love of the simple and primitive, as seen in children, peasants, savages, early men, animals, and Nature in general' (*Daily Chronicle*, 14 January 1913). Yet in a subsequent review his tone has become positive:

> The book is more than a mere anthology. It is as much an independent living book as "England's Helicon," or any of the other anthologies of the Elizabethan age which still maintain their original form. It represents an age; in the main, the youth of an age. It has been so well compiled that the individuality of the age is, if anything, clearer than that of the majority of men representing it. Perhaps only three men's work emerges new, beautiful, and complete above the rushing tide of the times, Messrs. Sturge Moore, Walter de la Mare, and W. H. Davies. But all three are men whose work had culminated or had taken an unmistakable direction before the accession of George the Fifth. They achieve what the others are still fervently and loudly pursuing—some form of magic, rapture, or beauty. (*The Bookman*, March 1913)

Thomas's abiding objection to the anthology's title was probably due to the fact that he had perceived ten years before Edward Marsh that English poetry 'was putting on a new strength and beauty.' He had consistently praised and promoted a number of future 'Georgians'—in particular W. H. Davies and Walter de la Mare—and reviewing a group of poets in 1903 that included both Sturge Moore and Masefield had declared: 'They fill us with respect for the poetry of the twentieth century,' and instituted his Elizabethan comparison: 'In short, we know of no other age that has abounded in lesser writers of verse with so much individuality. We have to look back as far as Tottel's Miscellany or "England's Helicon" for an assembly of contemporaneous versifiers anything like this.' (*Daily Chronicle*, 26 November 1903)

In his quest for a poet of commanding stature who would reap the harvest of this fertility Thomas did not adopt the official Georgian candidate, Rupert Brooke, although crediting him with potential in a review of *Poems* (1912): 'He is full of revolt, contempt, self-contempt, and yet of arrogance too. He reveals chiefly what he desires to be and to be thought. Now and then he gives himself away, as when, in three poems close together, he speaks of the scent of warm clover. Copies should be bought by everyone over forty who has never been under forty. It will be a revelation. Also, if they live yet a little longer, they may see Mr. Rupert Brooke a poet. He will not be a little one' (*Daily Chronicle*, 9 April 1912). Again, Thomas understood the originality of D. H. Lawrence's poetry better than most Georgians—better than Marsh who had 'a vehement correspondence with Lawrence about what I consider the formal deficiencies of his poems' (letter to Rupert Brooke, quoted by Hassall, p. 255). In April 1913 Thomas pronounced: 'The book of the moment in verse is Mr. D. H. Lawrence's (*Love Poems and Others*). He is remarkable for what he does not do and for what he does. Thus, he does not write smoothly, sweetly and with dignity; nor does he choose subjects, such as blackbirds at sunset, which ask to be so treated. For some time past it has been understood that verse is not best written in jerks of a line in length. Mr. Lawrence goes further, and at times seems bent on insulting rhyme ... Correspondingly, he writes of matters which cannot be subdued to conventional rhythm and rhyme ...' (*The Bookman*, April 1913)

Yet Thomas's impatience with certain aspects of Georgianism, his early recognition of Frost and Lawrence, by no means brought him into the left wing or Modernist camp.

He underwent a revulsion of attitude to Ezra Pound which seems to define the degree and kind of poetic experiment he was prepared to entertain. He initially hailed, though with reservations, Pound's *Personae* published in 1909, appreciating its 'brusque intensity of effect' and vital compound of faults and virtues: 'He is so possessed by his own strong conceptions, that he not only cannot think of wrapping them up in a conventional form, but he must ever show his disdain for it a little,—one of his poems is, in so many words, a revolt against the crepuscular spirit in modern poetry. But the disdain is the other side of a powerful love for something else, and it is usually either only implicit or entirely concealed.' Finally Thomas accepts the poetry as 'new,' as language 'worn new'; 'No remarkable melody; no golden worlds shot with meaning; a temperate use of images, and none far-fetched; no flattering of modern fashions, in descriptions of Nature, for example; no apostrophe, no rhetoric, nothing "Celtic." It is the old miracle that cannot be defined, nothing more than a subtle entanglement of words, so that they rise out of their graves and sing.' (*Daily Chronicle*, 7 June 1909)

But Pound, for Thomas, was a false dawn: 'Oh I do humble myself over Ezra Pound. He is not & cannot ever be very good. Certainly he is not what I mesmerized myself—out of pure love of praising the new poetry!—into saying he was & I am very much ashamed & only hope I never shall meet the man. My greatest humiliation is due to regret for cheapening praise & using the same words about such a man as about, say, Sturge Moore, though of course I did indicate the chaos of the work' (L.G.B., p. 187). Towards the end of 1909 a review of Pound's *Exultations* made public his disillusionment: 'having allowed the turbulent opacity of his peculiarities to sink down we believe that we see nearly nothing at all' (*Daily Chronicle*, 23 November 1909). *Maurice Maeter-*

linck (1911) shows Thomas unsympathetic to the French symbolists, important influences on Pound, the Imagists and the Modernist movement in general. Quoting a critic who had described symbolism as originating in 'an acuter perception of what all poets have always known, that words are insufficient if their power is bounded by their meaning,' Thomas comments: 'It is a little unkind to words to suppose that they can be bounded by their meaning, but apparently the symbolist must insist that his words are not only not so bounded, but have a further significance which is quite precise; otherwise there were no difference between the old and the new. It is a dangerous difference. For a poem of the old kind has a simple fundamental meaning which every sane reader can agree upon; above and beyond this each one builds as he can or must. In the new there is no basis of this kind; a poem means nothing unless its whole meaning has been grasped' (p. 21). In May 1914 Thomas wrote to Bottomley: 'What imbeciles the Imagistes are' (L.G.B., p. 233).

The Georgians themselves failed to maintain a vigorous creative and critical opposition to Modernism. The ebbing of their challenge may indeed have been due to built-in obsolescence or some evolutionary defect. Ross cites a failure to adapt which produced 'verse that was increasingly trivial, unreal, and irrelevant to the late war years and the violent post-war period' (p. 186). But it was the poets he characterises as 'neo-Georgian,' parasitic upon the first generation, who made the Georgian ethos after 1917 one of 'retrenchment, escape, and enervation' (p. 187). It might thus be alternatively argued that certain poets had already seized upon the real growth points in Georgianism and transfigured it in their individual consummations. Stead points out: 'It is common, since the Georgians are out of favour, for critics to insist of

any Georgian poet they admire that he did not really belong
to the movement' (p. 88). Lawrence was certainly a cuckoo in
the Georgian nest. But what of Graves, Rosenberg and
Sassoon within the anthology; of Owen and Thomas outside
it? Graves's classicism, which has provided a valuable
standard in twentieth-century poetry, is the apotheosis of a
number of Georgian virtues (whatever his later attitude to the
group). Quoting a letter of Wilfred Owen's in which he
boasts 'I am held peer by the Georgians' Stead comments:
'The work of a poet like Wilfred Owen proceeds naturally
out of the Georgian method'—i.e. 'a rejection of large themes
and of the language of rhetoric that accompanied them in the
nineteenth century; and an attempt to come to terms with
immediate experience, sensuous or imaginative, in a language
close to common speech' (p. 89). Stead calls Edward Thomas's
poems 'excellent examples of the common direction of what
was best in the original Georgian movement' (p. 101 n.);
while Press finds his 'virtues' 'precisely the virtues which
most of the Georgians aimed at, but seldom achieved' (p. 115).
Thomas's concreteness, fine eye for detail, denial of rhetoric,
and deeply implicit philosophy, in fact his whole infinitely
responsive procedure, developed out of the Georgian
aesthetic as well as from his own temperament.

Walter de la Mare and W. H. Davies would probably today
be judged the best of the Georgians. Thomas always named
them among his handful of chosen contemporary poets
(Robert Frost admired de la Mare), and letters as well as
reviews show him continuously involved with their work:
'O yes isn't Davies fine now? I was terribly excited over the
new book (*Nature Poems*, 1908). It was almost incredibly
good' (L.G.B., p. 179). '[De la Mare] is doing very good
work now, some of it very happy childish rhyming, most
delicate & new' (p. 203). In both poets Thomas detected the

'newness' he so rarely found as a reviewer before encountering it overwhelmingly in Robert Frost. 'Reverie has never made a more magical book than Mr. Walter de la Mare's third book of poems (*The Listeners and Other Poems*). For the most part, either they take the form of childish memories or their atmosphere is like that of overpowering memory. Never was child so tyrannous a father to the man.' Thomas goes on to observe that de la Mare recalls things 'always drowned, softened, reduced, and with a more or less distinctly sad sense of remoteness,' and that 'the dead in that country are more than the living.' He concludes: 'That when the poet speaks in his own person his melancholy should be overt cannot surprise anyone who realises how few of any man's hours can after all be given to reverie; how difficult or unlovely must appear the broken, scattered, or jangled things outside that province. He writes as an "exile" who would certainly not write if he were not an exile . . .' (*The Bookman*, August 1912). Thomas shared de la Mare's tendency to 'reverie,' preoccupation with memory, sense of a haunted landscape, the consciousness of 'exile' and 'solitude' which appears in the latter's *Napoleon*:

> 'What is the world, O soldiers?
> It is I:
> I, this incessant snow,
> This northern sky;
> Soldiers, this solitude
> Through which we go
> Is I.'

He responded not only to the 'melancholy' aspect of de la Mare's poetry but also to its 'Englishness,' and took the title of one section of *This England*, 'Her Sweet Three Corners,' from de la Mare's *Trees*:

Of all the trees in England,
    Her sweet three corners in,
Only the Ash, the bonnie Ash
    Burns fierce while it is green . . .

De la Mare, one of the 'very few living people' included in the anthology, was also represented by his *Epitaph* for the 'lady of the West Country.' If Thomas appreciated de la Mare's 'happy childish rhyming,' he must have relished his exploitation or invention of folk lore, fairy story and nursery rhyme. De la Mare's places and place names (half real, half magical), elves and witches, 'Old Nod, the Shepherd' and 'Old Tillie Turveycombe,' his inhabiting of an English child's imaginative world, may have partially guided Thomas towards his own more complex mythology.

Describing Thomas's first contact with the 'tramp-poet' W. H. Davies in 1905, Richard J. Stonesifer calls him 'the man who was to do more for [Davies] than anyone else' (*W. H. Davies: A Critical Biography*, Cape, 1963, p. 68). Thomas promoted Davies's poetry in reviews and to influential friends; found him a cottage near Elses farm where the Thomases were then living; gave or obtained for him books and financial aid (including the price of a new wooden leg); secured a publisher for *Autobiography of a Super-Tramp*. Thomas was sometimes irritated by Davies, but the latter, who dedicated his *New Poems* (1907) to Helen and Edward Thomas, suggests the real affection and affinity between the two poets in *Killed in Action* (*Edward Thomas*):

And we have known those days, when we
    Would wait to hear the cuckoo first;
When you and I, with thoughtful mind,
    Would help a bird to hide her nest,
    For fear of other hands less kind . . .

Thomas occasionally lamented Davies's lack of poetic as

well as personal sophistication, being disappointed by the long poems in *New Poems*: 'Perhaps they demand purely intellectual gifts in which he is not rich, and they certainly put a severe strain upon his constructive faculty which is weak; his poems either sing themselves through like an old air, or they break up and fall' (*Morning Post*, 3 January 1907). But he always recognised that it was the quality of 'singing themselves through like an old air' which mattered in Davies's poems; returned to his first perception of their freshness and traditionalism: 'His greatness rests upon a wide humanity, a fresh and unbiassed observation, and a noble use of the English tongue ... He can write commonplace and inaccurate English; but it is also natural to him to write, much as Wordsworth wrote, with the clearness, compactness and felicity which make a man think with shame how unworthily, through natural stupidity or uncertainty, he manages his native tongue' (review of Davies's first book, *The Soul's Destroyer*, *Daily Chronicle*, 21 October 1905). For Davies, as for Richard Jefferies and for Thomas, 'the clearness of the physical [was] allied to the penetration of the spiritual vision' (R.J., p. 44):

> The banks are stormed by Speedwell, that blue flower
> So like a little Heaven with one star out ...
>
> (*Seeking Beauty*)

Despite the grind of reviewing Thomas always retained his 'pure love of praising the new poetry,' his excitement in reading 'a fresh modern poet, straight from the press, before any one has praised it, and to know that it is good' (B.W., p. 44). His insight made him a poet in his criticism. It is likely also that his criticism helped to make him a poet. Frost expressed its role just a little perversely when he said 'Edward Thomas had about lost patience with the minor poetry it was his business to review.' Thomas had deeply absorbed the poetry of his own day, and, knowing the field, perhaps finally felt that he could pass it. Reviewing minor poets in 1902, he made a prophecy which proved to a considerable extent self-fulfilling:

... minor poetry is, we believe, significant, because it is abundantly prophetic of the future of poetry ... The youthfulness, the exuberance which distinguishes nearly all minor poetry succeeds in masking the new thoughts which are almost equally characteristic. In the minor poet himself these thoughts are seldom matured. They lie in a sort of life-in-death until the touch of a mighty hand grants them their full development. For the great poet comes at the end of a period, the resumé of a score of mediocrities, as Wordsworth was. We make no pretence of being able to create imaginatively the poet of the next age from the material in the books before us. We seem, nevertheless, to see in the best of them the beginnings of a path farther into the unknown.

(Daily Chronicle, 27 December 1902)

Appendix C

CONTENTS OF *POEMS* AND *LAST POEMS*

Poems was published by Selwyn and Blount in 1917 and the title-page reads: *Poems*/By/Edward Thomas/("Edward Eastaway")/With A Portrait/From A Photograph/By Duncan Williams/London/Selwyn & Blount/1917. A dedication: To/ Robert Frost appears on the next leaf. *Last Poems* was published by Selwyn and Blount in 1918 and the title-page reads: *Last Poems*/By/Edward Thomas/London:/Selwyn & Blount,/12, York Buildings, Adelphi, W.C.2./1918. Both volumes were printed at The Chapel River Press, Kingston, Surrey. C.P. 1920, C.P. 1928 and C.P. all preserve the order of these two collections, with the interpolation of a few additional poems, and print *Poems* and *Last Poems* consecutively. The tables of contents for the original volumes are as follows:

POEMS

The Trumpet, The Signpost, Tears, Two Pewits, The Manor Farm, The Owl, Swedes, Will You Come?, As the Team's Head-Brass, Thaw, Interval, Like the Touch of Rain, The Path, The Combe, If I Should Ever by Chance, What Shall I Give?, If I were to Own, And You, Helen, When First, Head and Bottle, After You Speak, Sowing, When We Two Walked, In Memoriam (Easter, 1915), Fifty Faggots, Women He Liked, Early One Morning, The Cherry Trees, It Rains, The Huxter, A Gentleman, The Bridge, Lob, Bright Clouds, As the Clouds that are so Light, Some Eyes Condemn, May the Twenty-third, The Glory, Melancholy, Adlestrop, The Green Roads,

The Mill-Pond, It Was Upon, Tall Nettles, Haymaking, How at Once, Gone, Gone Again, The Sun Used to Shine, October, The Long Small Room, Liberty, November, The Sheiling, The Gallows, Birds' Nests, Rain, 'Home,' There's Nothing Like the Sun, When He Should Laugh, An Old Song ('The sun set . . .'), *The Penny Whistle, Lights Out, Cock-Crow, Words.*

LAST POEMS

I Never Saw that Land Before, The Dark Forest, Celandine, The Ash Grove, Old Man, The Thrush, I Built Myself a House of Glass, February Afternoon, Digging ('What matter makes my spade . . .'), *Two Houses, The Mill-Water, A Dream, Sedge-Warblers, Under the Woods, What Will They Do?, Tonight, A Cat, The Unknown, Song, She Dotes, For These, March the Third, The New House, March, The Cuckoo, Over the Hills, Home* ('Often I had gone . . .'), *The Hollow Wood, Wind and Mist, The Unknown Bird, The Lofty Sky, After Rain, Digging* ('Today I think . . .'), *But These Things Also, April, The Barn, The Barn and the Down, The Child on the Cliffs, Good-Night, The Wasp Trap, July, A Tale, Parting, Lovers, That Girl's Clear Eyes* (Handel Street), *The Child in the Orchard, The Source, The Mountain Chapel, First Known when Lost, The Word, These Things that Poets Said, Home* ('Not the end . . .'), *Aspens, An Old Song* ('I was not apprenticed . . .'), *There Was a Time, Ambition, No One Cares Less than I, Roads, This is No Case of Petty Right or Wrong, The Chalk Pit, Health, Beauty, Snow, The New Year, The Brook, The Other, House and Man, The Gypsy, Man and Dog, A Private, Out in the Dark.*

Bibliography

Principal Publications of Thomas's Poetry in Book Form

Haymaking and *The Manor Farm* by 'Edward Eastaway' in *This England* (Oxford University Press, 1915), pp. 111–12.

Six Poems by 'Edward Eastaway' (The Pear Tree Press, Flansham, Sussex, 1916).

Eighteen poems by 'Edward Eastaway' in *An Annual of New Poetry* (Constable, 1917).

Poems (Selwyn & Blount, 1917). [P.]

Last Poems (Selwyn & Blount, 1918). [L.P.]

Up in the Wind in *In Memoriam: Edward Thomas* (The Morland Press, 1919).

Collected Poems (Selwyn & Blount, 1920). Includes *Poems*, *Last Poems* and *Up in the Wind*. [C.P. 1920]

Selected Poems, edited and introduced by Edward Garnett (The Gregynog Press, Newtown, Montgomeryshire, 1927).

Two Poems: The Lane and *The Watchers* (Ingpen & Grant, 1927).

Collected Poems (Ingpen & Grant, 1928). Includes C.P. 1920, *Two Poems*, *No One So Much As You* and *The Wind's Song*. [C.P. 1928]

Collected Poems (Faber and Faber, 1936 onwards). Includes same poems as C.P. 1928. [C.P.]

Collected Poems, fifth impression (Faber and Faber, 1949). Adds *P.H.T.*

Works of particular interest are marked with an asterisk.

The Woodland Life (William Blackwood and Sons, 1897). [T.W.L.]

Horae Solitariae (Duckworth, 1902). [H.S.]

Oxford (A. & C. Black, 1903).

Rose Acre Papers (S.C. Brown, Langham 1904).

Beautiful Wales (A. & C. Black, 1905). [B.W.]

The Heart of England (J. M. Dent, 1906). [H.E.]

Richard Jefferies (Hutchinson, 1909). References are to the edition published in the Aldine Library series (J. M. Dent, 1938). [R.J.]

The South Country (J. M. Dent, 1909). References are to the edition published in the Aldine Library series (J. M. Dent, 1938). [S.C.]

Windsor Castle (Blackie and Son, 1910).

Rest and Unrest (Duckworth, 1910). [R.U.]

Feminine Influence on the Poets (Martin Secker, 1910).

Rose Acre Papers (Duckworth, 1910). Contains two essays from *Rose Acre Papers* (1904) and twelve from *Horae Solitariae*. [R.A.P.]

Light and Twilight (Duckworth, 1911). [L.A.T.]

Maurice Maeterlinck (Methuen, 1911).

The Tenth Muse (Martin Secker, 1911). Consists of ch. VIII of *Feminine Influence on the Poets*, slightly revised.

Celtic Stories (Oxford, The Clarendon Press, 1911).

The Isle of Wight (Blackie and Son, 1911).

Lafcadio Hearn (Constable, 1912).

Norse Tales (Oxford, The Clarendon Press, 1912).

Algernon Charles Swinburne (Martin Secker, 1912).

George Borrow (Chapman & Hall, 1912).

The Country (B. T. Batsford, 1913).

The Icknield Way (Constable, 1913). [I.W.]

The Happy-Go-Lucky Morgans (Duckworth, 1913).

[H.G.L.M.]

Walter Pater (Martin Secker, 1913).

In Pursuit of Spring (Thomas Nelson and Sons, 1914). [I.P.S.]

Four-and-Twenty Blackbirds (Duckworth, 1915).

The Life of the Duke of Marlborough (Chapman & Hall, 1915).

Keats (T. C. & E. C. Jack, 1916).

A Literary Pilgrim in England (Methuen, 1917). [L.P.E.]

Cloud Castle and Other Papers (Duckworth, 1922).

The Last Sheaf (Jonathan Cape, 1928). [L.S.]

The Childhood of Edward Thomas (Faber and Faber, 1938). [C.O.E.T.]

The Prose of Edward Thomas, selected by Roland Gant with an introduction by Helen Thomas (The Falcon Press, 1948). [P.E.T.]

Some Books Introduced or Compiled by Thomas

The Temple and *A Priest to the Temple* by George Herbert (Everyman's Library, no. 309, J. M. Dent, 1908).

Words and Places by Isaac Taylor (Everyman's Library, no. 517, J. M. Dent, 1911).

Rural Rides by William Cobbett (Everyman's Library, nos. 638 and 639, J. M. Dent, 1912).

The Pocket Book of Poems and Songs for the Open Air (E. Grant Richards, 1907).

This England: An Anthology from her Writers (Oxford University Press, 1915). [T.E.]

BIBLIOGRAPHY

Suggestions for Further Reading

(i) Recommended for use in both schools and universities

WILLIAM COOKE, *Edward Thomas: A Critical Biography* (Faber, 1970). Most accurate and judicious biography to date. Traces the development from prose to poetry and re-examines Thomas's personal and poetic response to the First World War, while incorporating fine analysis of individual poems. Comprehensive bibliography of published and unpublished material. [Cooke]

H. COOMBES, *Edward Thomas* (Chatto, 1956). A full-scale discussion of Thomas's poetry and prose with valuable extended comment on a number of poems. [Coombes]

'Hardy, de la Mare, and Edward Thomas,' *The Pelican Guide to English Literature*, VII (Pelican, 1961, 138–53).

F. R. LEAVIS, *New Bearings in English Poetry* (Chatto, 1932 and Peregrine, 1963). Includes a brief but seminal assessment of Thomas's modernity. [References are to the Peregrine ed.]

JOHN PRESS, *A Map of Modern English Verse* (O.U.P. and Oxford Paperbacks, 1969). Interesting chapter on the Georgians which places Thomas in relation to them.

JAMES REEVES (ed.), *Georgian Poetry* (Penguin, 1962). Useful selection and introduction.

VERNON SCANNELL, *Edward Thomas* (*Writers and their Work*, no. 163; Longman's, 1963). Compact and perceptive study by a poet. Includes select bibliography. [Scannell]

C. K. STEAD, *The New Poetic: Yeats to Eliot* (Hutchinson, 1964 and Pelican, 1967). Stead's middle chapters set the Georgians and the literary context of Thomas's period in a fresh historical perspective. Concise and clear. [References are to the Pelican ed.]

HELEN THOMAS, *As It Was* (Heinemann, 1926) and *World*

Without End (Heinemann, 1931). Reprint of a combined edition (Faber, 1956). A moving and beautifully written account of the Thomases' relationship. [A.I.W., W.W.E.: references are to the 1956 ed.]

(ii) Recommended more particularly for university students

JOHN BURROW, 'Keats and Edward Thomas,' *Essays in Criticism*, VII (Oct. 1957), 404–15. A persuasive study of influence and similarity which illuminates a particular group of poems.

JOHN F. DANBY, 'Edward Thomas,' *Critical Quarterly*, I (Winter 1959), 308–17. A penetrating and succinct demonstration of how 'Edward Thomas is one of the genuine sources of strength in 20th century poetry.'

MACDONALD EMSLIE, 'Spectatorial Attitudes,' *A Review of English Literature*, V (Jan. 1964), 66–8. Analysis of *The Watchers* which raises wider issues.

D. W. HARDING, 'A Note on Nostalgia,' *Scrutiny* I (May 1932), 8–19. Investigates the nature of nostalgia and the degree to which it is exhibited by several writers, including Edward Thomas.

ELEANOR FARJEON, *Edward Thomas: The Last Four Years*, Book I of her *Memoirs* (O.U.P., 1958). Largely made up of Thomas's letters, interspersed with linking commentary. Covers the period of the poetry. [E.F.]

F. R. LEAVIS, 'Imagery and Movement,' *Scrutiny*, XIII (Sept. 1945), 119–34. Includes an analysis of *Cock-Crow*.

JOHN LEHMANN, 'Edward Thomas,' *The Open Night* (Longmans, 1952), 77–86. A general appreciation.

C. DAY LEWIS, 'The Poetry of Edward Thomas,' *Essays by Divers Hands* (transactions of the Royal Society of Literature), XXIII, ed. by Angela Thirkell (O.U.P., 1956), 75–92.

A fine assessment, which probes deeply into a number of individual poems.

ROLAND MATHIAS, 'Edward Thomas,' *Anglo-Welsh Review*, X (1960), 23–37. A reappraisal which takes Thomas's 'affinity with The Fifties in terms of sensibility' as its starting-point.

J. MIDDLETON MURRY, 'The Poetry of Edward Thomas,' *Aspects of Literature* (Collins, 1920), 29–38. Somewhat digressive and rhetorical but reaches the core and circumference of the poetry.

JOHN MOORE, *The Life and Letters of Edward Thomas* (Heinemann, 1939). Still the most readable if not the most unromanticised of the biographies. Includes letters not accessible elsewhere. [Moore]

R. GEORGE THOMAS, (ed.) *Letters from Edward Thomas to Gordon Bottomley* (O.U.P., 1968). Maps the years of personal and literary struggle. The letters are more revealing than those to Eleanor Farjeon. Professor Thomas's notes form a valuable guide to Thomas's reviewing and the writing of his prose books. Includes a bibliography of Thomas's prose and poetry, as well as a chronology of his life. [L.G.B.]

Edward Thomas (University of Wales Press, 1972). A concise general study.

'Edward Thomas, Poet and Critic,' *Essays and Studies*, XXI (1968), 118–36. Offers an integrated approach to Thomas.

Introduction to a war 'Diary of Edward Thomas' kept during the last few months of his life, *Anglo-Welsh Review*, XX (Autumn 1971), 8–32.

LAWRANCE THOMPSON (ed.), *Selected Letters of Robert Frost* (Cape, 1965). Contains letters to and about Thomas.

Robert Frost: The Early Years 1874–1915 (Cape, 1967). Includes an account of the relationship between Thomas and Frost.

425

BIBLIOGRAPHY

(iii) Recommended for advanced university students

EDWARD THOMAS, prose (see p. 421).

ROBERT P. ECKERT, *Edward Thomas: A Biography and A Bibliography* (Dent, 1937). Now out-of-date in some respects but still the only detailed bibliographical study of Thomas's writings. [Eckert]

ROBERT H. ROSS, *The Georgian Revolt* (Faber, 1967). This account of the 'Rise and Fall of a Poetic Ideal 1910–1922' thoroughly documents the attitudes which created and composed the Georgian movement, and relates it to other poetic movements of the time.

Index of First Lines

427

INDEX

Index of Titles

430